CCNP TSHOOT
Lab Manual

Cisco Networking Academy

Cisco Press

800 East 96th Street

Indianapolis, Indiana 46240 USA

CCNA TSHOOT Lab Manual
Cisco Networking Academy

Copyright© 2011 Cisco Systems, Inc.

Published by:
Cisco Press
800 East 96th Street
Indianapolis, IN 46240 USA

Printed in the United States of America

First Printing   November 2010

Library of Congress Cataloging-in-Publication Data available upon request.

ISBN-13: 978-1-58713-305-3

ISBN-10: 1-58713-305-9

Warning and Disclaimer

This book is designed to provide information about networking. Every effort has been made to make this book as complete and as accurate as possible, but no warranty or fitness is implied.

The information is provided on an "as is" basis. The authors, Cisco Press, and Cisco Systems, Inc. shall have neither liability nor responsibility to any person or entity with respect to any loss or damages arising from the information contained in this book or from the use of the discs or programs that may accompany it.

The opinions expressed in this book belong to the author and are not necessarily those of Cisco Systems, Inc.

Trademark Acknowledgments

All terms mentioned in this book that are known to be trademarks or service marks have been appropriately capitalized. Cisco Press or Cisco Systems, Inc., cannot attest to the accuracy of this information. Use of a term in this book should not be regarded as affecting the validity of any trademark or service mark.

Corporate and Government Sales

The publisher offers excellent discounts on this book when ordered in quantity for bulk purchases or special sales, which may include electronic versions and/or custom covers and content particular to your business, training goals, marketing focus, and branding interests. For more information, please contact: U.S. Corporate and Government Sales   1-800-382-3419   corpsales@pearsontechgroup.com

For sales outside the U.S. please contact: International Sales   international@pearsoned.com

Feedback Information

At Cisco Press, our goal is to create in-depth technical books of the highest quality and value. Each book is crafted with care and precision, undergoing rigorous development that involves the unique expertise of members from the professional technical community.

Readers' feedback is a natural continuation of this process. If you have any comments regarding how we could improve the quality of this book, or otherwise alter it to better suit your needs, you can contact us through email at feedback@ciscopress.com. Please make sure to include the book title and ISBN in your message.

We greatly appreciate your assistance.

Publisher	Paul Boger
Associate Publisher	Dave Dusthimer
Cisco Representative	Erik Ullanderson
Cisco Press Program Manager	Anand Sundaram
Executive Editor	Mary Beth Ray
Managing Editor	Sandra Schroeder
Editorial Assistant	Vanessa Evans
Cover Designer	Louisa Adair

Americas Headquarters	Asia Pacific Headquarters	Europe Headquarters
Cisco Systems, Inc.	Cisco Systems (USA) Pte. Ltd.	Cisco Systems International BV
San Jose, CA	Singapore	Amsterdam, The Netherlands

Cisco has more than 200 offices worldwide. Addresses, phone numbers, and fax numbers are listed on the Cisco Website at www.cisco.com/go/offices.

CCDE, CCENT, Cisco Eos, Cisco HealthPresence, the Cisco logo, Cisco Lumin, Cisco Nexus, Cisco StadiumVision, Cisco TelePresence, Cisco WebEx, DCE, and Welcome to the Human Network are trademarks; Changing the Way We Work, Live, Play, and Learn and Cisco Store are service marks; and Access Registrar, Aironet, AsyncOS, Bringing the Meeting To You, Catalyst, CCDA, CCDP, CCIE, CCIP, CCNA, CCNP, CCSP, CCVP, Cisco, the Cisco Certified Internetwork Expert logo, Cisco IOS, Cisco Press, Cisco Systems, Cisco Systems Capital, the Cisco Systems logo, Cisco Unity, Collaboration Without Limitation, EtherFast, EtherSwitch, Event Center, Fast Step, Follow Me Browsing, FormShare, GigaDrive, HomeLink, Internet Quotient, IOS, iPhone, iQuick Study, IronPort, the IronPort logo, LightStream, Linksys, MediaTone, MeetingPlace, MeetingPlace Chime Sound, MGX, Networkers, Networking Academy, Network Registrar, PCNow, PIX, PowerPanels, ProConnect, ScriptShare, SenderBase, SMARTnet, Spectrum Expert, StackWise, The Fastest Way to Increase Your Internet Quotient, TransPath, WebEx, and the WebEx logo are registered trademarks of Cisco Systems, Inc. and/or its affiliates in the United States and certain other countries.

All other trademarks mentioned in this document or website are the property of their respective owners. The use of the word partner does not imply a partnership relationship between Cisco and any other company. (0812R)

Contents

About This Lab Manual

This is the only authorized Lab Manual for the Cisco Networking Academy CCNP version 6 TSHOOT course

A CCNP certification equips students with the knowledge and skills needed to plan, implement, secure, maintain, and troubleshoot converged enterprise networks. The CCNP certification requires candidates to pass three 120-minute exams—ROUTE #642-902, SWITCH #642-813, and TSHOOT #642-832—that validate the key competencies of network engineers.

The Cisco Networking Academy curriculum consists of three experience-oriented courses that employ industry-relevant instructional approaches to prepare students for professional-level jobs: CCNP ROUTE: Implementing IP Routing, CCNP SWITCH: Implementing IP Switching, and CCNP TSHOOT: Maintaining and Troubleshooting IP Networks.

CCNP TSHOOT: Troubleshooting and Maintaining IP Networks

This course teaches students how to monitor and maintain complex, enterprise routed and switched IP networks. Skills learned include the planning and execution of regular network maintenance, as well as support and troubleshooting using technology based processes and best practices, based on systematic and industry recognized approaches. Extensive labs emphasize hands-on learning and practice to reinforce troubleshooting techniques. CCNP ROUTE and CCNP SWITCH are both prerequisites for this course.

The 12 comprehensive labs in this manual emphasize hands-on learning and practice to reinforce configuration skills.

Command Syntax Conventions

The conventions used to present command syntax in this book are the same conventions used in the IOS Command Reference. The Command Reference describes these conventions as follows:

- Boldface indicates commands and keywords that are entered literally as shown. In actual configuration examples and output (not general command syntax), boldface indicates commands that are manually input by the user (such as a show command).

- Italic indicates arguments for which you supply actual values.

- Vertical bars (|) separate alternative, mutually exclusive elements.

- Square brackets ([ ]) indicate an optional element.

- Braces ({ }) indicate a required choice.

- Braces within brackets ([{ }]) indicate a required choice within an optional element

Chapter 1 Planning Maintenance for Complex Networks

There are no labs for this chapter.

Chapter 2 Troubleshooting Processes for Complex Enterprise Networks

There are no labs for this chapter.

Chapter 3 Using Maintenance and Troubleshooting Tools and Applications

Lab 3-1, Assembling Maintenance and Troubleshooting Tools

Physical Topology

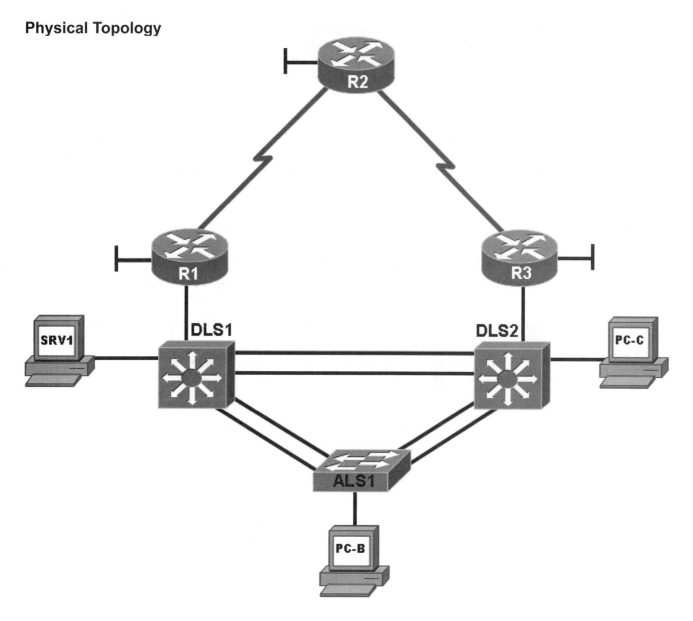

Objectives

- Assign responsibility for a device or set of devices to team members (optional).
- Load the baseline configuration for all devices in the topology.
- Use available tools to document key device configuration parameters, such as the interfaces in use, IP addressing, routing protocols, VLANs, logging mechanisms, and security measures.
- Document the physical topology to support future troubleshooting tasks.
- Document the logical topology to support future troubleshooting tasks.

Background

You have been employed as a network engineering consultant by a company that has made a recent acquisition. The documentation for the acquired company's network is incomplete and outdated, so you need to inventory their network architecture both logically and physically, per company documentation standards. This will help you learn about the design and implementation of their network and ensure that you have access to up-to-date and accurate network documentation to reference during future troubleshooting procedures.

In this lab, you survey the baseline TSHOOT network. No problems are introduced in this lab. This network will evolve over time as changes and enhancements are made. You will analyze and document the current topology and device configuration parameters to develop familiarity with the baseline configurations and network connections. You will review and fill out the provided documentation as you evaluate the network. You will assess and assemble tools that can be used for future maintenance and troubleshooting tasks.

Note: This lab uses Cisco 1841 routers with Cisco IOS Release 12.4(24)T and the Advanced IP Services image c1841-advipservicesk9-mz.124-24.T.bin. The switches are Cisco WS-C2960-24TT-L with the Cisco IOS image c2960-lanbasek9-mz.122-46.SE.bin and Catalyst 3560-24PS with the Cisco IOS image c3560-advipservicesk9-mz.122-46.SE.bin. Other routers (such as 2801 and 2811), switches (such as 2950 or 3550), and Cisco IOS Software versions can be used if they have comparable capabilities and features. Depending on the router or switch model and Cisco IOS Software version, the commands available and output produced might vary from what is shown in this lab.

Required Resources

- 3 routers (Cisco 1841 with Cisco IOS Release 12.4(24)T1 Advanced IP Service or comparable)
- 1 switch (Cisco 2960 with the Cisco IOS Release 12.2(46)SE C2960-LANBASEK9-M image or comparable)
- 2 switches (Cisco 3560 with the Cisco IOS Release 12.2(46)SE C3560-advipservicesK9-mz image or comparable)
- SRV1 (PC with static IP address): Windows XP, Vista, or Windows Server with RADIUS, TFTP, and syslog servers, plus an SSH client (PuTTY or comparable) and WireShark software
- PC-B (DHCP client): Windows XP or Vista (with SSH client and WireShark software)
- PC-C (DHCP client): Windows XP or Vista (with SSH client and WireShark software)
- Serial and Ethernet cables, as shown in the topology
- Rollover cables to configure the routers and switches via the console

Task 1: Assign Responsibility for Each Device (optional)

Step 1: Review the lab topology together with your team members.

Step 2: Assign responsibility for each device to a team member.

a. The team member who has primary responsibility for a device is in control of the console of that device and changes to the device. No other team member should access the console, make changes to the device, or execute disruptive actions, such as reloading or debugging, without permission from the responsible team member.

b. All team members can access all devices via Telnet or SSH for nondisruptive diagnostic action without permission of the responsible team member. Responsibilities can be reassigned during later labs if necessary.

c. If working in teams, you can document responsibilities in the Device Responsibilities table.

Device Responsibilities Table

Device	Description	Responsible Team Member
R1	Core Router 1	
R2	ISP Router	
R3	Core Router 2	
ALS1	Access Layer Switch 1	
DLS1	Distribution Layer Switch 1	
DLS2	Distribution Layer Switch 2	
SRV1	TFTP, syslog	
PC-B	User PC	
PC-C	User PC	

Task 2: Load the Baseline Device Configuration Files

Use the following procedure on each device in the network to load the baseline configuration. The procedure shown here is for a switch, but it is very similar to that of a router.

Note: The configs for this lab include `ip host` *name* *ip-addr* entries for all devices. This can be helpful in accessing devices using Telnet with this lab. The ip host entries are only provided in Lab 3-1 as the device IP addresses will change in subsequent labs.

Step 1: Verify the existence and location of the lab configuration files.

The lab configuration files for the course should be in flash under the tshoot directory for a given device. Use the `show flash` command to verify the presence of this directory. You can also verify the contents of the directory using the `cd` and `dir` commands. If the directory and files are not present, contact your instructor.

Note: When the `show flash` command is used on a switch, it lists the directories and files at the root directory but not the files within the directories. The following example uses the `cd` and `dir` commands on switch ALS1.

```
ALS1#show flash:

Directory of flash:/

    3  -rwx       916    Mar 1 1993 00:00:29 +00:00  vlan.dat
  619  -rwx      6582    Mar 1 1993 00:10:09 +00:00  config.text
    6  drwx       192    Oct 9 2009 13:00:50 +00:00  c2960-lanbasek9-mz.122-46.SE.bin
  622  drwx       128    Oct 9 2009 13:03:05 +00:00  tshoot
```

```
ALS1#cd tshoot
ALS1#dir
Directory of flash:/tshoot/

  623   -rwx       6582   Oct 9 2009 13:03:05 +00:00      Lab31-ALS1-Base-Cfg.txt
  624   -rwx       6578   Oct 9 2009 12:32:48 +00:00      Lab41-ALS1-TT-A-Cfg.txt
<output omitted>
```

Alternatively, you can see the contents of the directory by specifying its name using the dir command. For example:

```
ALS1#dir flash:/tshoot
Directory of flash:/tshoot/

    5  -rwx        6515   Oct 9 2009 14:39:42 +00:00  Lab31-ALS1-Base-Cfg.txt
```

Note: When the `show flash` command is used on a router, it lists the directories and the files within them. The following example uses only the `show flash` command on router R1. The tshoot directory and its contents are listed.

```
R1#show flash:
-#- --length-- -----date/time------ path
1    38266988 Sep 24 2009 17:47:14 c1841-advipservicesk9-mz.124-24.T1.bin
2           0 Oct 09 2009 12:32:06 tshoot
3        2288 Oct 09 2009 12:32:48 tshoot/Lab31-R1-Base-Cfg.txt
<output omitted>
```

Step 2: Erase the startup config from NVRAM.

```
ALS1#erase startup-config
Erasing the nvram filesystem will remove all configuration files! Continue?
[confirm]
[OK]
Erase of nvram: complete
```

Step 3: Delete the VLAN database from flash (switches only).

```
ALS1#delete vlan.dat
Delete flash:vlan.dat? [confirm]
```

Step 4: Reload the device, but do *not* save the system configuration if prompted.

```
ALS1#reload

System configuration has been modified. Save? [yes/no]: no
Proceed with reload? [confirm]
```

```
*Oct   1 00:29:28.704: %SYS-5-RELOAD: Reload requested by console. Reload
Reason:   Reload command.
```

Step 5: When the device restarts, do not enter the initial configuration dialog, but terminate autoinstall if prompted.

```
Press RETURN to get started!

          --- System Configuration Dialog ---

Would you like to enter the initial configuration dialog? [yes/no]: no

Would you like to terminate autoinstall? [yes]: Enter
```

Step 6: Copy the specified lab device configuration file from flash to the running config.

```
Switch>enable
Switch#copy flash:/tshoot/Lab31-ALS1-Base-Cfg.txt running-config
Destination filename [running-config]? Enter

ALS1#
```

Note: Although it is possible to copy the file to the startup config and reload the device, the RSA keys for SSH cannot be generated from the startup config.

Step 7: Copy the running config to the startup config.

Depending on the IOS version, AUTOSAVE may automatically save a copy of the running config to NVRAM for startup.

Note: AUTOSAVE does *not* copy the line con and vty configurations from the running config to the startup config. To ensure that the startup configuration is complete, you must copy manually.

```
ALS1#copy running-config startup-config
Building configuration...
[OK]
```

Note: If the device is rebooted at this point, you can log in with the username **admin** and the password **adminpa55**. To access privileged EXEC mode, use the **enable** password of **ciscoenpa55**.

Step 8: Repeat Steps 1 through 7 for the other devices in the network.

Step 9: Configure the PCs.

a. Configure SRV1 with the static IP address 10.1.50.1/24 and the default gateway 10.1.50.254.

b. Configure PC-B and PC-C as DHCP clients.

Step 10: Test basic network connectivity between devices.

a. Ping from PC-B to SRV1 at 10.1.50.1. Were the pings successful?

b. Ping from ALS1 to R2 at loopback 10.1.202.1. Were the pings successful?

_____

Note: If the pings are not successful, contact your instructor.

Task 3: Analyze and Document the Physical Lab Topology

Note: At this time, only examine and document the physical connections. Documenting the logical topology, such as subnets, IP addresses, and routing protocols, is addressed in Task 4 of this lab.

Step 1: Review the physical topology diagram on page 1 of the lab.

Step 2: Use Cisco Discovery Protocol and show commands to verify the Layer 1 and Layer 2 connections of the lab topology.

a. Use the `show cdp` command to discover the interfaces associated with the physical connections. Fill in the correct device and interface designators in the following Device Links table and label them on the physical topology diagram on the first page of the lab.

b. Review the configurations of the devices for using Layer 1 and Layer 2 features, such as trunks and EtherChannels. Fill in the information in the Device Links table and add it to the diagram. If a link is accounted for from one device to another, it is not necessary to repeat the entry from the other device. The first entry for ALS1, interface Fa0/1 is filled in as an example.

Which other commands could you use to identify Layer 1 and Layer 2 characteristics?

_____

_____

_____

Device Links Table

From Device	Interface	To Device	Interface	Layer 1 and 2 Features and Protocols Used
ALS1	Fa0/1	DLS1	Fa0/1	EtherChannel Po1, 802.1Q

From Device	Interface	To Device	Interface	Layer 1 and 2 Features and Protocols Used

c. Verify that all physical links shown in the diagram are operational. Which commands did you use?

_____

_____

Step 3: Map the VLANs used in the lab to the devices in the diagram.

Fill in the VLAN Definition table and label the physical topology diagram with the VLANs used for this topology. Identify all host devices that are members of each VLAN. The first entry for VLAN 10 is filled in as an example.

VLAN Definition Table

	Name	Description	VLAN Members
10	OFFICE	Office VLAN	ALS1, DLS1, DLS2, PC-B

Step 4: Analyze spanning tree for the Layer 2 switched domain.

a. Analyze the spanning tree characteristics of the Layer 2 switched portion of the network. Which type of spanning-tree mode is implemented?

_____

b. Which switch is the root switch for each VLAN, and what are the configured spanning-tree priorities?

_____

_____

_____

c. What is the resulting spanning-tree topology for VLANs that have client devices connected?

_____

_____

_____

_____

d. Which commands did you use to analyze the spanning-tree characteristics?

_____

_____

Step 5: Diagram the spanning tree for VLAN 10.

a. Label the STP role, port status, and direction for each port channel used in the physical topology diagram below.

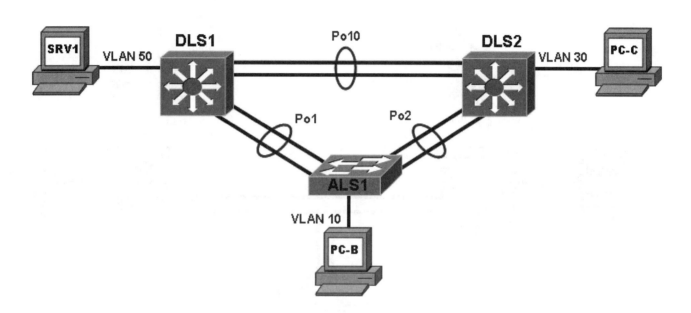

b   If working as a team, discuss your findings with your teammates to ensure that all team members understand the physical and data link aspects of the network design.

Student Notes

Use this space to make any additional notes regarding the physical configuration and the commands used.

_____

_____

_____

_____

_____

Task 4: Analyze and Document the Logical Lab Topology

Step 1: Review the logical lab diagram and the subnets.

Review the IP subnets in the Subnet table for the VLANs and WAN links that are used in the lab network. Router interface designations from the physical topology diagram are provided.

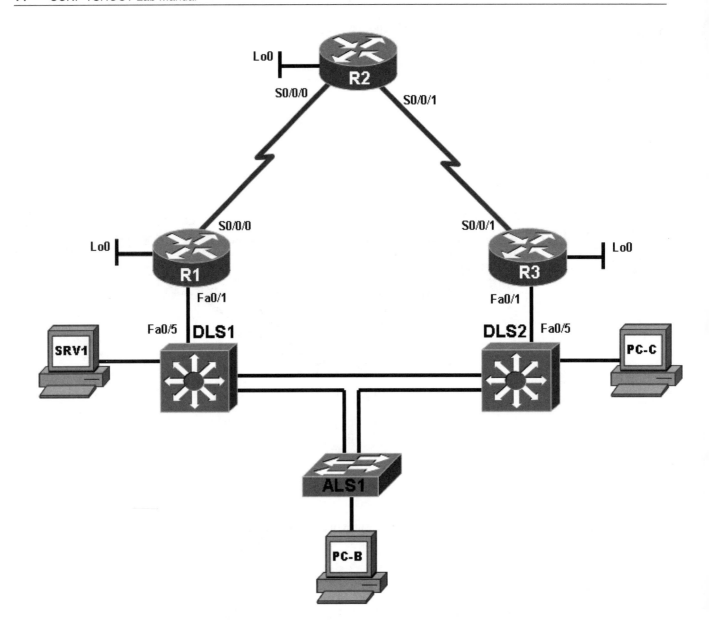

Subnet Table

Description	Subnet	Prefix	Devices
VLANs			
Office VLAN 10	10.1.10.0	/24	PC-B
Voice VLAN 20	10.1.20.0	/24	N/A
Guest VLAN 30	10.1.30.0	/24	PC-C
Servers VLAN 50	10.1.50.0	/24	SRV1
Management VLAN	10.1.100.0	/24	ALS1, DLS1, DLS2
WAN Links			
DLS1 – R1	10.1.2.0	/30	DLS1 and R1 FE link
DLS2 – R3	10.1.2.12	/30	DLS2 and R3 FE link
R1 – R2	10.1.1.0	/30	R1 and R2 serial link
R2 – R3	10.1.1.4	/30	R2 and R3 serial link

Step 2: Map the subnet scheme to the logical diagram.

In the previous step, the subnets were documented in the Subnet table. Now document the host portion of the addresses. To document the host part, research the routing tables and interface IP addresses of all the devices. Document the management VLAN and interface addresses in the IP Address table and on the logical topology diagram. Use only the number of the last octet for IP addresses in the diagram. The device names and interfaces are listed to help identify the IP addresses. The entry for ALS1 VLAN 100 is shown as an example. If an interface is not in use, indicate this in the Additional Information column. Account for all interfaces on the routers.

IP Address Table

Device Name Abbreviation	Interface	Network Address and Prefix	Additional Information
ALS1	Vlan 100	10.1.100.1/24	SVI
DLS1	Vlan 100		
DLS1	Fa0/5		
DLS2	Vlan 100		
DLS2	Fa0/5		
R1	Fa0/0		
R1	Fa0/1		
R1	S0/0/0		
R1	S0/0/1		
R1	Loopback 0		
R2	Fa0/0		
R2	Fa0/1		
R2	S0/0/0		
R2	S0/0/1		
R2	Loopback 0		
R3	Fa0/0		
R3	Fa0/1		
R3	S0/0/0		
R3	S0/0/1		
R3	Loopback 0		
SRV1	NIC		
PC-B	NIC		
PC-C	NIC		

Step 3: Analyze and document control plane logical configuration features.

Analyze the configurations of the devices for control plane features such as routing protocols, First Hop Redundancy Protocols (FHRPs), dynamic host configuration protocol (DHCP), and network address translation (NAT). Review, document, and discuss the following aspects of the logical network configuration.

a. Is dynamic or static routing being used?

b. If dynamic, which routing protocol?

_____

c. Are FHRPs in use, such as the Hot Standby Router Protocol (HSRP), Virtual Router Redundancy
    Protocol (VRRP), or Gateway Load Balancing Protocol (GLBP)? If yes, which one?

_____

d. What is the active router for all relevant VLANs?

_____

_____

e. From the PC-B command prompt, issue the **tracert** command to router R2 loopback 0 at 10.1.202.1.
    What path did the packets take?

_____

_____

_____

f. Are any access lists used to filter traffic on the network? If yes, describe their function.

_____

_____

g. Is DHCP in use? If yes, which DHCP server is used and for which VLANs present in the logical topology
    diagram?

_____

h. If working as a team, discuss your findings with your teammates to ensure that all team members
    understand the high-level design of the network.

_____

Notes

Use this space to make any additional notes regarding the logical configuration and the commands used.

_____

_____

_____

_____

_____

Task 5: Identify Troubleshooting and Maintenance Tools

Step 1: Analyze device configurations for troubleshooting and maintenance features.

Analyze the configurations of the devices for services that support troubleshooting and maintenance, such as syslog, Simple Network Management Protocol (SNMP), and other network management features.

Step 2: Document the troubleshooting and maintenance features.

a. Document the troubleshooting and maintenance applications or tools in use with the network devices in the Troubleshooting and Maintenance Tools table. An entry for system logging is provided as an example.

Troubleshooting and Maintenance Tools Table

Configured Feature	Devices	Target Server	Target Tool or Application
System message logging	All	SRV1	Syslog server

b. If working as a team, discuss your findings with your teammates to ensure that all team members know which maintenance and troubleshooting tools are available in the network.

Notes

Use this space to make any additional notes regarding troubleshooting and maintenance applications or tools.

_____

_____

_____

_____

_____

_____

Task 6: Identify the Security Measures Implemented

Step 1: Analyze device configurations for security-related features.

Analyze the configurations of your assigned devices for configuration options that help support a more secure network implementation, such as password security, login authentication, secure remote management, switch trunk and access port security, and VLANs. Record your entries in the Security Features table. An entry for password security is provided as an example.

Security Features Table

Security Feature Configured	Implementation Method or Commands
Password security	Enable secret, password encryption

Notes

Use this space to make any additional notes regarding security measures.

_____

_____

_____

_____

_____

_____

_____

Note: Reference configurations for all devices are provided at the end of the lab. These are not the full **show running-config** output. Only the nondefault commands used to configure the devices are included (along with **no shutdown** on interfaces).

Lab Debrief Notes

Use this space to make notes of the key learning points that you picked up during the lab debrief discussions with your instructor. This can include alternate solutions, methods, and processes, procedure and communication improvements, as well as key commands and tools.

Note: This is your primary opportunity to document a baseline of the lab network before starting the troubleshooting exercises. During the debrief session, ask your instructor for clarification of any aspects of the network design and configurations that are unclear to you.

_____

_____

_____

_____

_____

_____

_____

_____

_____

_____

_____

_____

Router Interface Summary Table

Router Interface Summary				
Router Model	Ethernet Interface #1	Ethernet Interface #2	Serial Interface #1	Serial Interface #2
1700	Fast Ethernet 0 (FA0)	Fast Ethernet 1 (FA1)	Serial 0 (S0)	Serial 1 (S1)
1800	Fast Ethernet 0/0 (FA0/0)	Fast Ethernet 0/1 (FA0/1)	Serial 0/0/0 (S0/0/0)	Serial 0/0/1 (S0/0/1)
2600	Fast Ethernet 0/0 (FA0/0)	Fast Ethernet 0/1 (FA0/1)	Serial 0/0 (S0/0)	Serial 0/1 (S0/1)
2800	Fast Ethernet 0/0 (FA0/0)	Fast Ethernet 0/1 (FA0/1)	Serial 0/0/0 (S0/0/0)	Serial 0/0/1 (S0/0/1)

Note: To find out how the router is configured, look at the interfaces to identify the type of router and how many interfaces the router has. Rather than try to list all the combinations of configurations for each router class, this table includes identifiers for the possible combinations of Ethernet and serial interfaces in the device. The table does not include any other type of interface, even though a specific router might contain one. An example of this is an ISDN BRI interface. The string in parenthesis is the legal abbreviation that can be used in Cisco IOS commands to represent the interface.

Device Configurations

Switch ALS1

```
!Lab 3-1 Switch ALS1 Baseline Config
!
hostname ALS1
!
service timestamps debug datetime msec
service timestamps log datetime msec
service password-encryption
!
logging buffered 16384
enable secret ciscoenpa55
!
username admin secret adminpa55
!
banner motd $*** Lab 3-1 Switch ALS1 Baseline Config ***$
!
no ip domain lookup
!
aaa new-model
aaa authentication login default local
aaa authentication login CONSOLE none
aaa authorization exec default local
!
system mtu routing 1500
!
vtp domain TSHOOT
vtp mode transparent
!
ip subnet-zero
ip domain-name tshoot.net
```

```
ip host R1 10.1.2.2 10.1.1.1 10.1.201.1
ip host R2 10.1.1.2 10.1.1.6 10.1.202.1
ip host R3 10.1.1.5 10.1.2.14 10.1.203.1
ip host ALS1 10.1.100.1
ip host DLS1 10.1.100.252 10.1.2.1
ip host DLS2 10.1.100.253 10.1.2.13
!
crypto key zeroize rsa
crypto key generate rsa general-keys modulus 1024
!
archive
 log config
  logging size 50
  notify syslog
  hidekeys
 path tftp://10.1.50.1/$h-archive-config
 write-memory
file prompt quiet

spanning-tree mode rapid-pvst
spanning-tree portfast default
!
interface Vlan1
 no ip address
 shutdown
!
vlan 10
 name OFFICE
!
vlan 20
 name VOICE
!
vlan 30
 name GUEST
!
vlan 100
 name MGMT
!
vlan 900
 name NATIVE
!
vlan 999
 name UNUSED
!
ip telnet source-interface Vlan100
ip ssh source-interface Vlan100
!
interface Port-channel1
 description Channel to DLS1
 no shutdown
 !
interface Port-channel2
 description Channel to DLS2
 no shutdown
!
interface FastEthernet0/1
 description Channel to DLS1
 switchport trunk native vlan 900
```

```
 switchport trunk allowed vlan 10,20,30,100
 switchport mode trunk
 switchport nonegotiate
 channel-group 1 mode on
 no shutdown
!
interface FastEthernet0/2
 description Channel to DLS1
 switchport trunk native vlan 900
 switchport trunk allowed vlan 10,20,30,100
 switchport mode trunk
 switchport nonegotiate
 channel-group 1 mode on
 no shutdown
!
interface FastEthernet0/3
 description Channel to DLS2
 switchport trunk native vlan 900
 switchport trunk allowed vlan 10,20,30,100
 switchport mode trunk
 switchport nonegotiate
 channel-group 2 mode on
 no shutdown
!
interface FastEthernet0/4
 description Channel to DLS2
 switchport trunk native vlan 900
 switchport trunk allowed vlan 10,20,30,100
 switchport mode trunk
 switchport nonegotiate
 channel-group 2 mode on
 no shutdown
!
interface FastEthernet0/5
 description Unused
 switchport access vlan 999
 switchport mode access
 switchport nonegotiate
 shutdown
!
interface FastEthernet0/6
 description Unused
 switchport access vlan 999
 switchport mode access
 switchport nonegotiate
 shutdown

interface FastEthernet0/7
 description Unused
 switchport access vlan 999
 switchport mode access
 switchport nonegotiate
 shutdown
!
interface FastEthernet0/8
 description Unused
 switchport access vlan 999
 switchport mode access
```

```
 switchport nonegotiate
 shutdown
!
interface FastEthernet0/9
 description Unused
 switchport access vlan 999
 switchport mode access
 switchport nonegotiate
 shutdown
!
interface FastEthernet0/10
 description Unused
 switchport access vlan 999
 switchport mode access
 switchport nonegotiate
 shutdown
!
interface FastEthernet0/11
 description Unused
 switchport access vlan 999
 switchport mode access
 switchport nonegotiate
 shutdown
!
interface FastEthernet0/12
 description Unused
 switchport access vlan 999
 switchport mode access
 switchport nonegotiate
 shutdown
!
interface FastEthernet0/13
 description Unused
 switchport access vlan 999
 switchport mode access
 switchport nonegotiate
 shutdown
!
interface FastEthernet0/14
 description Unused
 switchport access vlan 999
 switchport mode access
 switchport nonegotiate
 shutdown
!
interface FastEthernet0/15
 description Unused
 switchport access vlan 999
 switchport mode access
 switchport nonegotiate
 shutdown
!
interface FastEthernet0/16
 description Unused
 switchport access vlan 999
 switchport mode access
```

```
 switchport nonegotiate
 shutdown
!
interface FastEthernet0/17
 description Unused
 switchport access vlan 999
 switchport mode access
 switchport nonegotiate
 shutdown
!
interface FastEthernet0/18
 description To PC-B
 switchport access vlan 10
 switchport mode access
 switchport voice vlan 20
 spanning-tree portfast
 switchport port-security
 switchport port-security maximum 2
 switchport port-security violation shutdown
 switchport port-security mac-address sticky
 no shut
!
interface FastEthernet0/19
 description Unused
 switchport access vlan 999
 switchport mode access
 switchport nonegotiate
 shutdown
!
interface FastEthernet0/20
 description Unused
 switchport access vlan 999
 switchport mode access
 switchport nonegotiate
 shutdown
!
interface FastEthernet0/21
 description Unused
 switchport access vlan 999
 switchport mode access
 switchport nonegotiate
 shutdown
!
interface FastEthernet0/22
 description Unused
 switchport access vlan 999
 switchport mode access
 switchport nonegotiate
 shutdown
!
interface FastEthernet0/23
 description Unused
 switchport access vlan 999
 switchport mode access
 switchport nonegotiate
 shutdown
!
interface FastEthernet0/24
```

```
 description Unused
 switchport access vlan 999
 switchport mode access
 switchport nonegotiate
 shutdown
!
interface gigabitethernet0/1
 description Unused
 switchport access vlan 999
 switchport mode access
 switchport nonegotiate
 shutdown
!
interface gigabitethernet0/2
 description Unused
 switchport access vlan 999
 switchport mode access
 switchport nonegotiate
 shutdown
!
interface Vlan100
 ip address 10.1.100.1 255.255.255.0
 no shutdown
!
ip default-gateway 10.1.100.254
!
ip http server
ip http secure-server
!
logging source-interface Vlan100
logging 10.1.50.1
!
snmp-server community cisco RO
snmp-server community san-fran RW
snmp-server trap-source Vlan100
snmp-server location TSHOOT Lab Facility
snmp-server contact support@tshoot.net
snmp-server host 10.1.50.1 version 2c cisco
snmp-server enable traps vtp
snmp-server enable traps vlancreate
snmp-server enable traps vlandelete
snmp-server enable traps port-security
snmp-server enable traps vlan-membership
!
line con 0
 exec-timeout 60 0
 login authentication CONSOLE
 logging synchronous
line vty 0 4
 exec-timeout 60 0
 transport input telnet ssh
line vty 5 15
  no transport input
!
ntp source Vlan100
ntp server 10.1.202.1
end
```

Switch DLS1

```
!Lab 3-1 Switch DLS1 Baseline Config
!
hostname DLS1
!
service timestamps debug datetime msec
service timestamps log datetime msec
service password-encryption
!
logging buffered 16384
enable secret ciscoenpa55
!
username admin secret adminpa55

banner motd $*** Lab 3-1 Switch DLS1 Baseline Config ***$
!
no ip domain lookup
!
aaa new-model
aaa authentication login default local
aaa authentication login CONSOLE none
aaa authorization exec default local
!
system mtu routing 1500
!
vtp domain TSHOOT
vtp mode transparent
!
ip subnet-zero
ip routing
!
ip domain-name tshoot.net
ip host R1 10.1.2.2 10.1.1.1 10.1.201.1
ip host R2 10.1.1.2 10.1.1.6 10.1.202.1
ip host R3 10.1.1.5 10.1.2.14 10.1.203.1
ip host ALS1 10.1.100.1
ip host DLS1 10.1.100.252 10.1.2.1
ip host DLS2 10.1.100.253 10.1.2.13
!
ip dhcp excluded-address 10.1.10.252 10.1.10.254
ip dhcp excluded-address 10.1.20.252 10.1.20.254
ip dhcp excluded-address 10.1.30.252 10.1.30.254
!
ip dhcp pool OFFICE
   network 10.1.10.0 255.255.255.0
   default-router 10.1.10.254
   domain-name tshoot.net
!
ip dhcp pool VOICE
   network 10.1.20.0 255.255.255.0
   default-router 10.1.20.254
   domain-name tshoot.net
!
ip dhcp pool GUEST
   network 10.1.30.0 255.255.255.0
   default-router 10.1.30.254
   domain-name tshoot.net
```

```
!
crypto key zeroize rsa
crypto key generate rsa general-keys modulus 1024
!
errdisable recovery cause bpduguard
!
archive
 log config
  logging size 50
  notify syslog
  hidekeys
 path tftp://10.1.50.1/$h-archive-config
 write-memory
file prompt quiet
!
spanning-tree mode rapid-pvst
!
spanning-tree vlan 10,30,100 priority 24576
spanning-tree vlan 20,50 priority 28672
!
vlan 10
 name OFFICE
!
vlan 20
 name VOICE
!
vlan 30
 name GUEST
!
vlan 50
 name SERVERS
!
vlan 100
 name MGMT
!
vlan 900
 name NATIVE
!
vlan 999
 name UNUSED
!
ip telnet source-interface Vlan100
ip ssh source-interface Vlan100
!
interface Port-channel1
 description Channel to ALS1
 no shut
!
interface Port-channel10
 description Channel to DLS2
 no shut
!
interface FastEthernet0/1
 description Channel to ALS1
 switchport trunk encapsulation dot1q
 switchport trunk native vlan 900
 switchport trunk allowed vlan 10,20,30,100
 switchport mode trunk
```

```
 switchport nonegotiate
 channel-group 1 mode on
 no shut
!
interface FastEthernet0/2
 description Channel to ALS1
 switchport trunk encapsulation dot1q
 switchport trunk native vlan 900
 switchport trunk allowed vlan 10,20,30,100
 switchport mode trunk
 switchport nonegotiate
 channel-group 1 mode on
 no shut
!
interface FastEthernet0/3
 description Channel to DLS2
 switchport trunk encapsulation dot1q
 switchport trunk native vlan 900
 switchport trunk allowed vlan 10,20,30,50,100
 switchport mode trunk
 switchport nonegotiate
 channel-group 10 mode on
 no shut
!
interface FastEthernet0/4
 description Channel to DLS2
 switchport trunk encapsulation dot1q
 switchport trunk native vlan 900
 switchport trunk allowed vlan 10,20,30,50,100
 switchport mode trunk
 switchport nonegotiate
 channel-group 10 mode on
 no shut
!
interface FastEthernet0/5
 description FE to R1
 no switchport
 ip address 10.1.2.1 255.255.255.252
 speed 100
 duplex full
 spanning-tree bpduguard enable
 no shut
!
interface FastEthernet0/6
 description FE to SRV1
 switchport access vlan 50
 switchport mode access
 switchport nonegotiate
 spanning-tree portfast
 no shut
!
interface FastEthernet0/7
 description Unused
 switchport access vlan 999
 switchport mode access
 switchport nonegotiate
 shutdown
!
```

```
interface FastEthernet0/8
 description Unused
 switchport access vlan 999
 switchport mode access
 switchport nonegotiate
 shutdown
!
interface FastEthernet0/9
 description Unused
 switchport access vlan 999
 switchport mode access
 switchport nonegotiate
 shutdown
!
interface FastEthernet0/10
 description Unused
 switchport access vlan 999
 switchport mode access
 switchport nonegotiate
 shutdown
!
interface FastEthernet0/11
 description Unused
 switchport access vlan 999
 switchport mode access
 switchport nonegotiate
 shutdown
!
interface FastEthernet0/12
 description Unused
 switchport access vlan 999
 switchport mode access
 switchport nonegotiate
 shutdown
!
interface FastEthernet0/13
 description Unused
 switchport access vlan 999
 switchport mode access
 switchport nonegotiate
 shutdown
!
interface FastEthernet0/14
 description Unused
 switchport access vlan 999
 switchport mode access
 switchport nonegotiate
 shutdown
!
interface FastEthernet0/15
 description Unused
 switchport access vlan 999
 switchport mode access
 switchport nonegotiate
 shutdown
!
interface FastEthernet0/16
 description Unused
```

```
 switchport access vlan 999
 switchport mode access
 switchport nonegotiate
 shutdown
!
interface FastEthernet0/17
 description Unused
 switchport access vlan 999
 switchport mode access
 switchport nonegotiate
 shutdown
!
interface FastEthernet0/18
 description Unused
 switchport access vlan 999
 switchport mode access
 switchport nonegotiate
 shutdown
!
interface FastEthernet0/19
 description Unused
 switchport access vlan 999
 switchport mode access
 switchport nonegotiate
 shutdown
!
interface FastEthernet0/20
 description Unused
 switchport access vlan 999
 switchport mode access
 switchport nonegotiate
 shutdown
!
interface FastEthernet0/21
 description Unused
 switchport access vlan 999
 switchport mode access
 switchport nonegotiate
 shutdown
!
interface FastEthernet0/22
 description Unused
 switchport access vlan 999
 switchport mode access
 switchport nonegotiate
 shutdown
!
interface FastEthernet0/23
 description Unused
 switchport access vlan 999
 switchport mode access
 switchport nonegotiate
 shutdown
!
interface FastEthernet0/24
 description Unused
 switchport access vlan 999
 switchport mode access
```

```
 switchport nonegotiate
 shutdown
!
interface gigabitethernet0/1
 description Unused
 switchport access vlan 999
 switchport mode access
 switchport nonegotiate
 shutdown
!
interface gigabitethernet0/2
 description Unused
 switchport access vlan 999
 switchport mode access
 switchport nonegotiate
 shutdown
!
interface Vlan1
 no ip address
 shutdown

interface Vlan10
 ip address 10.1.10.252 255.255.255.0
 standby 10 ip 10.1.10.254
 standby 10 priority 110
 standby 10 preempt
!
interface Vlan20
 ip address 10.1.20.252 255.255.255.0
 standby 20 ip 10.1.20.254
 standby 20 preempt
!
interface Vlan30
 ip address 10.1.30.252 255.255.255.0
 standby 30 ip 10.1.30.254
 standby 30 priority 110
 standby 30 preempt
!
interface Vlan50
 ip address 10.1.50.252 255.255.255.0
 standby 50 ip 10.1.50.254
 standby 50 preempt
!
interface Vlan100
 ip address 10.1.100.252 255.255.255.0
 standby 100 ip 10.1.100.254
 standby 100 priority 110
 standby 100 preempt
!
router eigrp 1
 passive-interface default
 no passive-interface Fa0/5
 no auto-summary
 network 10.1.0.0 0.0.255.255
!
ip classless
ip http server
ip http secure-server
```

```
!
logging source-interface Vlan100
logging 10.1.50.1
!
snmp-server community cisco RO
snmp-server community san-fran RW
snmp-server trap-source Vlan100
snmp-server location TSHOOT Lab Facility
snmp-server contact support@tshoot.net
snmp-server host 10.1.50.1 version 2c cisco
snmp-server enable traps eigrp
snmp-server enable traps vtp
snmp-server enable traps vlancreate
snmp-server enable traps vlandelete
snmp-server enable traps port-security
snmp-server enable traps config
snmp-server enable traps hsrp
snmp-server enable traps vlan-membership
snmp-server enable traps errdisable
!
line con 0
 exec-timeout 60 0
 login authentication CONSOLE
 logging synchronous
line vty 0 4
 exec-timeout 60 0
 transport input telnet ssh
line vty 5 15
 no transport input
!
ntp source Vlan100
ntp server 10.1.202.1
end
```

Switch DLS2

```
!Lab 3-1 Switch DLS2 Baseline Config
!
hostname DLS2
!
service timestamps debug datetime msec
service timestamps log datetime
service password-encryption
!
logging buffered 16384
enable secret ciscoenpa55
!
username admin secret adminpa55
!
banner motd $*** Lab 3-1 Switch DLS2 Baseline Config ***$
!
no ip domain lookup
!
aaa new-model
aaa authentication login default local
aaa authentication login CONSOLE none
aaa authorization exec default local
!
```

```
system mtu routing 1500
!
vtp domain TSHOOT
vtp mode transparent
!
ip subnet-zero
ip routing
ip domain-name tshoot.net
ip host R1 10.1.2.2 10.1.1.1 10.1.201.1
ip host R2 10.1.1.2 10.1.1.6 10.1.202.1
ip host R3 10.1.1.5 10.1.2.14 10.1.203.1
ip host ALS1 10.1.100.1
ip host DLS1 10.1.100.252 10.1.2.1
ip host DLS2 10.1.100.253 10.1.2.13
!
crypto key zeroize rsa
crypto key generate rsa general-keys modulus 1024
!
errdisable recovery cause bpduguard
!
archive
 log config
  logging size 50
  notify syslog
  hidekeys
  path tftp://10.1.50.1/$h-archive-config
 write-memory
file prompt quiet
!
spanning-tree mode rapid-pvst
!
spanning-tree vlan 10,30,100 priority 28672
spanning-tree vlan 20,50 priority 24576

vlan 10
 name OFFICE
!
vlan 20
 name VOICE
!
vlan 30
 name GUEST
!
vlan 50
 name SERVERS
!
vlan 100
 name MGMT
!
vlan 900
 name NATIVE
!
vlan 999
 name UNUSED
!
ip telnet source-interface Vlan100
ip ssh source-interface Vlan100
!
```

```
interface Port-channel2
 description Channel to ALS1
 no shut

interface Port-channel10
 description Channel to DLS1
 no shut
!
interface FastEthernet0/1
 description Channel to ALS1
 switchport trunk encapsulation dot1q
 switchport trunk native vlan 900
 switchport trunk allowed vlan 10,20,30,100
 switchport mode trunk
 switchport nonegotiate
 channel-group 2 mode on
 no shut
!
interface FastEthernet0/2
 description Channel to ALS1
 switchport trunk encapsulation dot1q
 switchport trunk native vlan 900
 switchport trunk allowed vlan 10,20,30,100
 switchport mode trunk
 switchport nonegotiate
 channel-group 2 mode on
 no shut
!
interface FastEthernet0/3
 description Channel to DLS1
 switchport trunk encapsulation dot1q
 switchport trunk native vlan 900
 switchport trunk allowed vlan 10,20,30,50,100
 switchport mode trunk
 switchport nonegotiate
 channel-group 10 mode on
 no shut
!
interface FastEthernet0/4
 description Channel to DLS1
 switchport trunk encapsulation dot1q
 switchport trunk native vlan 900
 switchport trunk allowed vlan 10,20,30,50,100
 switchport mode trunk
 switchport nonegotiate
 channel-group 10 mode on
 no shut
!
interface FastEthernet0/5
 description FE to R3
 no switchport
 ip address 10.1.2.13 255.255.255.252
 speed 100
 duplex full
 spanning-tree bpduguard enable
 no shut
!
interface FastEthernet0/6
```

```
 description Unused
 switchport access vlan 999
 switchport mode access
 switchport nonegotiate
 shutdown
!
interface FastEthernet0/7
 description Unused
 switchport access vlan 999
 switchport mode access
 switchport nonegotiate
 shutdown
!
interface FastEthernet0/8
 description Unused
 switchport access vlan 999
 switchport mode access
 switchport nonegotiate
 shutdown
!
interface FastEthernet0/9
 description Unused
 switchport access vlan 999
 switchport mode access
 switchport nonegotiate
 shutdown
!
interface FastEthernet0/10
 description Unused
 switchport access vlan 999
 switchport mode access
 switchport nonegotiate
 shutdown
!
interface FastEthernet0/11
 description Unused
 switchport access vlan 999
 switchport mode access
 switchport nonegotiate
 shutdown
!
interface FastEthernet0/12
 description Unused
 switchport access vlan 999
 switchport mode access
 switchport nonegotiate
 shutdown
!
interface FastEthernet0/13
 description Unused
 switchport access vlan 999
 switchport mode access
 switchport nonegotiate
 shutdown
!
interface FastEthernet0/14
 description Unused
 switchport access vlan 999
```

```
 switchport mode access
 switchport nonegotiate
 shutdown
!
interface FastEthernet0/15
 description Unused
 switchport access vlan 999
 switchport mode access
 switchport nonegotiate
 shutdown
!
interface FastEthernet0/16
 description Unused
 switchport access vlan 999
 switchport mode access
 switchport nonegotiate
 shutdown
!
interface FastEthernet0/17
 description Unused
 switchport access vlan 999
 switchport mode access
 switchport nonegotiate
 shutdown
!
interface FastEthernet0/18
 description FE to PC-C
 switchport access vlan 30
 switchport mode access
 switchport nonegotiate
 spanning-tree portfast
 no shutdown
!
interface FastEthernet0/19
 description Unused
 switchport access vlan 999
 switchport mode access
 switchport nonegotiate
 shutdown
!
interface FastEthernet0/20
 description Unused
 switchport access vlan 999
 switchport mode access
 switchport nonegotiate
 shutdown
!
interface FastEthernet0/21
 description Unused
 switchport access vlan 999
 switchport mode access
 switchport nonegotiate
 shutdown
!
interface FastEthernet0/22
 description Unused
 switchport access vlan 999
 switchport mode access
```

```
 switchport nonegotiate
 shutdown
!
interface FastEthernet0/23
 description Unused
 switchport access vlan 999
 switchport mode access
 switchport nonegotiate
 shutdown
!
interface FastEthernet0/24
 description Unused
 switchport access vlan 999
 switchport mode access
 switchport nonegotiate
 shutdown
!
interface GigabitEthernet0/1
 description Unused
 switchport access vlan 999
 switchport mode access
 switchport nonegotiate
 shutdown
!
interface GigabitEthernet0/2
 description Unused
 switchport access vlan 999
 switchport mode access
 switchport nonegotiate
 shutdown
!
interface Vlan1
 no ip address
 shutdown
!
interface Vlan10
 ip address 10.1.10.253 255.255.255.0
 standby 10 ip 10.1.10.254
 standby 10 preempt
!
interface Vlan20
 ip address 10.1.20.253 255.255.255.0
 standby 20 ip 10.1.20.254
 standby 20 priority 110
 standby 20 preempt
!
interface Vlan30
 ip address 10.1.30.253 255.255.255.0
 standby 30 ip 10.1.30.254
 standby 30 preempt
!
interface Vlan50
 ip address 10.1.50.253 255.255.255.0
 standby 50 ip 10.1.50.254
 standby 50 priority 110
 standby 50 preempt
!
interface Vlan100
```

```
 ip address 10.1.100.253 255.255.255.0
 standby 100 ip 10.1.100.254
 standby 100 preempt
!
!
router eigrp 1
 passive-interface default
 no passive-interface Fa0/5
 no auto-summary
 network 10.1.0.0 0.0.255.255
!
ip classless
ip http server
ip http secure-server
!
!
logging source-interface Vlan100
logging 10.1.50.1
!
snmp-server community cisco RO
snmp-server community san-fran RW
snmp-server trap-source Vlan100
snmp-server location TSHOOT Lab Facility
snmp-server contact support@tshoot.net
snmp-server enable traps eigrp
snmp-server enable traps vtp
snmp-server enable traps vlancreate
snmp-server enable traps vlandelete
snmp-server enable traps port-security
snmp-server enable traps hsrp
snmp-server enable traps vlan-membership
snmp-server enable traps errdisable
snmp-server host 10.1.50.1 version 2c cisco
!
line con 0
 exec-timeout 60 0
 login authentication CONSOLE
 logging synchronous
line vty 0 4
 exec-timeout 60 0
 transport input telnet ssh
line vty 5 15
 no transport input
!
ntp source Vlan100
ntp server 10.1.202.1
end
```

Router R1

```
!Lab 3-1 Router R1 Baseline Config
!
hostname R1
!
service timestamps debug datetime msec
service timestamps log datetime msec
service password-encryption
!
```

```
logging buffered 16384 debugging
enable secret ciscoenpa55
!
username admin secret adminpa55
!
banner motd $*** Lab 3-1 Router R1 Baseline Config ***$
!
no ip domain lookup
!
aaa new-model
aaa authentication login default local
aaa authentication login CONSOLE none
aaa authorization exec default local
!
ip domain name tshoot.net
ip host R1 10.1.2.2 10.1.1.1 10.1.201.1
ip host R2 10.1.1.2 10.1.1.6 10.1.202.1
ip host R3 10.1.1.5 10.1.2.14 10.1.203.1
ip host ALS1 10.1.100.1
ip host DLS1 10.1.100.252 10.1.2.1
ip host DLS2 10.1.100.253 10.1.2.13
!
crypto key zeroize rsa
crypto key generate rsa general-keys modulus 1024
!
file prompt quiet
archive
 log config
  logging size 50
  notify syslog
  hidekeys
 path tftp://10.1.50.1/$h-archive-config
 write-memory
!
ip telnet source-interface Loopback0
ip ssh source-interface Loopback0
!
interface Loopback0
 ip address 10.1.201.1 255.255.255.255
!
interface FastEthernet0/0
 no ip address
 shutdown
!
interface FastEthernet0/1
 description FE to DLS1
 ip address 10.1.2.2 255.255.255.252
 ip flow ingress
 speed 100
 full-duplex
 no shutdown
!
interface Serial0/0/0
 description WAN link to R2 - 128k leased line
 ip address 10.1.1.1 255.255.255.252
 ip flow ingress
 encapsulation ppp
 clock rate 128000
```

```
  no shutdown
!
interface Serial0/0/1
 description WAN link to R3 (not used)
 no ip address
 shutdown
!
router eigrp 1
 passive-interface default
 no passive-interface FastEthernet0/1
 no passive-interface Serial0/0/0
 network 10.1.1.0 0.0.0.3
 network 10.1.2.0 0.0.0.3
 network 10.1.201.1 0.0.0.0
 no auto-summary
!
ip http server
no ip http secure-server
!
ip flow-export source Loopback0
ip flow-export version 5
ip flow-export destination 10.1.50.1 9996
!
logging source-interface Loopback0
logging 10.1.50.1
!
snmp-server community cisco RO
snmp-server community san-fran RW
snmp-server trap-source Loopback0
snmp-server location TSHOOT Lab Facility
snmp-server contact support@tshoot.net
snmp-server enable traps eigrp
snmp-server enable traps flash insertion removal
snmp-server enable traps config
snmp-server enable traps cpu threshold
snmp-server host 10.1.50.1 version 2c cisco
!
line con 0
 exec-timeout 60 0
 login authentication CONSOLE
 logging synchronous
line vty 0 4
 exec-timeout 60 0
 transport input telnet ssh
!
ntp source Loopback0
ntp update-calendar
ntp server 10.1.202.1
end
```

Router R2

```
!Lab 3-1 Router R2 Baseline Config
!
service timestamps debug datetime msec
service timestamps log datetime msec
service password-encryption
!
```

```
Hostname R2
!
logging buffered 16384 debugging
enable secret ciscoenpa55
!
username admin secret adminpa55
!
banner motd $*** Lab 3-1 Router R2 Baseline Config ***$
!
no ip domain lookup
ip host R1 10.1.2.2 10.1.1.1 10.1.201.1
ip host R2 10.1.1.2 10.1.1.6 10.1.202.1
ip host R3 10.1.1.5 10.1.2.14 10.1.203.1
ip host ALS1 10.1.100.1
ip host DLS1 10.1.100.252 10.1.2.1
ip host DLS2 10.1.100.253 10.1.2.13
!
aaa new-model
aaa authentication login default local
aaa authentication login CONSOLE none
aaa authorization exec default local
!
ip domain name tshoot.net
!
crypto key zeroize rsa
crypto key generate rsa general-keys modulus 1024
!
file prompt quiet
archive
 log config
  logging size 50
  notify syslog
  hidekeys
 path tftp://10.1.50.1/$h-archive-config
 write-memory
!
!
ip telnet source-interface Loopback0
ip ssh source-interface Loopback0
!
interface Loopback0
 ip address 10.1.202.1 255.255.255.255
!
interface FastEthernet0/0
 no ip address
 shutdown
!
interface FastEthernet0/1
 description optional connection for PC-C w/ static address
 no ip addr
 shutdown
!
interface Serial0/0/0
 description WAN link to R1 - 128k leased line
 ip address 10.1.1.2 255.255.255.252
 encapsulation ppp
 no shutdown
```

```
!
interface Serial0/0/1
 description WAN link to R3 - 128k leased line
 ip address 10.1.1.6 255.255.255.252
 clock rate 128000
 encapsulation ppp
 no shutdown
!
router eigrp 1
 passive-interface default
 no passive-interface Serial0/0/0
 no passive-interface Serial0/0/1
 network 10.1.1.0 0.0.0.3
 network 10.1.1.4 0.0.0.3
 network 10.1.202.1 0.0.0.0
 no auto-summary
!
ip http server
no ip http secure-server
!
logging source-interface Loopback0
logging 10.1.50.1
snmp-server community cisco RO
snmp-server community san-fran RW
snmp-server trap-source Loopback0
snmp-server location TSHOOT Lab Facility
snmp-server contact support@tshoot.net
snmp-server enable traps eigrp
snmp-server enable traps flash insertion removal
snmp-server enable traps config
snmp-server enable traps cpu threshold
snmp-server host 10.1.50.1 version 2c cisco
!
line con 0
 exec-timeout 60 0
 login authentication CONSOLE
 logging synchronous
line vty 0 4
 exec-timeout 60 0
 transport input telnet ssh
!
ntp master 3
 end
```

Router R3

```
!Lab 3-1 Router R3 Baseline Config
!
service timestamps debug datetime msec
service timestamps log datetime msec
service password-encryption
!
hostname R3
!
!
logging buffered 16384 debugging
enable secret ciscoenpa55
!
```

```
username admin secret adminpa55
!
banner motd $*** Lab 3-1 Router R3 Baseline Config ***$
!
aaa new-model
aaa authentication login default local
aaa authentication login CONSOLE none
aaa authorization exec default local
!
no ip domain lookup
ip domain-name tshoot.net
ip host R1 10.1.2.2 10.1.1.1 10.1.201.1
ip host R2 10.1.1.2 10.1.1.6 10.1.202.1
ip host R3 10.1.1.5 10.1.2.14 10.1.203.1
ip host ALS1 10.1.100.1
ip host DLS1 10.1.100.252 10.1.2.1
ip host DLS2 10.1.100.253 10.1.2.13
!
crypto key zeroize rsa
crypto key generate rsa general-keys modulus 1024
!
file prompt quiet
archive
 log config
  logging size 50
  notify syslog
  hidekeys
 path tftp://10.1.50.1/$h-archive-config
 write-memory
!
ip telnet source-interface Loopback0
ip ssh source-interface Loopback0
!
interface Loopback0
 ip address 10.1.203.1 255.255.255.255
!
interface FastEthernet0/0
 no ip address
 shutdown

interface FastEthernet0/1
 description FE to DLS2
 ip address 10.1.2.14 255.255.255.252
 ip flow ingress
 speed 100
 full-duplex
 no shutdown
!
interface Serial0/0/0
 description WAN link to R1 - (Not used)
 no ip address
 clock rate 128000
 encapsulation ppp
 shutdown
!
interface Serial0/0/1
 description WAN link to R2 - 128k leased line
 ip address 10.1.1.5 255.255.255.252
```

```
 ip flow ingress
 encapsulation ppp
 no shutdown
!
router eigrp 1
 passive-interface default
 no passive-interface FastEthernet0/1
 no passive-interface Serial0/0/1
 network 10.1.1.4 0.0.0.3
 network 10.1.2.12 0.0.0.3
 network 10.1.203.1 0.0.0.0
 no auto-summary
!
ip http server
no ip http secure-server
!
ip flow-export source Loopback0
ip flow-export version 5
ip flow-export destination 10.1.50.1 9996
!
logging source-interface Loopback0
logging 10.1.50.1
!
snmp-server community cisco RO
snmp-server community san-fran RW
snmp-server trap-source Loopback0
snmp-server location TSHOOT Lab Facility
snmp-server contact support@tshoot.net
snmp-server enable traps eigrp
snmp-server enable traps flash insertion removal
snmp-server enable traps config
snmp-server enable traps cpu threshold
snmp-server host 10.1.50.1 version 2c cisco
!
line con 0
 exec-timeout 60 0
 login authentication CONSOLE
 logging synchronous
line vty 0 4
 exec-timeout 60 0
transport input telnet ssh
!
ntp source Loopback0
ntp update-calendar
ntp server 10.1.202.1
end
```

Chapter 4 Maintaining and Troubleshooting Campus Switched Solutions

Lab 4-1, Layer 2 Connectivity and Spanning Tree

Physical Topology

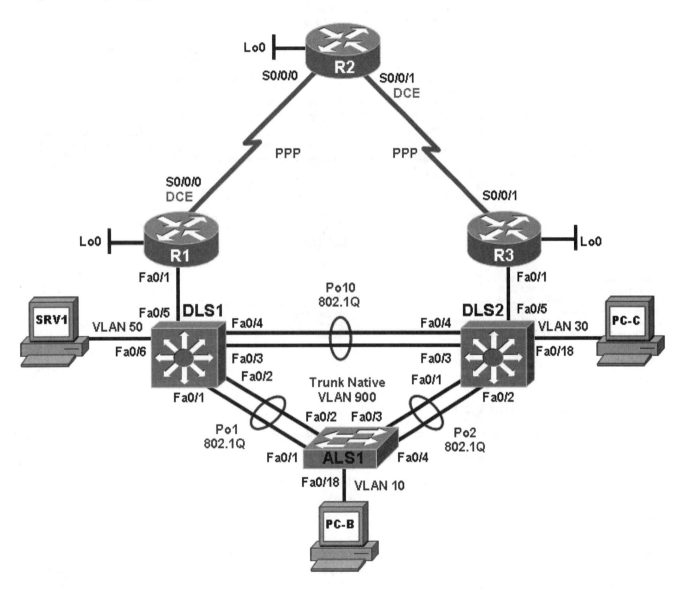

Logical Topology

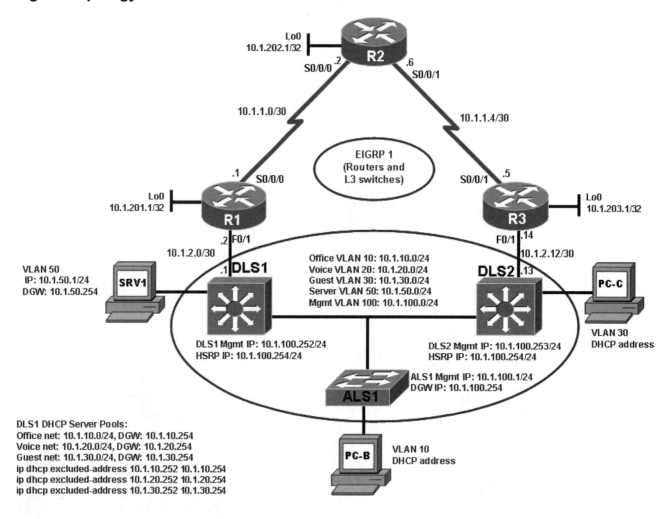

Objectives

- Load the device configuration files for each trouble ticket.

- Diagnose and resolve Layer 2 connectivity problems.

- Diagnose and resolve spanning-tree problems.

- Document the troubleshooting progress, configuration changes, and problem resolution.

Background

User computers, servers, and printers all connect to the access layer of the hierarchical model. With hundreds or thousands of hosts attached, access devices such as Layer 2 switches are a common source of networking issues. Physical and data-link problems at the access layer can include hardware, cabling, VLAN assignment, spanning tree, trunking protocol, or port security issues.

In this lab, you will troubleshoot various Layer 2 problems. For each task or trouble ticket, the scenario and symptoms are described. While troubleshooting, you will discover the cause of the problem, correct it, and then document the process and results.

Physical and Logical Topology Diagrams

The physical and logical topologies, including interface designations and IP addresses, are provided to assist the troubleshooting effort.

Lab Structure

This lab is divided into two main sections.

Section 1—Trouble Tickets and Troubleshooting Logs

This section includes multiple tasks. Each task is associated with a trouble ticket (TT) and introduces one or more errors on one or more devices. If time is a consideration, each task or trouble ticket can be performed independently.

Section 2—Troubleshooting Reference Information

This section provides general Layer 2 troubleshooting information that can be applied to any of the trouble tickets in this lab. Sample troubleshooting flows are provided, along with examples of useful commands and output. If time permits, it is recommended that you read through Section 2 prior to starting on the trouble tickets.

Note: This lab uses Cisco 1841 routers with Cisco IOS Release 12.4(24)T1 and the Advanced IP Services image c1841-advipservicesk9-mz.124-24.T1.bin. The switches are Cisco WS-C2960-24TT-L with the Cisco IOS image c2960-lanbasek9-mz.122-46.SE.bin and Catalyst 3560-24PS with the Cisco IOS image c3560-advipservicesk9-mz.122-46.SE.bin. Other routers (such as 2801 and 2811), switches (such as 2950 or 3550), and Cisco IOS Software versions can be used if they have comparable capabilities and features. Depending on the router or switch model and Cisco IOS Software version, the commands available and output produced might vary from what is shown in this lab.

Note: Any changes made to the baseline configurations or topology (other than errors introduced) are noted in the trouble ticket so that you are aware of them prior to beginning the troubleshooting process.

Required Resources

- 3 routers (Cisco 1841 with Cisco IOS Release 12.4(24)T1 Advanced IP Service or comparable)
- 1 switch (Cisco 2960 with the Cisco IOS Release 12.2(46)SE C2960-LANBASEK9-M image or comparable)
- 2 switches (Cisco 3560 with the Cisco IOS Release 12.2(46)SE C3560-advipservicesK9-mz image or comparable)
- SRV1 (Windows PC with a static IP address) with TFTP and syslog servers, plus an SSH client (PuTTY or comparable) and WireShark software
- PC-B (Windows PC—DHCP client) with PuTTY and WireShark software
- PC-C (Windows PC—DHCP client) with PuTTY and WireShark software
- Serial and Ethernet cables

Section 1—Trouble Tickets and Troubleshooting Logs

Task 1: Trouble Ticket Lab 4-1 TT-A

Step 1: Review trouble ticket Lab 4-1 TT-A.

Late yesterday afternoon, access switch ALS1 failed, and you discovered that the power supply was not working. A junior colleague was tasked with replacing ALS1 with a comparable switch.

When you arrived this morning, you asked him how things went. He told you that he had stayed late trying to reconfigure ALS1, but was not entirely successful. Users on VLAN 10 have started to complain that they cannot get access to the network server SRV1, and you are unable to use Telnet to connect to ALS1 from SRV1. In addition, syslog messages from ALS1 are not being received on SRV1.

Your task is to diagnose the issues and restore switch ALS1 as a fully functional access switch on the network.

Step 2: Load the device trouble ticket configuration files for TT-A.

Using the procedure described in Lab 3-1, verify that the lab configuration files are present in flash. Load the configuration files indicated in the Device Configuration File table.

Note: The following device access methods are in effect after loading the configuration files:

- Console access requires no username or password.
- Telnet and SSH require username **admin** and password **adminpa55**.
- The enable password is **ciscoenpa55**.

Device Configuration File Table

Device Name	File to Load	Notes
ALS1	Lab41-ALS1-TT-A-Cfg.txt	
DLS1	Lab41-DLS1-TT-A-Cfg.txt	
DLS2	Lab41-DLS2-TT-A-Cfg.txt	
R1	Lab41-R1-TT-A-Cfg.txt	
R2	Lab41-R2-TT-A-Cfg.txt	
R3	Lab41-R3-TT-A-Cfg.txt	
SRV1	N/A	Static IP: 10.1.50.1 Default gateway: 10.1.50.254
PC-B	N/A	DHCP (release and renew after loading device configurations)
PC-C	N/A	DHCP (release and renew after loading device configurations)

Step 3: Configure SRV1 and start the syslog and TFTP servers.

Ensure that SRV1 has static IP address 10.1.50.1 and default gateway 10.1.50.254.

Start the syslog server on SRV1, which is the syslog server for the entire network. When the network is properly configured, all devices send syslog messages to SRV1.

Start the TFTP server on SRV1, which is the archive server for the entire network. When the network is properly configured, all devices send archives of their running configurations to this server whenever the running config is copied to the startup config. Ensure that the default TFTP directory on SRV1 is set to the directory where you want to store the archives.

Step 4: Release and renew the DHCP leases on PC-B and PC-C.

Ensure that PC-B and PC-C are configured as DHCP clients.

After loading all TT-A device configuration files, issue the **ipconfig /release** and **ipconfig /renew** commands on PC-B and PC-C.

Note: Problems introduced into the network by the trouble ticket might prevent one or both of these PCs from acquiring an IP address. Do not assign either PC a static address.

Step 5: Outline the troubleshooting approach and validation steps.

Use this space to identify your troubleshooting approach and the key steps to verify that the problem is resolved. Troubleshooting approaches to select from include the follow-the-path, spot-the-differences, bottom-up, top-down, divide-and-conquer, shoot-from-the-hip, and move-the-problem methods.

Note: In addition to a specific approach, you can use the generic troubleshooting process described in the course, which can be found at the beginning of Section 2 of this lab.

_____

_____

_____

_____

_____

_____

Step 6: Record the troubleshooting process and configuration changes.

Note: Section 2 of this lab includes sample troubleshooting flows, useful commands, and examples of output.

Use this log to document your actions and results during the troubleshooting process. List the commands you used to gather information and, as you progress, record your thoughts as to what you think the problem might be and what actions you will take to correct the problems.

Device	Actions and Results

Device	Actions and Results

Step 7: Document trouble ticket debrief notes.

Use this space to make notes of the key learning points that you picked up during the discussion of this trouble ticket with your instructor. The notes can include problems encountered, solutions applied, useful commands employed, alternate solutions, methods, and processes, and procedure and communication improvements.

_____

_____

_____

_____

_____

_____

_____

Task 2: Trouble Ticket Lab 4-1 TT-B

Step 1: Review trouble ticket Lab 4-1 TT-B.

After an equipment failure, a network technician was asked to configure bundled Ethernet links between the ALS1 access switch and the two distribution layer switches in the network (DLS1 and DLS2). Shortly after the changes were made, users on ALS1 were unable to access the Internet (simulated by Lo0 on R2). You have been asked to look into the problem and have determined that you are able to ping the Internet from SRV1.

Your task is to diagnose the issues, allow hosts on ALS1 to connect to the Internet via DLS1 or DLS2, and verify that the switching environment redundant paths are functional.

Note: To simulate an Internet connection, you can ping the R2 Lo0 address at 10.1.202.1. Alternately, you can use the PC browser to connect to 10.1.202.1. You will then be prompted for a login to the router management GUI by R2. Enter the username **admin** and enable password **ciscoenpa55**.

Step 2: Load the device trouble ticket configuration files for TT-B.

Using the procedure described in Lab 3-1, verify that the lab configuration files are present in flash. Load the configuration files indicated in the Device Configuration File table.

Note: See Task 1, Step 2 for device access methods, usernames, and passwords after the configuration files have been loaded.

Device Configuration File Table

Device Name	File to Load	Notes
ALS1	Lab41-ALS1-TT-B-Cfg.txt	
DLS1	Lab41-DLS1-TT-B-Cfg.txt	
DLS2	Lab41-DLS2-TT-B-Cfg.txt	
R1	Lab41-R1-TT-B-Cfg.txt	
R2	Lab41-R2-TT-B-Cfg.txt	
R3	Lab41-R3-TT-B-Cfg.txt	
SRV1	N/A	Static IP: 10.1.50.1 Default gateway: 10.1.50.254
PC-B	N/A	DHCP (release and renew after loading device configurations)
PC-C	N/A	DHCP (release and renew after loading device configurations)

Step 3: Configure SRV1 and start the syslog and TFTP servers as described in Task 1.

Step 4: Reboot PC-B and PC-C or release and renew the DHCP lease as described in Task 1.

Step 5: Outline the troubleshooting approach and validation steps.

Use this space to identify your troubleshooting approach and the key steps to verify that the problem is resolved. Troubleshooting approaches to select from include the follow-the-path, spot-the-differences, bottom-up, top-down, divide-and-conquer, shoot-from-the-hip, and move-the-problem methods.

Note: In addition to a specific approach, you can use the generic troubleshooting process described at the beginning of Section 2 of this lab.

_____

_____

_____

_____

_____

Step 6: Record the troubleshooting process and configuration changes.

Note: Section 2 of this lab includes sample troubleshooting flows, useful commands, and examples of output.

Use this log to document your actions and results during the troubleshooting process. List the commands you used to gather information. As you progress, record what you think the problem might be and what actions you will take to correct the problem.

Device	Actions and Results

Step 7: Document trouble ticket debrief notes.

Use this space to make notes of the key learning points that you picked up during the discussion of this trouble ticket with your instructor. The notes can include problems encountered, solutions applied, useful commands employed, alternate solutions, methods and processes, and procedure and communication improvements.

_____

_____

_____

_____

_____

_____

_____

Task 3: Trouble Ticket Lab 4-1 TT-C

Step 1: Review trouble ticket Lab 4-1 TT-C.

This morning, the help desk received a call from an external consultant that needed access to the SRV1 guest account (simulated by ping). Her PC, PC-C, was plugged into one of the outlets that is patched to the guest VLAN on switch DLS2. However, she has not been able to get an IP address and cannot get onto the network.

Your task is to diagnose and solve this problem, making sure that the consultant gets access to SRV1.

Step 2: Load the device trouble ticket configuration files for TT-C.

Using the procedure described in Lab 3-1, verify that the lab configuration files are present in flash. Load the configuration files indicated in the Device Configuration File table.

Note: See Task 1, Step 2 for device access methods, usernames, and passwords after you have loaded the configuration files.

Device Configuration File Table

Device Name	File to Load	Notes
ALS1	Lab41-ALS1-TT-C-Cfg.txt	
DLS1	Lab41-DLS1-TT-C-Cfg.txt	
DLS2	Lab41-DLS2-TT-C-Cfg.txt	
R1	Lab41-R1-TT-C-Cfg.txt	
R2	Lab41-R2-TT-C-Cfg.txt	
R3	Lab41-R3-TT-C-Cfg.txt	
SRV1	N/A	Static IP: 10.1.50.1 Default gateway: 10.1.50.254
PC-B	N/A	DHCP (release and renew after loading the device configurations)
PC-C	N/A	DHCP (release and renew after loading the device configurations)

Step 3: Configure SRV1 and start the syslog and TFTP servers, as described in Task 1.

Step 4: Reboot PC-B and PC-C or release and renew the DHCP lease, as described in Task 1.

Step 5: Outline the troubleshooting approach and validation steps.

Use this space to identify your troubleshooting approach and the key steps to verify that the problem is resolved. Troubleshooting approaches to select from include the follow-the-path, spot-the-differences, bottom-up, top-down, divide-and-conquer, shoot-from-the-hip, and move-the-problem methods.

Note: In addition to a specific approach, you can use the generic troubleshooting process described at the beginning of Section 2 of this lab.

_____

_____

_____

_____

_____

_____

Step 6: Record the troubleshooting process and configuration changes.

Note: Section 2 of this lab includes sample troubleshooting flows, useful commands, and examples of output.

Use this log to document your actions and results during the troubleshooting process. List the commands you used to gather information. As you progress, record your thoughts as to what you think the problem might be and which actions you take to correct the problem.

Device	Actions and Results

Step 7: Document trouble ticket debrief notes.

Use this space to make notes of the key learning points that you picked up during the discussion of this trouble ticket with your instructor. The notes can include problems encountered, solutions applied, useful commands employed, alternate solutions and methods, and procedure and communication improvements.

_____

_____

Section 2—Troubleshooting Reference Information

General Troubleshooting Process

As a general guideline, you can use the following general troubleshooting process described in the course:

1. Define the problem (symptoms).

2. Gather information.

3. Analyze the information.

4. Propose a hypothesis (possible cause).

5. Test the hypothesis.

6. Eliminate or accept the hypothesis.

7. Solve the problem.

8. Document the problem.

Command Summary

The table lists useful commands for this lab. The sample output is shown on following pages.

Command	Key Information Displayed
`clear arp-cache`	Clears ARP entries and resets aging.
`show arp`	Displays the IP address, MAC address, and interface.
`show interfaces status`	Displays link status, speed, duplex, trunk or VLAN membership, and interface descriptions.
`show cdp neighbors (detail)`	Displays device ID and type and confirms that a link is operational at the data link layer in both directions, including the sending and receiving ports. The **detail** option gives the remote device IP address.
`show spanning-tree vlan` *vlan#*	Displays all essential parameters that affect the topology, such as root port, designated ports, port state, and port type, as well as the spanning-tree mode implemented.
`show spanning-tree inconsistentports`	Displays a more detailed description of the type of port inconsistency and what might be causing it.
`show spanning-tree summary`	Displays the spanning-tree mode and the VLANs for which this switch is the root bridge. VLANs are listed along with the number of ports in various STP states.
`show mac address-table address` *mac-addr*	Displays the MAC address and interface entry in the table for the specified host.
`show mac-address-table interface` *intf-id*	Displays all MAC addresses that were learned on the specified port.
`show vlan brief`	Displays an overview of all existing VLANs and the ports within them. Trunk ports are not listed.

`show vlan id` `vlan#`	Displays whether the VLAN exists and, if so, which ports are assigned to it. Includes trunk ports on which the VLAN is allowed.
`show interfaces` `type/#`	Displays interface status, IP address/prefix, load, duplex, speed and packet statistics and errors.
`show interfaces trunk`	Displays all trunk ports, the operational status, trunk encapsulation, and native VLAN, as well as the list of allowed VLANs, active VLANs, and the VLANs in Spanning Tree Forwarding state for the trunk.
`show interfaces` `type/#` `switchport`	Checks all VLAN-related parameters for a specific interface (access ports and trunk ports).
`show etherchannel summary`	Displays port channels, the member ports, and flags indicating status.

Lab 4-1 Sample Troubleshooting Flows

The figure illustrates an example of a method that you could follow to diagnose and resolve Layer 2 problems.

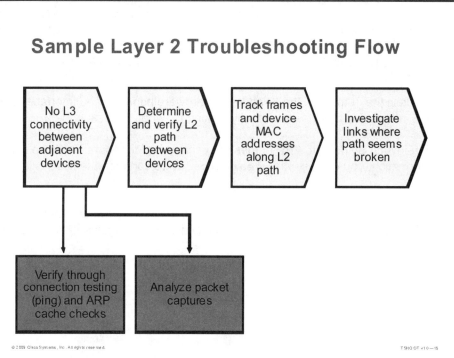

Sample Layer 2 Troubleshooting Flow

TSHOOT v1.0—15

Usually, you start troubleshooting the Layer 2 connectivity between devices because you have discovered that there is no Layer 3 connectivity between two adjacent Layer 2 hosts, such as two hosts in the same VLAN or a host and its default gateway. The following are typical symptoms that could lead you to start examining Layer 2 connectivity:

- Failing pings between adjacent devices. (This can also be caused by a host-based firewall that is blocking pings.)

- Address Resolution Protocol (ARP) failures. After clearing the ARP cache and triggering a connection attempt (for instance, by using ping), ARP entries show up as incomplete or are missing.

- Packets are not being received, which is shown by using a packet sniffer on the receiving host.

Confirm or Deny Layer 3 Connectivity

```
DLS1#ping 10.1.2.2

Type escape sequence to abort.
Sending 5, 100-byte ICMP Echos to 10.1.2.2, timeout is 2 seconds:
.....
Success rate is 0 percent (0/5)

DLS1#clear arp-cache


DLS1#show arp
Protocol   Address          Age (min)   Hardware Addr    Type   Interface
Internet   10.1.10.1                0   0007.e963.ce53   ARPA   Vlan10
Internet   10.1.2.1                 -   0017.5a5b.b442   ARPA   FastEthernet0/5
Internet   10.1.50.1                0   0007.e963.ce53   ARPA   Vlan50
Internet   10.1.100.1               0   001b.0c6d.8f41   ARPA   Vlan100
Internet   10.1.100.254             -   0000.0c07.ac64   ARPA   Vlan100
Internet   10.1.100.253             0   0017.5a53.a3c1   ARPA   Vlan100
Internet   10.1.100.252             -   0017.5a5b.b441   ARPA   Vlan100
Internet   10.1.50.252              -   0017.5a5b.b446   ARPA   Vlan50
Internet   10.1.50.254              -   0000.0c07.ac32   ARPA   Vlan50
Internet   10.1.20.252              -   0017.5a5b.b444   ARPA   Vlan20
Internet   10.1.30.252              -   0017.5a5b.b445   ARPA   Vlan30
Internet   10.1.10.252              -   0017.5a5b.b443   ARPA   Vlan10
```

The most relevant fields in the output are the IP address, hardware address, and interface fields, because these give you the essential information that you are usually looking for when you issue the **show arp** command.

The age field is also relevant. By default, ARP entries are cached for four hours. To make sure that you are looking at current information, you can use the **clear arp-cache** command to flush existing entries from the cache.

If there is a "-" in the age field instead of a number, this entry is local to the switch. These entries represent locally configured IP and MAC addresses, and the switch will respond to ARP requests for these entries.

Sample Layer 2 Troubleshooting Flow

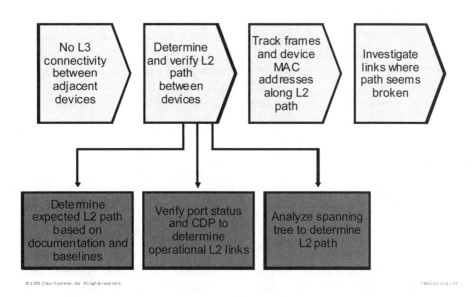

If you have determined that the problem is most likely a Layer 2 or Layer 1 problem, you want to reduce the scope of the potential failures. You can diagnose Layer 2 problems with the following common troubleshooting method:

- Determine the Layer 2 path. Based on documentation, baselines, and knowledge of your network in general, the first step is to determine the path that you would expect frames to follow between the affected hosts. Determining the expected traffic path beforehand helps you in two ways: It gives you a starting point for gathering information about what is actually happening on the network, and it makes it easier to spot abnormal behavior. The second step in determining the Layer 2 path is to follow the expected path and verify that the links on the expected path are actually up and forwarding traffic. If the actual traffic path is different from your expected path, this step might give you clues about the particular links or protocols that are failing and the cause of these failures.

- Track the flow of traffic across the Layer 2 path. By following the expected Layer 2 path and verifying that frames actually flow along that path, you can likely find the spot where the connectivity is failing.

- When you have found the spot where the connectivity is failing, examine the link or links where the path is broken. Now you can apply targeted troubleshooting commands to find the root cause of the problem. Even if you cannot find the underlying cause of the problem yourself, by reducing the scope of the problem, you have a better-defined problem that can be escalated to the next level of support.

Although there are many different approaches to troubleshooting Layer 2 problems, the elements mentioned above will most likely be part of any methodical approach. These elements are not necessarily executed in the presented order. Determining the expected path and verifying the actual path often go hand-in-hand.

To determine the traffic path between the affected hosts, you can combine knowledge from the following sources:

- **Documentation and baselines:** Documentation that was written during design and implementation usually contains information about the intended traffic paths between the hosts. If the documentation does not provide this information, you can usually reconstruct the expected flow of traffic by analyzing network diagrams and configurations.

- **Link status across the path:** A very straightforward check after you have determined the expected path of the traffic is to verify that all ports and links in the path are operational.

- **Spanning-tree topology:** In Layer 2 networks that have a level of redundancy built into the topology, analyze the operation of Spanning Tree Protocol (STP) to determine which of the available links will be used.

Verify Link Status

```
DLS1#show interfaces status

Port     Name                Status        Vlan      Duplex   Speed Type
Fa0/1    Channel to ALS1     connected     trunk     a-full   a-100 10/100BaseTX
Fa0/2    Channel to ALS1     connected     trunk     a-full   a-100 10/100BaseTX
Fa0/3    Channel to DLS2     connected     trunk     a-full   a-100 10/100BaseTX
Fa0/4    Channel to DLS2     connected     trunk     a-full   a-100 10/100BaseTX
Fa0/5    FE to R1            notconnect    routed    full       100 10/100BaseTX
Fa0/6    FE to SRV1          connected     50        a-full   a-100 10/100BaseTX
Fa0/7    Unused              disabled      999       auto      auto 10/100BaseTX
<output omitted>
Fa0/24   Unused              disabled      999       auto      auto 10/100BaseTX
Gi0/1    Unused              disabled      999       auto      auto Not Present
Gi0/2    Unused              disabled      999       auto      auto Not Present
Po1      Channel to ALS1     connected     trunk     a-full   a-100
Po10     Channel to DLS2     connected     trunk     a-full   a-100
```

To determine link status on switches, the **show interfaces status** command is useful because it gives a brief overview of all the interfaces on the switch as well as contains important elements, such as link status, speed, duplex, trunk or VLAN membership, and interface descriptions. If the link is up, the Status field shows "connected." If it is down up, "notconnect" is in the Status field. If the link has been administratively shut down, the status is "disabled."

```
DLS1#show cdp neighbors
Capability Codes: R - Router, T - Trans Bridge, B - Source Route Bridge
                  S - Switch, H - Host, I - IGMP, r - Repeater, P - Phone

Device ID         Local Intrfce    Holdtme    Capability   Platform   Port ID
R1.tshoot.net     Fas 0/5          151          R S I      1841       Fas 0/1
ALS1.tshoot.net   Fas 0/2          153            S I      WS-C2960-  Fas 0/2
ALS1.tshoot.net   Fas 0/1          153            S I      WS-C2960-  Fas 0/1
DLS2.tshoot.net   Fas 0/4          172          R S I      WS-C3560-  Fas 0/4
DLS2.tshoot.net   Fas 0/3          172          R S I      WS-C3560-  Fas 0/3
```

If the Cisco Discovery Protocol is enabled between the switches and routers, you can use the **show cdp neighbor** command to confirm that a link is operational at the data link layer in both directions. Also, it is essential in uncovering cabling problems because it records both the sending and receiving ports, as can be seen in the output above.

Analyze Spanning Tree

```
ALS1#show spanning-tree vlan 10

VLAN0010
  Spanning tree enabled protocol rstp
  Root ID    Priority    24586
             Address     0017.5a5b.b400
             Cost        12
             Port        56 (Port-channel1)
             Hello Time   2 sec  Max Age 20 sec  Forward Delay 15 sec

  Bridge ID  Priority    32778  (priority 32768 sys-id-ext 10)
             Address     001b.0c6d.8f00
             Hello Time   2 sec  Max Age 20 sec  Forward Delay 15 sec
```

```
        Aging Time 300

Interface              Role Sts Cost       Prio.Nbr Type
------------------     ---- --- ---------  -------- --------------------------------

Fa0/18                 Desg FWD 19         128.18   P2p Edge
Po1                    Root FWD 12         128.56   P2p
Po2                    Altn BLK 12         128.64   P2p
```

To analyze the spanning-tree topology and the consequences that STP has for the Layer 2 path, the **show spanning-tree vlan** *vlan-id* command is a good starting point. It lists all essential parameters that affect the topology, such as the root port, designated ports, port state, and port type.

Typical values for the port status field are BLK (blocking) and FWD (forwarding). You might also see LIS or LTN (listening), and LRN (learning) while STP is converging.

The states LBK (loopback), DWN (down), or BKN (broken) typically indicate problems. If the value is BKN, the Type field indicates what is causing the broken status. Possible values are ROOT_Inc, LOOP_Inc, PVID_Inc, TYPE_Inc, or PVST_Inc. To get a more detailed description of the type of inconsistency and what might be causing it, you can examine the output of the **show spanning-tree inconsistentports** command. Interface Type and information includes:

- P2p or Shr to indicate the link type (typically based on duplex status – P2p is full-duplex and Shr is half-duplex or shared Ethernet).

- Edge for edge (PortFast) ports.

- Bound for boundary ports when this switch is running 802.1s (MST) and the other switch is running a different spanning-tree variety. The output also indicates which other type of STP was detected on the port.

- Peer for peer ports when this switch is running Per VLAN Spanning Tree Plus (PVST+) or Per VLAN Rapid Spanning Tree Plus (PVRST+) and the other switch is running a different standard variety of STP (802.1D or 802.1s MST).

Sample Layer 2 Troubleshooting Flow

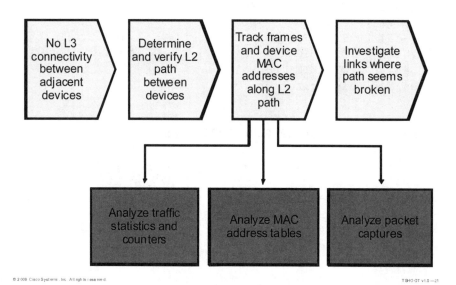

After you have determined the Layer 2 path between the two affected hosts, you can start tracking the traffic between the hosts as it is being switched along the path. The most direct approach to tracking the traffic is to capture packets at set points along the path by using a packet sniffer. Tracking packets in real time is a fairly intensive procedure, and technical limitations might restrict the links where traffic captures could be collected. However, it is the most definitive proof that traffic is or is not flowing along specific paths and links. A less labor-intensive method is to track the flow of traffic by analyzing MAC address tables or traffic statistics. These methods are less direct, because you are not looking at the actual traffic itself but at traces left by the passing of frames.

In a network that has not yet gone into production, packet statistics can help you see where traffic is flowing. On live networks, the test traffic that you are generating will be lost against the background of the live traffic patterns in most cases. However, if the switches that you are using have the capability to track packet statistics for access lists, you might be able to write an access list that matches the specific traffic that you are interested in and isolate the traffic statistics for that type of traffic.

A method of tracing traffic that can be used under all circumstances is analyzing the process of MAC address learning along the Layer 2 path. When a switch receives a frame on a particular port and for a particular VLAN, it records the source MAC address of that frame together with the port and VLAN in the MAC address table. Therefore, if the MAC address of the source host is recorded in a switch but not on the next switch in the path, it indicates a communication problem between these switches for the VLAN concerned, and the link between these switches should be examined.

Analyze MAC Address Tables

```
DLS1#show mac address-table

        Mac Address Table
-------------------------------------------

Vlan    Mac Address       Type        Ports
----    -----------       --------    -----
 <Output omitted>
  50    0000.0c07.ac32    STATIC      CPU
  50    0007.e963.ce53    DYNAMIC     Fa0/6
  50    0017.5a53.a385    DYNAMIC     Po10
  50    0017.5a53.a3c6    DYNAMIC     Po10
  10    0000.0c07.ac0a    DYNAMIC     Po10
  10    000b.db04.a5cd    DYNAMIC     Po1
  20    0000.0c07.ac14    DYNAMIC     Po10
  20    0017.5a53.a385    DYNAMIC     Po10
  30    0000.0c07.ac1e    DYNAMIC     Po10
 100    0000.0c07.ac64    STATIC      CPU
 100    0017.5a53.a3c1    DYNAMIC     Po10
 100    001b.0c6d.8f41    DYNAMIC     Po1
Total Mac Addresses for this criterion: 32


DLS1#show mac address-table address 0000.0c07.ac0a
        Mac Address Table
-------------------------------------------

Vlan    Mac Address       Type        Ports
----    -----------       --------    -----
  10    0000.0c07.ac0a    DYNAMIC     Po10
Total Mac Addresses for this criterion: 1
```

You can use the `show mac-address-table` command to check the content of the MAC address table. Because this table usually contains hundreds to thousands of entries, you can narrow the results to find what you are looking for by using command options.

If you are looking for the MAC address of a specific host, use the `show mac-address-table address` *mac-address* option.

Another useful option is `show mac-address-table interface` *intf-id*, which shows which MAC addresses were learned on a specific port.

Sample Layer 2 Troubleshooting Flow

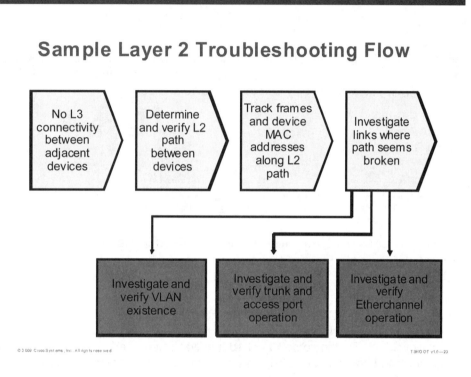

After you have found the spot in the Layer 2 path where one switch is learning the source MAC address and the next switch is not, examine the link between those two switches carefully.

When trying to determine what could cause the MAC address not to be learned on the next switch, consider the following questions:

- Does the VLAN exist on the next switch?

- Is there an operational trunk between the two switches?

- Is the VLAN allowed on the trunk between the switches?

- If an EtherChannel is between the switches, is the EtherChannel fully operational?

Verify VLAN Existence

`ALS1#`**`show vlan brief`**

```
VLAN Name                             Status    Ports
---- -------------------------------- --------- -------------------------------
1    default                          active
10   OFFICE                           active    Fa0/18
20   VOICE                            active    Fa0/18
30   GUEST                            active
```

```
100   MGMT                            active
900   NATIVE                          active
999   UNUSED                          active    Fa0/5, Fa0/6, Fa0/7, Fa0/8
                                                Fa0/9, Fa0/10, Fa0/11, Fa0/12
                                                Fa0/13, Fa0/14, Fa0/15, Fa0/16
                                                Fa0/17, Fa0/19, Fa0/20, Fa0/21
                                                Fa0/22, Fa0/23, Fa0/24, Gi0/1
                                                Gi0/2
1002  fddi-default                    act/unsup
1003  token-ring-default              act/unsup
1004  fddinet-default                 act/unsup
1005  trnet-default                   act/unsup
```

To get a quick overview of all existing VLANs, use the **show vlan brief** command. However, this command does not list the trunk ports. For instance, in the sample output above, trunk ports F0/1, F0/2, F0/3, and F0/4 are not listed. FastEthernet 0/18 is listed as the only port in VLANs 10 and 20.

```
ALS1#show vlan id 10

VLAN Name                             Status    Ports
---- -------------------------------- --------- -------------------------------
10   OFFICE                           active    Fa0/18, Po1, Po2

VLAN Type  SAID       MTU   Parent RingNo BridgeNo Stp  BrdgMode Trans1 Trans2
---- ----- ---------- ----- ------ ------ -------- ---- -------- ------ ------
10   enet  100010     1500  -      -      -        -    -        0      0
```

To verify the existence of a particular VLAN on a switch, use the **show vlan id** *vlan-id* command. This command shows you whether the VLAN exists and which ports are assigned to it. This command includes trunk ports that the VLAN is allowed on. For the same VLAN 10 that was referenced in the previous output, you now see interface port channel 1 and port channel 2 listed as ports that are associated with VLAN 10.

Verify Trunk Operation

```
ALS1#show interfaces trunk

Port        Mode                 Encapsulation Status       Native vlan
Po1         on                   802.1q        trunking     900
Po2         on                   802.1q        trunking     900

Port        Vlans allowed on trunk
Po1         10,20,30,100
Po2         10,20,30,100

Port        Vlans allowed and active in management domain
Po1         10,20,30,100
Po2         10,20,30,100

Port        Vlans in spanning tree forwarding state and not pruned
Po1         10,30,100
Po2         20
```

The easiest way to get an overview of trunk operation is by using the **show interface trunk** command. Not only does it list trunk status, trunk encapsulation, and the native VLAN, but it also lists the allowed VLANs, active VLANs, and VLANs in Spanning Tree Forwarding state for the trunk. The last list can be very helpful in determining whether frames for a particular VLAN will be forwarded on a trunk.

For instance, in the example, you can see that both interface port channel 1 and port channel 2 allow VLANs 10, 20, 30, and 100, but VLANs 10, 30, and 100 are forwarded on port channel 1, while VLAN 20 is forwarded on port channel 2.

Verify VLAN Port Status

```
ALS1#show interfaces fastEthernet 0/18 switchport
Name: Fa0/18
Switchport: Enabled
Administrative Mode: static access
Operational Mode: static access
Administrative Trunking Encapsulation: dot1q
Operational Trunking Encapsulation: native
Negotiation of Trunking: Off
Access Mode VLAN: 10 (OFFICE)
Trunking Native Mode VLAN: 1 (default)
Administrative Native VLAN tagging: enabled
Voice VLAN: 20 (VOICE)
Administrative private-vlan host-association: none
Administrative private-vlan mapping: none
Administrative private-vlan trunk native VLAN: none
Administrative private-vlan trunk Native VLAN tagging: enabled
Administrative private-vlan trunk encapsulation: dot1q
Administrative private-vlan trunk normal VLANs: none
Administrative private-vlan trunk associations: none
Administrative private-vlan trunk mappings: none

<Output Omitted>
```

To check all VLAN-related parameters for a specific interface, use the **show interface** *intf-id* **switchport** command. This command applies to access ports as well as trunk ports. For instance, in the example output, the port is configured as a static access port in VLAN 10, and VLAN 20 is assigned to the port as a voice VLAN.

Verify EtherChannel Operation

```
ALS1#show etherchannel summary
Flags:  D - down         P - bundled in port-channel
        I - stand-alone  s - suspended
        H - Hot-standby (LACP only)
        R - Layer3       S - Layer2
        U - in use       f - failed to allocate aggregator

        M - not in use, minimum links not met
        u - unsuitable for bundling
        w - waiting to be aggregated
        d - default port


Number of channel-groups in use: 2
Number of aggregators:           2

Group  Port-channel  Protocol    Ports
------+-------------+-----------+------------------------------------
```

```
1       Po1(SU)              -         Fa0/1(P)    Fa0/2(P)
2       Po2(SU)              -         Fa0/3(P)    Fa0/4(P)
```

When an EtherChannel is configured between the switches and you suspect that EtherChannel operation could be causing the communication failure between the switches, you can verify this by using the **show etherchannel summary** command. Although the command output is fairly self-explanatory, the typical things to look for is the lowercase "s" flag, which indicates that a physical interface is suspended because of incompatibility with the other ports in the channel or the uppercase "D" flag, which indicates that an interface (physical or port channel) is down.

Reflection Questions

1. Which lab trouble tickets did you have the most difficulty with? _____

_____

_____

_____

2. Would you change anything about the process that you used now that you see the resolution of the problem?

_____

_____

_____

3. Which commands did you find most useful in diagnosing Layer 1 and Layer 2 issues? Add these to your toolbox for future use. Which commands did you find least useful?

_____

_____

_____

Lab 4-1: References

If you need more information on the commands and their options, refer to the following references:

- Command References for Cisco Catalyst LAN Switches
Go to http://www.cisco.com/en/US/products/hw/switches/index.html. Then select Campus LAN and the product family that you are working with. The Command References are under the "Reference Guides" section.

- Virtual LANs and VLAN Trunking Protocol Troubleshooting Tech Notes

www.cisco.com/en/US/tech/tk389/tk689/tsd_technology_support_troubleshooting_technotes_list.html

- Spanning Tree Protocol Troubleshooting Tech Notes

www.cisco.com/en/US/tech/tk389/tk621/tsd_technology_support_troubleshooting_technotes_list.html

- EtherChannel Troubleshooting Tech Notes
www.cisco.com/en/US/tech/tk389/tk213/tsd_technology_support_troubleshooting_technotes_list.html

Router Interface Summary Table

Router Interface Summary				
Router Model	Ethernet Interface #1	Ethernet Interface #2	Serial Interface #1	Serial Interface #2
1700	Fast Ethernet 0 (FA0)	Fast Ethernet 1 (FA1)	Serial 0 (S0)	Serial 1 (S1)
1800	Fast Ethernet 0/0 (FA0/0)	Fast Ethernet 0/1 (FA0/1)	Serial 0/0/0 (S0/0/0)	Serial 0/0/1 (S0/0/1)
2600	Fast Ethernet 0/0 (FA0/0)	Fast Ethernet 0/1 (FA0/1)	Serial 0/0 (S0/0)	Serial 0/1 (S0/1)
2800	Fast Ethernet 0/0 (FA0/0)	Fast Ethernet 0/1 (FA0/1)	Serial 0/0/0 (S0/0/0)	Serial 0/0/1 (S0/0/1)
Note: To find out how the router is configured, look at the interfaces to identify the type of router and how many interfaces the router has. Rather than try to list all the combinations of configurations for each router class, this table includes identifiers for the possible combinations of Ethernet and serial interfaces in the device. The table does not include any other type of interface, even though a specific router might contain one. An example of this is an ISDN BRI interface. The string in parenthesis is the legal abbreviation that can be used in Cisco IOS commands to represent the interface.				

Lab 4-2, Layer 3 Switching and First-Hop Redundancy

Physical Topology

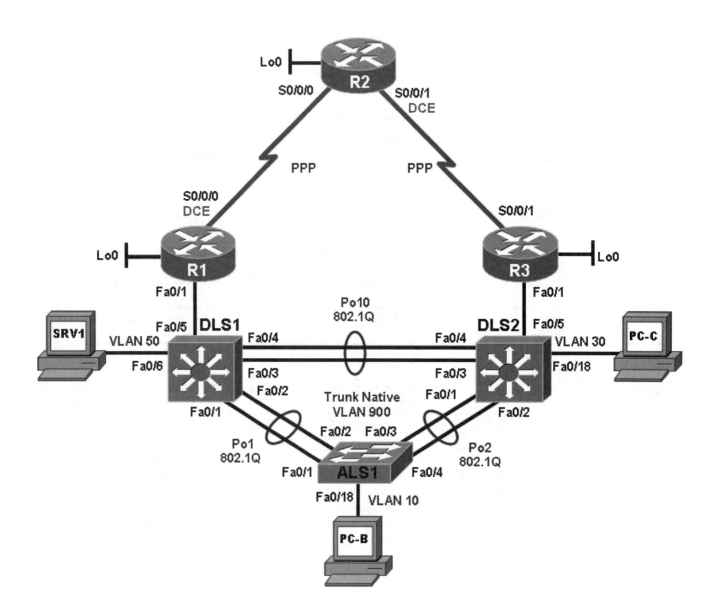

Logical Topology

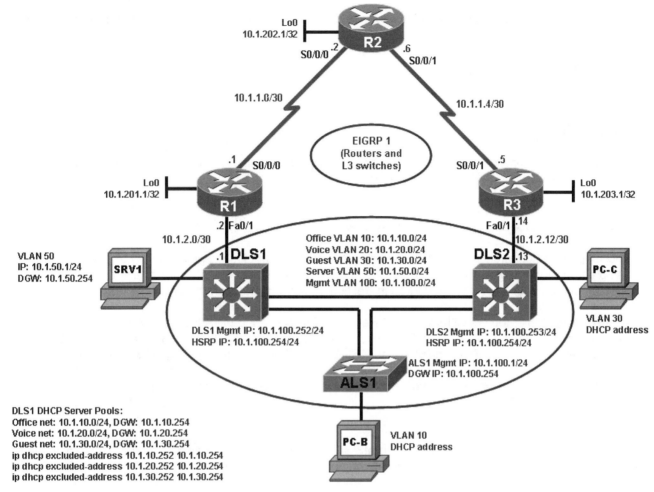

Objectives

- Load the trouble ticket device configuration files for each trouble ticket.
- Diagnose and resolve problems related to switch virtual interfaces and multilayer switching.
- Diagnose and resolve problems related to First Hop Redundancy Protocols.
- Document troubleshooting progress, configuration changes, and problem resolution.

Background

Multilayer (Layer 3) switches have the capability to act as switches and routers when using switch virtual interfaces (SVIs), routed interfaces, and routing protocols. Layer 3 switches allow you to create SVIs or logical interfaces that represent a VLAN. They can also support routed physical interfaces. These versatile switches are frequently used as part of the LAN switch fabric and can be configured with a First Hop Redundancy Protocol (FHRP). Two or more Layer 3 switches (or routers) can provide redundant paths to the network edge for local hosts. A host is configured with a virtual default gateway address. If one of the gateways goes down, the other can take over for the client without the client's knowledge. Examples of FHRPs discussed in this course are Hot Standby Router Protocol (HSRP), Virtual Router Redundancy Protocol (VRRP), and Gateway Load Balancing Protocol (GLBP).

In this lab, you will troubleshoot problems related to Layer 3 switching and FHRPs, such as HSRP, including HSRP authentication. For each task or trouble ticket, the scenario and problem symptom is described. While troubleshooting, you will discover the cause of the problem, correct it, and then document the process and results.

Physical and Logical Topology Diagrams

The physical and logical topologies, including interface designations and IP addresses, are provided to assist the troubleshooting effort.

Lab Structure

This lab is divided into two main sections.

Section 1—Trouble Tickets and Troubleshooting Logs

This section includes multiple tasks. Each task is associated with a trouble ticket (TT) and introduces one or more errors on one or more devices. If time is a consideration, each task or trouble ticket can be performed independently.

Section 2—Troubleshooting Reference Information

This section provides general Layer 2 troubleshooting information that can be applied to any trouble ticket in this lab. Sample troubleshooting flows are provided, along with examples of useful commands and output. If time permits, it is recommended that you read through Section 2 prior to starting on the trouble tickets.

This lab uses Cisco 1841 routers with Cisco IOS Release 12.4(24)T1 and the Advanced IP Services image c1841-advipservicesk9-mz.124-24.T1.bin. The switches are Cisco WS-C2960-24TT-L with the Cisco IOS image c2960-lanbasek9-mz.122-46.SE.bin and Catalyst 3560-24PS with the Cisco IOS image c3560-advipservicesk9-mz.122-46.SE.bin. Other routers (such as 2801 and 2811), switches (such as 2950 or 3550), and Cisco IOS Software versions can be used if they have comparable capabilities and features. Depending on the router or switch model and Cisco IOS Software version, the commands available and output produced might vary from what is shown in this lab.

Note: Any changes made to the baseline configurations or topology (other than errors introduced) are noted in the trouble ticket so that you are aware of them prior to beginning the troubleshooting process.

Required Resources

- 3 routers (Cisco 1841 with Cisco IOS Release 12.4(24)T1 Advanced IP Service or comparable)

- 1 switch (Cisco 2960 with the Cisco IOS Release 12.2(46)SE C2960-LANBASEK9-M image or comparable)

- 2 switches (Cisco 3560 with the Cisco IOS Release 12.2(46)SE C3560-advipservicesK9-mz image or comparable)

- SRV1 (Windows PC with a static IP address) with TFTP and syslog servers plus an SSH client (PuTTY or comparable) and WireShark software.

- PC-B (Windows PC—DHCP client) with PuTTY and WireShark software available

- PC-C (Windows PC—DHCP client) with PuTTY and WireShark software available

- Serial and Ethernet cables

Section 1—Trouble Tickets and Troubleshooting Logs

Task 1: Trouble Ticket Lab 4-2 TT-A

Step 1: Review trouble ticket Lab 4-2 TT-A.

Upon arriving at the office this morning, you find the following ticket in the system:

Switch ALS1 has been showing CRC errors on a group of eight ports for several days. It was suspected that hardware was the cause. During yesterday evening's maintenance window, the switch was replaced with a similar switch from the lab. After this replacement, clients could connect, and no errors were shown on the ports. However, making a backup of the ALS1 configuration to server SRV1 did not work, and no syslog messages from ALS1 are being received by SRV1. The switch is not reachable via Telnet or SSH from server SRV1. There was no time for further research yesterday so, because there is no impact to users, it was decided to leave the switch and pick up this issue the next day.

Your task is to diagnose the issue and restore connectivity between switch ALS1 and server SRV1. After resolving the problem, make a backup of the configuration to server SRV1.

Step 2: Load the device trouble ticket configuration files for TT-A.

Using the procedure described in Lab 3-1, verify that the lab configuration files are present in flash. Load the proper configuration files indicated in the Device Configuration File table.

Note: The following device access methods are in effect after loading the configuration files:

* Console access requires no username or password.

* Telnet and SSH require the username **admin** and password **adminpa55**.

* The **enable** password is **ciscoenpa55**.

Device Configuration File Table

Device Name	File to Load	Notes
ALS1	Lab42-ALS1-TT-A-Cfg.txt	
DLS1	Lab42-DLS1-TT-A-Cfg.txt	
DLS2	Lab42-DLS2-TT-A-Cfg.txt	
R1	Lab42-R1-TT-A-Cfg.txt	
R2	Lab42-R2-TT-A-Cfg.txt	
R3	Lab42-R3-TT-A-Cfg.txt	
SRV1	N/A	Static IP: 10.1.50.1 Default gateway: 10.1.50.254
PC-B	N/A	DHCP (release and renew after loading device configurations)
PC-C	N/A	DHCP (release and renew after loading device configurations)

Step 3: Configure SRV1 and start the syslog and TFTP servers.

a.   Ensure that SRV1 has the static IP address 10.1.50.1 and default gateway 10.1.50.254.

b.   Start the syslog server on SRV1, which is the syslog server for the entire network. When the network is properly configured, all devices send syslog messages to SRV1.

c.   Start the TFTP server on SRV1, which is the archive server for the entire network. When the network is properly configured, all devices send archives of their running configurations to this server whenever the running config is copied to the startup config. Ensure that the default TFTP directory on SRV1 is set to the directory where you want to store the archives.

Step 4: Release and renew the DHCP leases on PC-B and PC-C.

a.   Ensure that PC-B and PC-C are configured as DHCP clients.

b.   After loading all TT-A device configuration files, issue the **ipconfig /release** and **ipconfig /renew** commands on PC-B and PC-C. You might need to repeat this process after the TT problems have been resolved.

   Note: Problems introduced into the network by the trouble ticket might prevent one or both of the PCs from acquiring an IP address. Do not assign either PC a static address.

Step 5: Outline the troubleshooting approach and validation steps.

Use this space to identify the troubleshooting approach that you plan to take and the key steps involved to verify that the problem is resolved. Troubleshooting approaches to select from include the follow-the-path, spot-the-differences, bottom-up, top-down, divide-and-conquer, shoot-from-the-hip, and move-the-problem methods.

Note: In addition to a specific approach, you can use the generic troubleshooting process described at the beginning of Section 2 of this lab.

_____

_____

_____

_____

_____

_____

Step 6: Record the troubleshooting process and configuration changes.

Note: Section 2 of this lab includes sample troubleshooting flows, useful commands, and examples of output.

Use this log to document your actions and results during the troubleshooting process. List the commands you used to gather information. As you progress, record your thoughts as to what you think the problem might be and which actions you take to correct the problem.

Device	Actions and Results

Step 7: Document trouble ticket debrief notes.

Use this space to make notes of the key learning points that you picked up during the discussion of this trouble ticket with your instructor. The notes can include problems encountered, solutions applied, useful commands employed, alternate solutions, methods and processes, and procedure and communication improvements.

_____

_____

_____

_____

_____

_____

_____

Task 2: Trouble Ticket Lab 4-2 TT-B

Step 1: Review trouble ticket Lab 4-2 TT-B.

During last Friday's maintenance window, a series of failover tests at headquarters and the branch offices were executed. It was discovered during a reboot of switch DLS1 that connectivity between clients in OFFICE VLAN 10 and the Internet was lost. After router DLS1 came back online, the clients regained connectivity. This was not the expected behavior, because the network provides gateway first-hop redundancy for clients in the OFFICE VLAN to ensure correct failover during outages.

If one of the HSRP switches fails, the hosts on the OFFICE VLAN should still be able to access the Internet (by pinging R2 Lo0 10.1.202.1 during the outage).

Step 2: Load the device trouble ticket configuration files for TT-B.

Using the procedure described in Lab 3-1, verify that the lab configuration files are present in flash. Load the proper configuration files indicated in the Device Configuration File table.

Note: See Task 1, Step 2 for device access methods, usernames, and passwords after the configuration files have been loaded.

Note: You can test the simulated Internet access by opening a browser and entering the IP address of the R2 Lo0 interface 10.1.202.1. You will be prompted for a username and password. You can gain access to the router GUI management interface by entering username **admin** and the enable password **ciscoenpa55**.

Device Configuration File Table

Device Name	File to Load	Notes
ALS1	Lab42-ALS1-TT-B-Cfg.txt	
DLS1	Lab42-DLS1-TT-B-Cfg.txt	
DLS2	Lab42-DLS2-TT-B-Cfg.txt	
R1	Lab42-R1-TT-B-Cfg.txt	
R2	Lab42-R2-TT-B-Cfg.txt	
R3	Lab42-R3-TT-B-Cfg.txt	
SRV1	N/A	Static IP: 10.1.50.1 Default gateway: 10.1.50.254
PC-B	N/A	DHCP (release and renew after loading device configurations)
PC-C	N/A	DHCP (release and renew after loading device configurations)

Step 3: Configure SRV1 and start the syslog and TFTP servers, as described in Task 1.

Step 4: Release and renew the DHCP leases on PC-B and PC-C, as described in Task 1.

Step 5: Outline the troubleshooting approach and validation steps.

Use this space to identify the troubleshooting approach that you plan to take and the key steps involved to verify that the problem is resolved. Troubleshooting approaches to select from include the follow-the-path, spot-the-differences, bottom-up, top-down, divide-and-conquer, shoot-from-the-hip, and move-the-problem methods.

Note: In addition to a specific approach, you can use the generic troubleshooting process described at the beginning of Section 2 of this lab.

_____

_____

_____

_____

_____

Step 6: Record the troubleshooting process and configuration changes.

Note: Section 2 of this lab includes sample troubleshooting flows, useful commands, and examples of output.

Use this log to document your actions and results during the troubleshooting process. List the commands you used to gather information. As you progress, record your thoughts as to what you think the problem might be and which actions you take to correct the problem.

Device	Actions and Results

Step 7: Document trouble ticket debrief notes.

Use this space to make notes of the key learning points that you picked up during the discussion of this trouble ticket with your instructor. The notes can include problems encountered, solutions applied, and useful commands employed. It can also include alternate solutions, methods, and procedures and communication improvements.

_____

_____

_____

_____

_____

_____

_____

Task 3: Trouble Ticket Lab 4-2 TT-C

Step 1: Review trouble ticket Lab 4-2 TT-C.

Your company has decided to use Message Digest 5 (MD5)-based authentication between the HSRP routers. A colleague of yours was asked to test the authentication using VLAN 100 MGMT (to avoid impact on end users) between DLS1 and DLS2. He started to configure the test late this afternoon but then left on vacation. Your task is to review and verify the implementation of HSRP authentication in VLAN 100 and fix any issues that remain.

Step 2: Load the device trouble ticket configuration files for TT-C.

Using the procedure described in Lab 3-1, verify that the lab configuration files are present in flash. Load the configuration files indicated in the Device Configuration File table.

Note: See Task 1, Step 2 for device access methods, usernames, and passwords after you have loaded the configuration files.

Device Configuration File Table

Device Name	File to Load	Notes
ALS1	Lab42-ALS1-TT-C-Cfg.txt	
DLS1	Lab42-DLS1-TT-C-Cfg.txt	
DLS2	Lab42-DLS2-TT-C-Cfg.txt	
R1	Lab42-R1-TT-C-Cfg.txt	
R2	Lab42-R2-TT-C-Cfg.txt	
R3	Lab42-R3-TT-C-Cfg.txt	
SRV1	N/A	Static IP: 10.1.50.1 Default gateway: 10.1.50.254
PC-B	N/A	DHCP
PC-C	N/A	DHCP

Step 3: Configure SRV1 and start the syslog and TFTP servers, as described in Task 1.

Step 4: Release and renew the DHCP leases on PC-B and PC-C, as described in Task 1.

Step 5: Outline the troubleshooting approach and validation steps.

Use this space to identify the troubleshooting approach you plan to take and the key steps to verify that the problem is resolved. Troubleshooting approaches to select from include the follow-the-path, spot-the-differences, bottom-up, top-down, divide-and-conquer, shoot-from-the-hip, and move-the-problem methods.

Note: In addition to a specific approach, you can use the generic troubleshooting process described at the beginning of Section 2 of this lab.

_____

_____

_____

_____

_____

_____

Step 6: Record the troubleshooting process and configuration changes.

Note: Section 2 of this lab includes sample troubleshooting flows, useful commands, and examples of output.

Use this log to document your actions and results during the troubleshooting process. List the commands you used to gather information. As you progress, record your thoughts as to what you think the problem might be and which actions you take to correct the problem.

Note: You might need to issue the **ipconfig /release** and **ipconfig /renew** commands on DHCP clients after the network device problems are resolved.

Device	Actions and Results

Step 7: Document trouble ticket debrief notes.

Use this space to make notes of the key learning points that you picked up during the discussion of this trouble ticket with your instructor. The notes can include the problems encountered, solutions applied, and useful commands employed. It could also include alternate solutions, methods, and procedures and communication improvements.

_____

_____

_____

_____

_____

_____

_____

Section 2—Troubleshooting Reference Information

General Troubleshooting Process

As a general guideline, you can use the following general troubleshooting process described in the course:

1. Define the problem (symptoms).
2. Gather information.
3. Analyze the information.
4. Propose a hypothesis (possible cause).
5. Test the hypothesis.
6. Eliminate or accept the hypothesis.
7. Solve the problem.
8. Document the problem.

Commands Summary

The table lists useful commands. The sample output is shown on the following pages.

Command	Key Information Displayed
`show spanning-tree vlan` *vlan#*	Displays all essential parameters that affect the topology, such as the root port, designated ports, port state, and port type, as well as the spanning-tree mode being implemented.
`show vlan brief`	Displays a quick overview of all existing VLANs and the ports within them. Trunk ports are not listed.
`show vlan id` *vlan#*	Displays whether the VLAN exists and which ports are assigned to it. Includes the trunk ports on which the VLAN is allowed.
`show interfaces vlan` *vlan#*	Displays the SVI status, IP address, and statistics.
`show ip route` *ip-addr*	Displays the routing table information for a particular destination address.
`show ip arp` *ip-addr*	Displays the ARP table information for an IP address, including age, hardware address, and interface.
`show interfaces` *type/#* | `include bia`	Displays the MAC address of an interface on one output line.
`show ip cef` *ip-addr* `detail`	Displays the next hop and interface used for a particular destination address from the Cisco Express Forwarding table.
`show adjacency` *int-type/#* `detail`	Displays the information contained in the adjacency table for a next-hop IP address or interface.
`show platform forward`	Displays the hardware ternary content addressable memory (TCAM) information and exact forwarding behavior for a Layer 2 or Layer 3 switched frame. **Note:** Specific to the Catalyst 3560 and 3750 series of switches.
`show standby vlan` *vlan#* `brief`	Verify active and standby roles and IP addresses for a particular VLAN for HSRP routers.
`debug standby packets`	Displays real-time messages exchanged between HSRP routers.

Lab 4-2 Sample Troubleshooting Flows

Troubleshooting Multilayer Switching

The figure illustrates an example of a method that you could follow to diagnose and resolve problems related to multilayer switching.

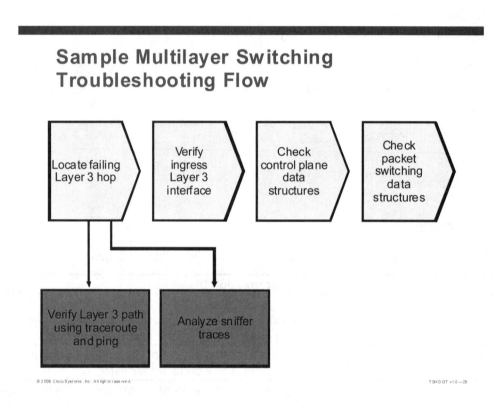

What is multilayer switching? In essence, a multilayer switch is a switch that is capable of switching Ethernet frames based on information in the Layer 2 and Layer 3 headers. Troubleshooting Layer 2 switching was covered in the previous lab exercise. This troubleshooting flow focuses on troubleshooting the process of switching Ethernet frames based on Layer 3 information.

Under which kind of circumstances do you start troubleshooting the multilayer switching process? Troubleshooting multilayer switching is just one of the steps in the bigger picture of troubleshooting network connectivity along a Layer 3 path. After you have determined—by using tools like traceroute or ping or through analysis of packet captures—that a particular hop in the Layer 3 path seems to be the point where packets start to get dropped and that hop is a multilayer switch, or when you are troubleshooting performance problems and you want to find the exact physical links on which packets travel, then start tracing and verifying the Layer 3 forwarding behavior of the multilayer switch that you suspect to be the cause of the problem.

Sample Multilayer Switching Troubleshooting Flow

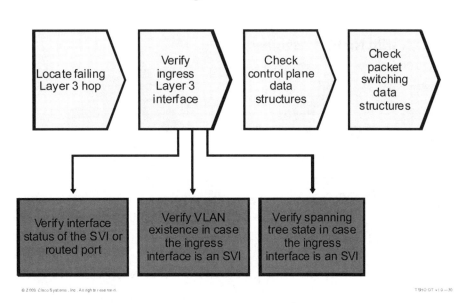

© 2009 Cisco Systems, Inc. All rights reserved.   TSHOOT v1.0—30

Layer 3 packet switching generally consists of three major steps:

1. Receive the packet on a Layer 3 interface. This interface can either be a routed port or an SVI.

2. Perform a lookup in the hardware packet-switching data structures. Multilayer switches store packet-forwarding information in special TCAM data structures. The information contained in these data structures is compiled from the Cisco Express Forwarding data structures in the main memory of the route processor. These data structures are, in turn, derived from control plane tables, such as the routing table and the ARP cache.

3. Rewrite the frame and switch it to the outbound interface based on the information found in the TCAM.

Consequently, a straightforward approach to troubleshooting a Layer3 switching problem is to verify the components that are involved in this process. First, verify the ingress Layer 3 interface, then the control plane data structures and, subsequently, the packet-forwarding data structures. (Alternatively, you can perform these steps in the reverse order.)

If the ingress interface is a routed port, the first step in this process is simple because the Layer 3 and Layer 2 ports are identical. Verifying the physical interface status and the configured IP address and subnet mask for that interface is sufficient to determine the status of the Layer 3 ingress interface. However, if the ingress interface is an SVI, its status is not directly related to any particular physical interface.

Verify SVI Status (Missing VLAN)

```
DLS1#show vlan id 100
VLAN id 100 not found in current VLAN database
```

```
DLS1#show interfaces vlan 100
Vlan100 is down, line protocol is down
  Hardware is EtherSVI, address is 0017.5a5b.b441 (bia 0017.5a5b.b441)
  Internet address is 10.1.100.252/24
```

```
<Output Omitted>
```

A VLAN interface or SVI is up if there is at least one interface in the spanning-tree forwarding state for that VLAN.

This implies that if an SVI is down, you should verify VLAN existence, VLAN port assignments, and the spanning-tree state for the SVI.

In the output above, you can see that a missing VLAN results in a VLAN interface that is in state "down, line protocol is down."

Verify SVI Status (VLAN with No Port Assigned)

```
DLS1#show vlan id 100

VLAN Name                             Status    Ports
---- -------------------------------- --------- -------------------------------
100  MGMT                             active

VLAN Type  SAID       MTU   Parent RingNo BridgeNo Stp  BrdgMode Trans1 Trans2
---- ----- ---------- ----- ------ ------ -------- ---- -------- ------ ------
100  enet  100100     1500  -      -      -        -    -        0      0


DLS1#show interfaces vlan 100
Vlan100 is up, line protocol is down
  Hardware is EtherSVI, address is 0017.5a5b.b441 (bia 0017.5a5b.b441)
  Internet address is 10.1.100.252/24

<Output Omitted>
```

When the VLAN exists but no ports are assigned to that VLAN, the status of the SVI changes to "up, line protocol is down."

Verify SVI Status (VLAN with No Port in Spanning-Tree Forwarding State)

```
DLS1#show spanning-tree vlan 100

<Output Omitted>

Interface          Role Sts Cost      Prio.Nbr Type
------------------ ---- --- --------- -------- -------------------------------

Po1                Desg LRN 12        128.56   P2p
Po10               Desg LRN 12        128.128  P2p

DLS1#show interfaces vlan 100
Vlan100 is up, line protocol is down
  Hardware is EtherSVI, address is 0017.5a5b.b441 (bia 0017.5a5b.b441)
  Internet address is 10.1.100.252/24

<Output Omitted>
```

Finally, if ports are assigned to the VLAN and at least one of these physical ports (trunk or access port) is up, one more condition needs to be met: The spanning-tree state for at least one of the ports needs to be forwarding. Under normal circumstances, if there is at least one interface assigned to a VLAN, an interface is in spanning-tree forwarding state. Either the switch is the root for the VLAN and all the ports assigned to the VLAN are designated ports and therefore forwarding, or the switch is not the root and it has a root port that is in forwarding state.

As a result, when you are troubleshooting a multilayer switching problem and you find that the ingress interface is an SVI and it is down, there is an underlying Layer 2 problem for that VLAN and you need to initiate a Layer 2 troubleshooting process.

Sample Multilayer Switching Troubleshooting Flow

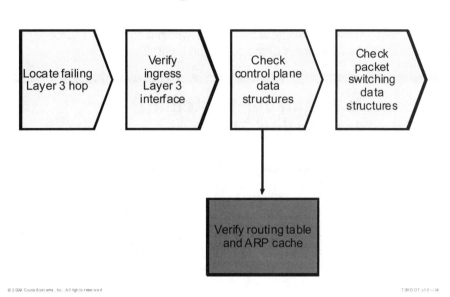

Verify the Routing Table and ARP Cache

The next step in this process is to verify that the control plane information that is necessary to forward the packets is present. The two control plane data structures that are relevant to multilayer switching are the routing table and the ARP cache.

In this sample troubleshooting flow, the multilayer switching data structures for an Internet Control Message Protocol (ICMP) echo request traveling from source IP address 10.1.50.1 to destination IP address 10.1.202.1 is verified by using various **show** commands.

```
DLS1#show ip route 10.1.202.1
Routing entry for 10.1.202.1/32
  Known via "eigrp 1", distance 90, metric 2300416, type internal
  Redistributing via eigrp 1
  Last update from 10.1.2.2 on FastEthernet0/5, 02:41:16 ago
  Routing Descriptor Blocks:
  * 10.1.2.2, from 10.1.2.2, 02:41:16 ago, via FastEthernet0/5
      Route metric is 2300416, traffic share count is 1
      Total delay is 25100 microseconds, minimum bandwidth is 1544 Kbit
      Reliability 255/255, minimum MTU 1500 bytes
      Loading 1/255, Hops 2

DLS1#show ip arp 10.1.2.2
Protocol  Address          Age (min)  Hardware Addr   Type   Interface
Internet  10.1.2.2               162  001b.530d.60b1  ARPA   FastEthernet0/5
DLS1#show interfaces FastEthernet 0/5 | include bia
  Hardware is Fast Ethernet, address is 0017.5a5b.b442 (bia 0017.5a5b.b442)
```

In the output, you can see that a route is found in the routing table for the destination IP address 10.1.202.1, and the next hop and outbound interface for packets with that destination are listed.

If the routing table does not contain an entry (specific prefix or default route) for the destination, the problem is not a packet-switching problem but a routing problem, and you should initiate a process to troubleshoot the routing operation on the control plane.

The ARP cache provides the destination MAC address for the next hop. If an ARP entry for the destination is missing or listed as incomplete, either the next hop listed in the route is not valid, or there is a Layer 2 problem between the multilayer switch and the next hop. In both cases, the problem is not really a multilayer switching problem, and you should investigate the routing operation on the control plane and the Layer 2 connectivity to the next hop first.

The final element that the router needs to rewrite a frame and switch it out is the source MAC address of the frame, which corresponds to the MAC address of the outbound Layer 3 interface.

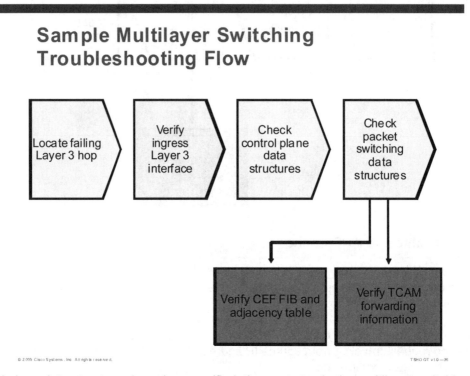

When the control plane data structures have been verified, the next step in the multilayer switching troubleshooting process is to verify the data structures in software and hardware that are used to forward packets.

All recent Layer 3 switches use the Cisco Express Forwarding technology as the foundation for the multilayer switching process. The switches combine the information from the control plane data structure, such as the routing table and the ARP cache, into two different data structures: the Forwarding Information Base (FIB) and the adjacency table. These two data structures are stored in the main memory of the route processor. They are only used to forward packets that are not handled in hardware.

However, based on the information in the FIB and adjacency table, the hardware TCAM is populated, and the resulting TCAM information is what is eventually used to forward frames in hardware.

To verify the correct operation of the multilayer switching process, first verify that the control plane information is accurately reflected in the software FIB and adjacency table. Next, verify that the information from the FIB and adjacency table is correctly compiled into the TCAM.

Verify the FIB and Adjacency Table

```
DLS2#show ip cef 10.1.202.1
10.1.202.1/32
   nexthop 10.1.2.14 FastEthernet0/5

DLS2#show adjacency fastEthernet 0/5 detail
Protocol Interface              Address
IP       FastEthernet0/5        10.1.2.14(19)
                                0 packets, 0 bytes
```

```
epoch 0
sourced in sev-epoch 0
Encap length 14
001B530D6029 00175A53A3C2 0800
L2 destination address byte offset 0
L2 destination address byte length 6
Link-type after encap: ip
ARP
```

The `show ip cef` command can be used in a similar way as the `show ip route` command. When you specify a destination IP address as an option to the command, it lists the entry in the Cisco Express Forwarding FIB that matches that IP address. It also shows the next-hop IP address and egress interface, which serve as a pointer to the adjacency table.

The `show adjacency` command can be used to display the information contained in the adjacency table. The next-hop IP address or interface can be specified to select specific adjacencies. Adding the `detail` keyword to the command shows the frame rewrite information for packets that are switched through that adjacency. The frame rewrite information lists the complete Ethernet header. For the example in the output, this consists of the destination MAC address 001B.530D.6029 (which is the same MAC address that was listed as the MAC address of next hop 10.1.2.14 in the ARP cache), followed by the source MAC address 0017.5A53.A3C2 (which equals the MAC address of the egress interface F0/5), and finally, the Ethertype 0x0800 (which indicates that the protocol contained in the Ethernet frame is IP version 4).

The information displayed in these `show` commands should accurately reflect the information in the routing table and ARP cache.

Verify the Hardware TCAM Information

```
DLS2#show platform forward fa0/3 vlan 50 0017.5a5b.b405 0017.5a53.a385 ip 10.1.50.1
10.1.202.1 icmp 8 0
Ingress:
Global Port Number: 129, lpn: 4 Asic Number: 0
Source Vlan Id: Real 50, Mapped 5. L2EncapType 0, L3EncapType 0

<Output Omitted>

Egress: Asic 0, switch 1
        CPU queues: 7 14.
Source Vlan Id: Real 50, Mapped 5. L2EncapType 0, L3EncapType 0
portMap 0x1000, non-SPAN portMap 0x1000

<Output Omitted>

Port       Vlan       SrcMac          DstMac     Cos   Dscpv
Fa0/5      1006 0017.5a53.a385   0017.5a53.a3c2
```

Note: The `show platform forward` command shown in the above output is specific to the Catalyst 3560 and 3750 series of switches. Consult the documentation for the platform that you are working with to find similar commands to examine the content of the hardware forwarding data structures for the platform.

The `show platform forward` command consults the hardware TCAM information and displays the exact forwarding behavior for a Layer 2 or Layer 3 switched frame.

This command displays the exact forwarding behavior for a packet, taking into account all features that affect packet forwarding, including Cisco Express Forwarding load balancing, EtherChannel load balancing, and packet filtering using access control lists. Therefore, you must specify the exact content of all the relevant fields in the header of the packet.

In the example command output above, the following fields are specified:

- **Ingress interface:** In the example interface, FastEthernet 0/3 is specified as the ingress interface for the packet.

- **Ingress VLAN:** It is not necessary to specify this parameter if the port is an access port. For trunk ports, you must specify the VLAN that the frame is tagged with when it enters the ingress interface. VLAN 50 is specified as the ingress VLAN.

- **Source MAC address:** The source MAC address of the frame when it enters the switch needs to be specified. In the example, the address is 0017.5A5B.B405. This is the MAC address of the egress interface of the previous hop (DLS1 Fa0/3 MAC).

- **Destination MAC address:** The destination MAC address of the frame when it enters the switch needs to be specified. In the example, the address is 0017.5A53.A385 (DLS2 Fa0/3 MAC). For a Layer 3 switched packet, this address is the MAC address of the ingress Layer 3 interface (routed port or SVI).

- **Protocol:** This is not necessary for Layer 2 switched frames. For Layer 3 switching, the Layer 3 protocol that is used and the major fields in that protocol's header must be specified. In the example, IP is listed as the protocol.

- **Source IP address:** When IP is specified as the Layer 3 protocol, the source IP address of the packet must be specified. In the example, it is 10.1.50.1.

- **Destination IP address:** When IP is specified as the Layer 3 protocol, the destination IP address of the packet must be specified. In the example, it is 10.1.202.1.

- **IP protocol:** When IP is specified as the Layer 3 protocol, the protocol in the IP header, for example, TCP, UDP, or ICMP, must be specified. In the example, ICMP is specified because the example represents an ICMP echo request packet.

- **ICMP type and code:** When ICMP is specified as the protocol, the ICMP type and code values must be specified. When TCP or UDP is specified as the protocol, additional header fields that are appropriate for those protocols, such as source and destination port numbers, must be specified. In the example, ICMP type 8 and code 0 are specified to represent an echo request packet.

This command is very powerful because it shows you exactly how frames will be forwarded based on all features that affect forwarding behavior, such as load balancing, EtherChannel, and access control lists. Also, if a frame is dropped instead of forwarded, the command lists the reason why the frame is dropped.

What should you do if somewhere in this chain of verifying the control plane, you find an inconsistency between the software and hardware packet-forwarding data structures?

The process of building the FIB and adjacency table from the routing table and ARP cache, and subsequently populating the TCAM based on the FIB and adjacency table, is internal to the Cisco IOS software and not configurable. Whenever you find an instance where the information in these data structures is not consistent, open a case with the Cisco Technical Assistance Center (provided that you have a valid support contract for your device) to investigate and resolve the issue. As a workaround, you can try to clear the control plane data structures, such as the routing table and the ARP cache, for the particular entries that you are troubleshooting. This triggers both the control plane and the packet-forwarding data structures to be repopulated for those entries and, in certain cases, this might resolve the inconsistencies. However, this is only a workaround, not a real solution, because it only addresses the symptoms of the problem and not the underlying cause.

Troubleshooting First Hop Redundancy Protocols

The figure illustrates an example of a method that you could follow to diagnose and resolve problems related to FHRPs, such as HSRP, VRRP, and GLBP.

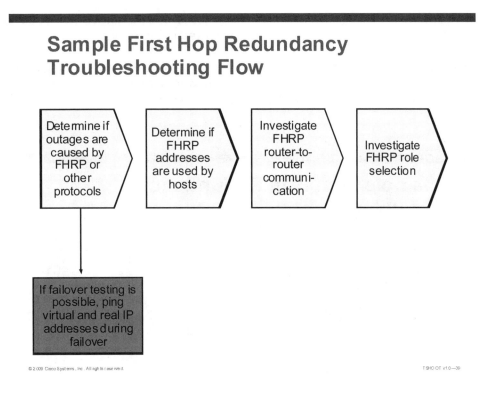

The most common reason to start troubleshooting FHRP behavior is because during an outage or a test, network connectivity is lost for longer than expected when a redundant device or link is temporarily disabled. In redundantly configured IP networks, a number of different protocols usually need to reconverge to recover from a failure. The FHRP that is used is just one of the protocols that could be the cause of the loss of connectivity. Other protocols that need to converge as well—and could be the cause of the problem—are routing protocols and Spanning Tree Protocol (STP).

So how do you determine if the FHRP is the problem?

If you have the opportunity to execute failover tests (for instance, during a scheduled maintenance window), a good way to determine if the problem is caused by the FHRP or by another protocol is by sending multiple continuous pings from a client that is using the virtual router as its default gateway. Ping to the virtual and real IP addresses of the routers that participate in the FHRP, and ping to an IP address of a host that is one or more router hops removed from the client. Observe and compare the behavior of the pings while you force a failover by disabling a device or a link.

Based on the observed differences between the ping responses, you can draw conclusions about the likelihood that the problem is related to the FHRP or to any other protocols that are involved in the convergence. Here are a few examples:

- If you observe that the pings to the real IP address of the redundant router and the virtual IP address of the FHRP both fail at the same time and resume at the same time when you disable the primary router, assume that the problem is not related to the FHRP (because the FHRP does not affect the pings to the real IP address). The most likely cause in this scenario is the Layer 2 convergence for the VLAN, so you should start a Layer 2 troubleshooting procedure.

- If you observe that the pings to the real IP address of the redundant router do not suffer any packet loss, but pings to the virtual IP address fail, this strongly suggests that there is a problem with the FHRP.

- If you observe that the pings to the real IP address of the redundant router and to the virtual IP address do not suffer packet loss, but the ping to the host further out in the network fails, this might indicate an issue with the routing protocol. Alternatively, it could indicate that the client is using the primary router address as its default gateway rather than the virtual IP address.

There are too many possible scenarios, combinations of ping results, and conclusions to list, but important clues can be gained in any scenario by comparing the differences between several pings during a failover.

If you have to troubleshoot without the opportunity to force failover for testing purposes, you might need to assume that the FHRP is the cause of the problem and carefully verify its implementation and operation, even if you cannot determine beforehand if this might be the cause of the problem.

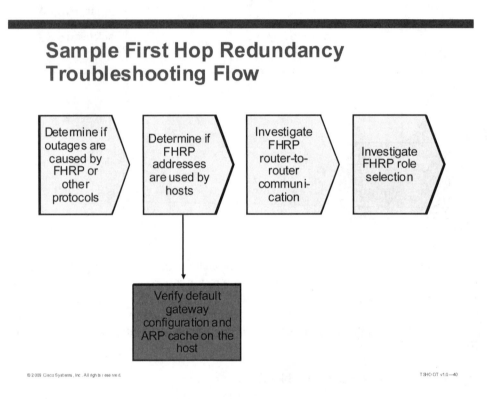

Before starting to troubleshoot the FHRP itself, verify if the client is correctly using the virtual IP address and MAC address of the FHRP as its default gateway. This involves verifying the default gateway configuration (whether statically configured or learned via DHCP) and the ARP cache on the client to verify that both the virtual IP address and the virtual MAC address on the client match the expected values for the FHRP that is in use.

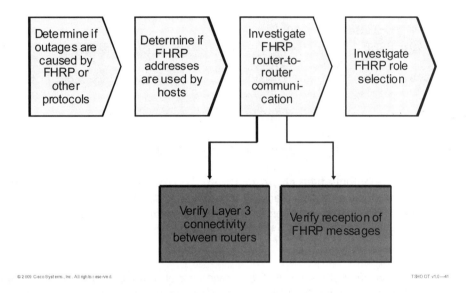

Sample First Hop Redundancy Troubleshooting Flow

Many problems with FHRPs are caused by underlying problems in the Layer 3 connectivity between the routers. Therefore, a good next-step in the troubleshooting process is to verify that there is Layer 3 connectivity between all routers that are participating in the FHRP. Ping from each of the participating routers to the IP addresses of the other participating routers. If one of these pings fail, start a troubleshooting process to diagnose and resolve the Layer 3 connectivity issues between the routers before further investigating the FHRP.

When you have confirmed that there is Layer 3 connectivity between the participating routers in general, you must verify the proper transmission and reception of FHRP packets. To limit potential disruption, always use **show** commands to gather information before using **debug** commands.

Verify Reception of FHRP Messages

```
DLS1#show standby vlan 100 brief
                     P indicates configured to preempt.
                     |
Interface   Grp  Pri P State  Active          Standby         Virtual IP
Vl100       100  110 P Active local           10.1.100.253    10.1.100.254


DLS2#show standby vlan 100 brief
                     P indicates configured to preempt.
                     |
Interface   Grp  Pri P State    Active          Standby       Virtual IP
Vl100       100  100 P Standby  10.1.100.252    local         10.1.100.254
```

This example shows how to confirm proper transmission and reception of HSRP messages. For GLBP or VRRP, the procedure is similar, although the command output is slightly different.

To confirm the proper reception of HSRP messages on all routers in the group, verify that all routers list an active and a standby router and that these roles are listed in a consistent way across all the routers. The **show standby brief** command is concise and still shows the most relevant information. As you can see in the example, switch DLS2 lists the IP address of switch DLS1 as the active router. As the standby router, it lists "local" to indicate that it considers itself to be the standby router. On switch DLS1, the situation is the opposite: The address of switch DLS2 is listed as the standby address, while the active router is listed as local. While you are verifying these roles, this is also a good opportunity to confirm that both the standby group number and the virtual IP address are configured in a consistent manner. Misconfiguration of these parameters is a common cause of HSRP problems.

```
DLS1#debug standby packets

DLS1#show logging | include Grp 100
Oct 26 15:29:00.049: HSRP: Vl100 Grp 100 Hello  in  10.1.100.253 Standby pri 100 vIP
10.1.100.254
Oct 26 15:29:01.659: HSRP: Vl100 Grp 100 Hello  out 10.1.100.252 Active  pri 110 vIP
10.1.100.254
```

Note: If you used Telnet, you cannot see the debug messages without using the **terminal monitor** command.

If you find inconsistencies in the output of the **show standby brief** commands, such as a missing standby router on one of the routers or multiple routers claiming the active or standby role for a group, this strongly suggests that there is a problem with the reception or interpretation of the HSRP messages on the routers. A **debug** command can now be used to investigate the transmission and reception of HSRP messages to gather more clues about the failure.

Before enabling a debug, first verify that the CPU of the device is not running at such high levels that adding the load of a debug would risk overloading the CPU. Secondly, it is always good to have a fallback plan to stop the debug when it unexpectedly starts to affect the performance of the device. For instance, you could open a second connection to the device and before you enable the debug in your primary session, type the **undebug all** command in the secondary session, but do not confirm it by pressing the Enter key yet. Another fallback scenario is to schedule a timed reload within a short time by using the **reload in** command. If you lose your connection to the device as a result of your debug, you can be assured that it will reload shortly and you will be able to reconnect to it. And finally, you should always refer to your organization's policies before executing any commands on a device that put the operation of the network at risk.

The **debug standby packets** command displays all HSRP packets sent or received by the device. This can quickly generate a lot of output, especially if you have configured many different HSRP groups or if you have tuned the hello timer to be shorter than the default value of three seconds. To make it easier to select the packets that you are interested in, you could use the technique shown in the example above. Instead of logging the debug output to the console or virtual terminal session, you can capture the output in a buffer in the device's RAM and then display the buffer's content by using the **show logging** command. The output of the command can then be filtered by using a regular expression to select the HSRP group that you are interested in.

In the example above, the output reveals that hellos are sent by this router and received from the other router. Just like the **show** commands in the previous output examples, execute the **debug** command on both routers to spot possible differences in behavior between the devices.

Do not forget to disable the debug by using the **no debug** command after you have gathered the information that you were interested in.

If these debugs reveal that HSRP protocol packets are not properly received on any router, check if access lists are blocking the packets. Given that you have already verified the Layer 3 connectivity between the devices, this problem should be on a higher layer.

Sample First Hop Redundancy Troubleshooting Flow

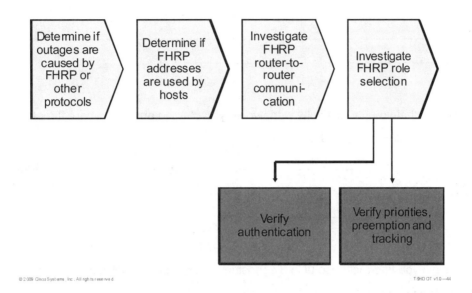

After you have established that FHRP messages are sent and received properly on all routers and still the FHRP does not perform as expected, the problem must be related to the role selection and transferring roles between routers during failover. You might need to verify two potential problem areas.

If the FHRP is using authentication and there is a mismatch between the authentication parameters, the devices will not accept each other's messages as valid when they are received. A typical symptom is that more than one router considers itself to be the active router for a group.

For all FHRPs, role selection is influenced by two parameters: priority and preemption. Tracking objects such as interfaces and routes can further alter these priorities. If an unexpected router is selected for the primary role at any point in the process, carefully analyze the priorities configured on the different devices and how they are affected by potential tracking options. However, to properly determine how properties behave during a failover, you must be able to force a failover, which means that you might need to postpone this type of testing until a regularly scheduled maintenance interval.

Reflection Questions

1. Which lab trouble tickets did you have the most difficulty with? _____

_____

_____

_____

2. For the trouble tickets that you had difficulty with, would you change anything about the process that you used now that you see the resolution of the problem? _____

_____

_____

_____

3. Which commands did you find most useful in diagnosing Layer 3 and HSRP issues? Add these to your toolbox for future use. Which commands did you find least useful?

_____

_____

_____

References

If you need more information on the commands and their options, see the following references:

- Command References for Cisco Catalyst LAN Switches
  Go to http://www.cisco.com/en/US/products/hw/switches/index.html. Then select product category (Campus LAN) and the model you are working with (for example 3560-E). The Command References for various IOS releases are under the "Reference Guides" section.

- Virtual LANs and VLAN Trunking Protocol Troubleshooting Tech Notes
  www.cisco.com/en/US/tech/tk389/tk689/tsd_technology_support_troubleshooting_technotes_list.html

- Layer 3 Switching and Forwarding Troubleshooting Tech Notes
  www.cisco.com/en/US/tech/tk389/tk815/tsd_technology_support_troubleshooting_technotes_list.html

Router Interface Summary Table

Router Interface Summary				
Router Model	Ethernet Interface #1	Ethernet Interface #2	Serial Interface #1	Serial Interface #2
1700	Fast Ethernet 0 (FA0)	Fast Ethernet 1 (FA1)	Serial 0 (S0)	Serial 1 (S1)
1800	Fast Ethernet 0/0 (FA0/0)	Fast Ethernet 0/1 (FA0/1)	Serial 0/0/0 (S0/0/0)	Serial 0/0/1 (S0/0/1)
2600	Fast Ethernet 0/0 (FA0/0)	Fast Ethernet 0/1 (FA0/1)	Serial 0/0 (S0/0)	Serial 0/1 (S0/1)
2800	Fast Ethernet 0/0 (FA0/0)	Fast Ethernet 0/1 (FA0/1)	Serial 0/0/0 (S0/0/0)	Serial 0/0/1 (S0/0/1)

Note: To find out how the router is configured, look at the interfaces to identify the type of router and how many interfaces the router has. Rather than try to list all the combinations of configurations for each router class, this table includes identifiers for the possible combinations of Ethernet and serial interfaces in the device. The table does not include any other type of interface, even though a specific router might contain one. An example of this is an ISDN BRI interface. The string in parenthesis is the legal abbreviation that can be used in Cisco IOS commands to represent the interface.

Chapter 5 Maintaining and Troubleshooting Routing Solutions

Lab 5-1, Layer 3 Connectivity and EIGRP

Physical Topology

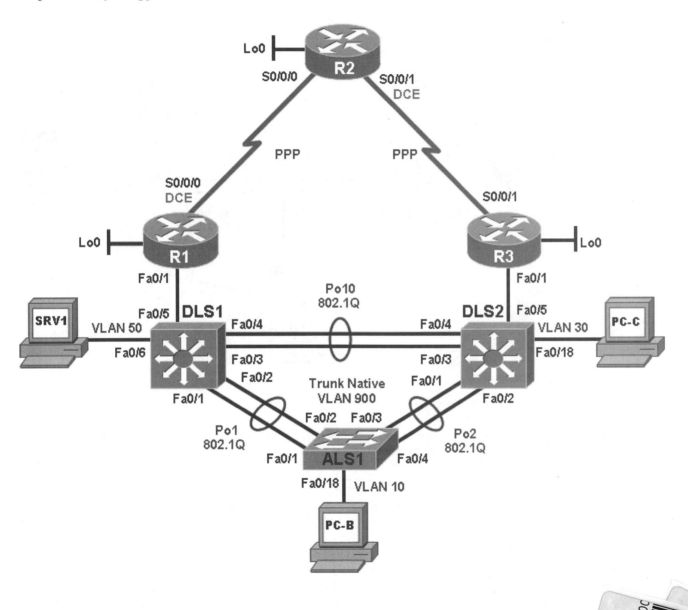

Logical Topology

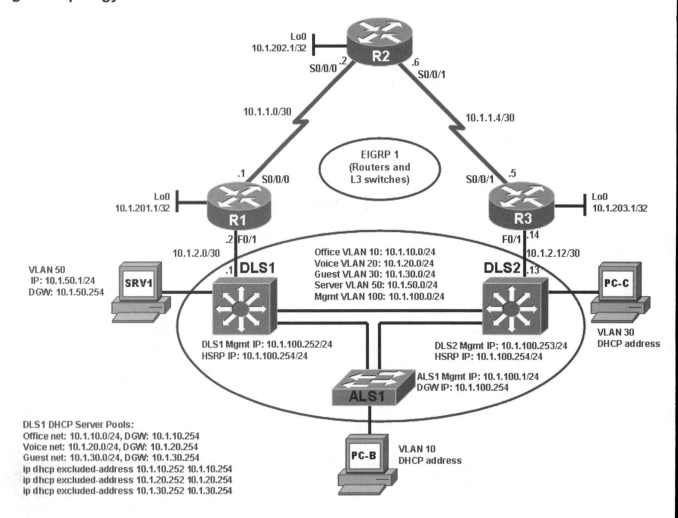

Objectives

- Load the trouble ticket device configuration files for each trouble ticket.

- Diagnose and resolve problems related to network layer connectivity.

- Diagnose and resolve problems related to EIGRP.

- Document troubleshooting progress, configuration changes, and problem resolution.

Background

Because of the complexity of modern networks, Layer 3 routing issues are quite common and can also be difficult to troubleshoot. One of the most widely used enterprise routing protocols is Enhanced Interior Gateway Routing Protocol (EIGRP). It is a Cisco proprietary distance vector, classless routing protocol that was released in 1992 with Cisco IOS Release 9.21. EIGRP has features that are not commonly found in other distance vector routing protocols, such as the following:

- Reliable Transport Protocol (RTP)

- Bounded updates

- Diffusing Update Algorithm (DUAL)

- Establishing adjacencies

- Neighbor and topology tables

In this lab, you will troubleshoot problems related to Layer 3 connectivity and routing problems related to EIGRP.

For each task or trouble ticket, the trouble scenario and problem symptom are described. While troubleshooting, you will discover the cause of the problem, correct it, and then document the process and results.

Physical and Logical Topology Diagrams

The physical and logical topologies, including the interface designations and IP addresses, are provided to assist the troubleshooting effort.

Lab Structure

This lab is divided into two main sections.

Section 1—Trouble Tickets and Troubleshooting Logs

This section includes multiple tasks. Each task is associated with a trouble ticket (TT) and introduces one or more errors on one or more devices. If time is a consideration, each task or trouble ticket can be performed independently.

Section 2—Troubleshooting Reference Information

This section provides general Layer 3 and EIGRP troubleshooting information that can be applied to any trouble ticket in this lab. Sample troubleshooting flows are provided, along with examples of useful commands and output. If time permits, it is recommended that you read through Section 2 prior to starting on the trouble tickets.

Note: This lab uses Cisco 1841 routers with Cisco IOS Release 12.4(24)T1 and the Advanced IP Services image c1841-advipservicesk9-mz.124-24.T1.bin. The switches are Cisco WS-C2960-24TT-L with the Cisco IOS image c2960-lanbasek9-mz.122-46.SE.bin and Catalyst 3560-24PS with the Cisco IOS image c3560-advipservicesk9-mz.122-46.SE.bin. Other routers (such as 2801 and 2811), switches (such as 2950 or 3550), and Cisco IOS Software versions can be used if they have comparable capabilities and features. Depending on the router or switch model and Cisco IOS Software version, the commands available and output produced might vary from what is shown in this lab.

Required Resources

- 3 routers (Cisco 1841 with Cisco IOS Release 12.4(24)T1 Advanced IP Service or comparable)
- 1 switch (Cisco 2960 with the Cisco IOS Release 12.2(46)SE C2960-LANBASEK9-M image or comparable)
- 2 switches (Cisco 3560 with the Cisco IOS Release 12.2(46)SE C3560-advipservicesk9-mz image or comparable)
- SRV1 (Windows PC with a static IP address) with TFTP and syslog servers, plus an SSH client (PuTTY or comparable) and WireShark software
- PC-B (Windows PC—DHCP client) with PuTTY and WireShark software
- PC-C (Windows PC—DHCP client) with PuTTY and WireShark software
- Serial and Ethernet cables

Section 1—Trouble Tickets and Troubleshooting Logs

Task 1: Trouble Ticket Lab 5-1 TT-A

Step 1: Review trouble ticket Lab 5-1 TT-A.

Your company is interested in implementing an IP-based closed circuit television (CCTV) solution. Currently, different solutions and vendors are being evaluated. One of the vendors has offered to implement a pilot to show the capabilities of their solution. To keep the traffic associated with the CCTV solution separate from the regular network traffic, it will be implemented using a new VLAN (VLAN 70 corresponding to subnet 10.1.70.0/24). There must be communication between the test server (PC-C) and the office users on the LAN. In addition, branch workers on the R2 LAN (simulated by Lo0) must be able to access the internal CCTV server.

The vendor will come in tomorrow to install the client and server software. The network team has been asked to make sure that the new VLAN has been implemented and that there is IP connectivity between the local test client (PC-B) and the CCTV test server (PC-C) in the CCTV VLAN. You must also verify that there is connectivity between the remote test client (Lo0 on R2) and the CCTV test server. The test server requires a static IP address. One of your colleagues implemented the static address yesterday afternoon, but did not have time to test the implementation.

You have the following tasks:

- Configure the CCTV test server (PC-C).

- Verify the CCTV VLAN device configurations for the pilot.

- Ensure that the local and remote test clients can communicate with the CCTV test server before the vendor arrives to implement the CCTV pilot.

- Verify Hot Standby Router Protocol (HSRP) redundancy for CCTV VLAN 70.

Step 2: Load the device trouble ticket configuration files for TT-A.

Using the procedure described in Lab 3-1, verify that the lab configuration files are present in flash. Load the configuration files indicated in the Device Configuration File table.

Note: The following device access methods are in effect after loading the configuration files:

- Console access requires no username or password.

- Telnet and SSH require username **admin** and password **adminpa55**.

- The enable password is **ciscoenpa55**.

Device Configuration File Table

Device Name	File to Load	Notes
ALS1	Lab51-ALS1-TT-A-Cfg.txt	
DLS1	Lab51-DLS1-TT-A-Cfg.txt	
DLS2	Lab51-DLS2-TT-A-Cfg.txt	
R1	Lab51-R1-TT-A-Cfg.txt	
R2	Lab51-R2-TT-A-Cfg.txt	
R3	Lab51-R3-TT-A-Cfg.txt	

SRV1	N/A	Static IP: 10.1.50.1 Default gateway: 10.1.50.254
PC-B	N/A	DHCP (test CCTV client)
PC-C	N/A	Static (test CCTV server)

Step 3: Configure the CCTV server IP address.

Configure the test server PC-C with a static IP address in the CCTV test VLAN subnet 10.1.70.0/24. According to the test plan, the default gateway should be the last usable IP address in the subnet.

Note: After this TT is completed, restore PC-C to its status as a DHCP client in VLAN 30.

Step 4: Release and renew the DHCP lease on PC-B.

Ensure that PC-B is configured as a DHCP client in the OFFICE VLAN.

After loading all TT-A device configuration files, issue the **ipconfig /release** and **ipconfig /renew** commands on PC-B.

Step 5: Outline the troubleshooting approach and validation steps.

Use this space to identify your troubleshooting approach and the key steps to verify that the problem is resolved. Troubleshooting approaches to select from include: follow-the-path, spot-the-differences, bottom-up, top-down, divide-and-conquer, shoot-from-the-hip, and move-the-problem.

Note: In addition to a specific approach, you can use the generic troubleshooting process described at the beginning of Section 2 of this lab.

_____

_____

_____

_____

_____

Step 6: Record the troubleshooting process and configuration changes.

Note: Section 2 of this lab includes sample troubleshooting flows, useful commands, and examples of output.

Use this log to document your actions and results during the troubleshooting process. List the commands you used to gather information. As you progress, record what you think the problem might be and which actions you will take to correct the problem.

Device	Actions and Results

Device	Actions and Results

Step 7: Document trouble ticket debrief notes.

Use this space to make notes of the key learning points that you picked up during the discussion of this trouble ticket with your instructor. The notes can include problems encountered, solutions applied, useful commands employed, alternate solutions, methods and processes, and procedure and communication improvements.

_____

_____

_____

_____

_____

_____

Task 2: Trouble Ticket Lab 5-1 TT-B

Step 1: Review trouble ticket Lab 5-1 TT-B.

You receive an emergency call and are told that a short circuit caused a small fire in the server room. Routers R1 and R3, which were mounted in the same rack, were damaged. Luckily, you had two comparable spare routers in storage. When you arrive at the office, two of your colleagues have already installed the replacement routers, cabled them, and tried to restore the routers by cutting and pasting the configurations from the console. However, the routers are not operational when you come in.

You receive a call from the network administrator at the branch office (LAN simulated by R2 Lo0) asking about the loss of the WAN. His users cannot access server SRV1 at the central site. He has started to troubleshoot. You tell him what happened and ask him not to do anything until you have resolved the problem at the central site.

Your task is to check the configuration of routers R1 and R3 and restore the configurations as necessary to regain connectivity between the branch office and the central site across the WAN.

Step 2: Load the device trouble ticket configuration files for TT-B.

Using the procedure described in Lab 3-1, verify that the lab configuration files are present in flash. Load the configuration files indicated in the Device Configuration File table.

Note: See Task 1, Step 2 for device access methods, usernames, and passwords after the configuration files have been loaded.

Device Configuration File Table

Device Name	File to Load	Notes
ALS1	Lab51-ALS1-TT-B-Cfg.txt	
DLS1	Lab51-DLS1-TT-B-Cfg.txt	
DLS2	Lab51-DLS2-TT-B-Cfg.txt	
R1	Lab51-R1-TT-B-Cfg.txt	
R2	Lab51-R2-TT-B-Cfg.txt	
R3	Lab51-R3-TT-B-Cfg.txt	
SRV1	N/A	Static IP: 10.1.50.1 Default gateway: 10.1.50.254
PC-B	N/A	DHCP (release and renew after loading device configurations)
PC-C	N/A	DHCP (release and renew after loading device configurations)

Step 3: Configure SRV1 and start the syslog and TFTP servers, as described in Task 1.

Step 4: Release and renew the DHCP leases on PC-B and PC-C, as described in Task 1.

Step 5: Outline the troubleshooting approach and validation steps.

Use this space to identify your troubleshooting approach and the key steps to verify that the problem is resolved. Troubleshooting approaches to select from include: follow-the-path, spot-the-differences, bottom-up, top-down, divide-and-conquer, shoot-from-the-hip, and move-the-problem.

Note: In addition to a specific approach, you can use the generic troubleshooting process described at the beginning of Section 2 of this lab.

_____

_____

_____

_____

_____

Step 6: Record the troubleshooting process and configuration changes.

Note: Section 2 of this lab includes sample troubleshooting flows, useful commands, and examples of output.

Use this log to document your actions and results during the troubleshooting process. List the commands you used to gather information. As you progress, record what you think the problem might be and which actions you will take to correct the problem.

Device	Actions and Results

Device	Actions and Results

Step 7: Document trouble ticket debrief notes.

Use this space to make notes of the key learning points that you picked up during the discussion of this trouble ticket with your instructor. The notes can include problems encountered, solutions applied, useful commands employed, alternate solutions, methods and procedure, and procedure and communication improvements.

_____

_____

_____

_____

_____

_____

_____

Task 3: Trouble Ticket Lab 5-1 TT-C

Step 1: Review trouble ticket Lab 5-1 TT-C.

A user on VLAN 10 (PC-B) called the help desk this morning because she does not have Internet access. When she tried to open a website (simulated by another Loopback Lo1 on R2 with address 209.165.200.225/30), she received an error message from her browser saying that it cannot display the web page. She can reach the internal server SRV1 without any problems.

One of your colleagues was working with the ISP to make some changes to the routing model used to access the ISP and the Internet. The ISP does not run EIGRP on its router. The colleague has called in sick today, but made some notes in the log about the ISP not running EIGRP on its router and not wanting R2 to attempt to establish an EIGRP neighbor relationship.

Your task is to diagnose and solve this problem and make sure that the user regains connectivity to the Internet.

Step 2: Load the device trouble ticket configuration files for TT-C.

Using the procedure described in Lab 3-1, verify that the lab configuration files are present in flash. Load the proper configuration files indicated in the Device Configuration File table.

Note: See Task 1, Step 2 for device access methods, usernames, and passwords after the configuration files have been loaded.

Device Configuration File Table

Device Name	File to Load	Notes
ALS1	Lab51-ALS1-TT-C-Cfg.txt	
DLS1	Lab51-DLS1-TT-C-Cfg.txt	
DLS2	Lab51-DLS2-TT-C-Cfg.txt	
R1	Lab51-R1-TT-C-Cfg.txt	
R2	Lab51-R2-TT-C-Cfg.txt	
R3	Lab51-R3-TT-C-Cfg.txt	
SRV1	N/A	Static IP: 10.1.50.1 Default gateway: 10.1.50.254
PC-B	N/A	DHCP
PC-C	N/A	DHCP

Step 3: Configure SRV1 and start the syslog and TFTP servers, as described in Task 1.

Step 4: Release and renew the DHCP leases on PC-B and PC-C, as described in Task 1.

Step 5: Outline the troubleshooting approach and validation steps.

Use this space to identify your troubleshooting approach and the key steps to verify that the problem is resolved. Troubleshooting approaches to select from include: follow-the-path, spot-the-differences, bottom-up, top-down, divide-and-conquer, shoot-from-the-hip, and move-the-problem.

Note: In addition to a specific approach, you can use the generic troubleshooting process described at the beginning of Section 2 of this lab.

_____

_____

_____

_____

_____

_____

Step 6: Record the troubleshooting process and configuration changes.

Note: Section 2 of this lab includes sample troubleshooting flows, useful commands, and examples of output.

Use this log to document your actions and results during the troubleshooting process. List the commands you used to gather information. As you progress, record what you think the problem might be and which actions you will take to correct the problems.

Device	Actions and Results

Step 7: Document trouble ticket debrief notes.

Use this space to make notes of the key learning points that you picked up during the discussion of this trouble ticket with your instructor. The notes can include problems encountered, solutions applied, useful commands employed, alternate solutions and methods, and procedure and communication improvements.

_____

_____

_____

_____

_____

_____

_____

Task 4: Trouble Ticket Lab 5-1 TT-D

Step 1: Review trouble ticket Lab 5-1 TT-D.

A contract worker called the help desk to report that he could not access the ISP email server (simulated by Lo0 on R2). He was working at a PC that is attached to a port in the GUEST VLAN (PC-C). You checked with the ISP and discovered that they had an unplanned outage, and the WAN link from R2 to R3 had gone down temporarily. Users in the OFFICE VLAN did not experience any loss of connectivity to the email server during the WAN link outage. Your expectation, if one of the WAN links went down, was that users in the GUEST VLAN would still be able to reach the server because of the redundancy in the network design.

Your colleague will replicate this scenario during the maintenance window this evening. You have agreed to help her diagnose the problem and propose a plan that can account for an outage in one of the WAN links to R2 so that guest users do not lose connectivity to the ISP mail server.

Your plan is to simulate the R3-to-R2 WAN link going down. You do not have administrative control over ISP router R2. You will test connectivity, determine the cause of the problem, and recommend which configuration changes to the devices could correct the issue.

Step 2: Load the device trouble ticket configuration files for TT-D.

Using the procedure described in Lab 3-1, verify that the lab configuration files are present in flash. Load the proper configuration files indicated in the Device Configuration File table.

Note: See Task 1, Step 2 for device access methods, usernames, and passwords after the configuration files have been loaded.

Device Configuration File Table

Device Name	File to Load	Notes
ALS1	Lab51-ALS1-TT-D-Cfg.txt	
DLS1	Lab51-DLS1-TT-D-Cfg.txt	
DLS2	Lab51-DLS2-TT-D-Cfg.txt	
R1	Lab51-R1-TT-D-Cfg.txt	
R2	Lab51-R2-TT-D-Cfg.txt	
R3	Lab51-R3-TT-D-Cfg.txt	
SRV1	N/A	Static IP: 10.1.50.1 Default gateway: 10.1.50.254
PC-B	N/A	DHCP
PC-C	N/A	DHCP

Step 3: Configure SRV1 and start the syslog and TFTP servers, as described in Task 1.

Step 4: Release and renew the DHCP leases on PC-B and PC-C, as described in Task 1.

Step 5: Outline the troubleshooting approach and validation steps.

Use this space to identify your troubleshooting approach and the key steps to verify that the problem is resolved. Troubleshooting approaches to select from include: follow-the-path, spot-the-differences, bottom-up, top-down, divide-and-conquer, shoot-from-the-hip, and move-the-problem.

Note: In addition to a specific approach, you can use the generic troubleshooting process described at the beginning of Section 2 of this lab.

_____

_____

_____

_____

_____

_____

Step 6: Record the troubleshooting process and configuration changes.

Note: Section 2 of this lab includes sample troubleshooting flows, useful commands, and examples of output.

Use this log to document your actions and results during the troubleshooting process. List the commands you used to gather information. As you progress, record what you think the problem might be and which actions you will take to correct the problems.

Device	Actions and Results

Step 7: Document trouble ticket debrief notes.

Use this space to make notes of the key learning points that you picked up during the discussion of this trouble ticket with your instructor. The notes can include problems encountered, solutions applied, useful commands employed, alternate solutions and methods, and procedure and communication improvements.

_____

_____

_____

_____

Task 5: Trouble Ticket Lab 5-1 TT-E

Step 1: Review trouble ticket Lab 5-1 TT-E.

A tech support intern on VLAN 30 (PC-C) called the help desk this Monday morning to report problems accessing certain areas of the network. It appears that the routers, R1, R2, and R3, are either down or unreachable.

Your company is in the process of testing various security measures to protect the network. Over the weekend, your IT staff worked on a project to secure EIGRP by implementing MD5 authentication. The staff was instructed to test the configuration over the weekend and reverse the implementation in the event that there were connectivity problems.

Your task is to ensure that the R1, R2 and R3 routers are online and reachable.

Step 2: Load the device trouble ticket configuration files for TT-E.

Using the procedure described in Lab 3-1, verify that the lab configuration files are present in flash. Load the proper configuration files indicated in the Device Configuration File table.

Note: See Task 1, Step 2 for device access methods, usernames, and passwords after the configuration files have been loaded.

Device Configuration File Table

Device Name	File to Load	Notes
ALS1	Lab51-ALS1-TT-E-Cfg.txt	
DLS1	Lab51-DLS1-TT-E-Cfg.txt	
DLS2	Lab51-DLS2-TT-E-Cfg.txt	
R1	Lab51-R1-TT-E-Cfg.txt	
R2	Lab51-R2-TT-E-Cfg.txt	
R3	Lab51-R3-TT-E-Cfg.txt	
SRV1	N/A	Static IP: 10.1.50.1 Default gateway: 10.1.50.254
PC-B	N/A	DHCP
PC-C	N/A	DHCP

Step 3: Configure SRV1 and start the syslog and TFTP servers, as described in Task 1.

Step 4: Release and renew the DHCP leases on PC-B and PC-C, as described in Task 1.

Step 5: Outline the troubleshooting approach and validation steps.

Use this space to identify your troubleshooting approach and the key steps to verify that the problem is resolved. Troubleshooting approaches to select from include: follow-the-path, spot-the-differences, bottom-up, top-down, divide-and-conquer, shoot-from-the-hip, and move-the-problem.

Note: In addition to a specific approach, you can use the generic troubleshooting process described at the beginning of Section 2 of this lab.

_____

_____

_____

_____

_____

_____

Step 6: Record the troubleshooting process and configuration changes.

Note: Section 2 of this lab includes sample troubleshooting flows, useful commands, and examples of output.

Use this log to document your actions and results during the troubleshooting process. List the commands you used to gather information. As you progress, record what you think the problem might be and which actions you will take to correct the problems.

Device	Actions and Results

Step 7: Document trouble ticket debrief notes.

Use this space to make notes of the key learning points that you picked up during the discussion of this trouble ticket with your instructor. The notes can include problems encountered, solutions applied, useful commands employed, alternate solutions and methods, and procedure and communication improvements.

_____

_____

_____

_____

_____

_____

Section 2 – Troubleshooting Reference Information

General Troubleshooting Process

As a general guideline, you can use the following general troubleshooting process described in the course:

1. Define the problem (symptoms).
2. Gather information.
3. Analyze the information.
4. Propose a hypothesis (possible cause).
5. Test the hypothesis.
6. Eliminate or accept the hypothesis.
7. Solve the problem.
8. Document the problem.

Command Summary

The table lists useful commands for this lab. Sample output is shown on the following pages.

Command	Key Information Displayed
`show spanning-tree vlan` *vlan#*	Displays all essential parameters that affect the topology, such as the root port, designated ports, port state, and port type, as well as the spanning-tree mode being implemented.
`show vlan brief`	Displays a quick overview of all existing VLANs and the ports within them. Trunk ports are not listed.
`show vlan id` *vlan#*	Displays whether the VLAN exists and which ports are assigned to it. Includes the trunk ports on which the VLAN is allowed.
`show ip interface vlan` *vlan#*	Displays the SVI status, IP address, statistics, and IP Cisco Express Forwarding (CEF) information.
`show ip route` *ip-addr*	Displays the routing table information for a particular destination address.
`show ip cef` *ip-addr* `detail`	Displays the next hop and interface used for a particular destination address from the CEF table.
`show ip cef exact-route src-`*ip-*`addr dest-`*ip-addr*	Displays the next hop and interface used for a particular destination address from the CEF table.
`show adjacency` *int-type/#* `detail`	Displays information contained in the adjacency table for a next-hop IP address or interface.
`show standby vlan` *vlan#* `brief`	Verify active and standby roles and IP addresses for a particular VLAN for HSRP routers.
`show standby brief`	Verify active and standby roles and IP addresses for all VLANs on an HSRP router.
`show ip eigrp interfaces`	Displays interfaces that are participating in the EIGRP routing process. An interface does not need to be operational to be listed in the output.
`show ip eigrp neighbors`	Displays the EIGRP neighbor table to verify that all expected neighbor relationships are operational.

`show ip eigrp topology` *ip-addr* *net-mask*	Displays the EIGRP topology, which contains all routes that were received from all neighbors for a particular prefix.
`debug eigrp packets`	Displays real-time messages exchanged between EIGRP routers. **Caution:** Produces large amounts of output.
`debug ip eigrp` *as#* `neighbor` *ip-addr*	Displays real-time messages exchanged for a particular neighbor.
`debug ip eigrp`	Displays the processing of routing events by the router. **Caution:** Produces large amounts of output.

Lab 5-1 Sample Troubleshooting Flows

Troubleshooting IP Connectivity

The figure illustrates an example of a method that you could follow to diagnose and resolve problems related to IP connectivity.

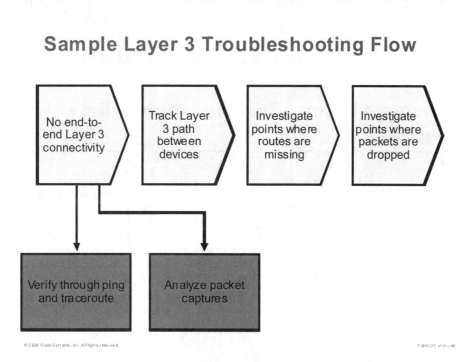

Layer 3 is a common starting point for many troubleshooting procedures. An often applied method is the divide-and-conquer approach. When a user reports a problem concerning connectivity to a certain service or application running on a server, a good first step is to determine if there is end-to-end IP connectivity between the client and the server. If this is the case, you can focus on the higher layers of the Open Systems Interconnection (OSI) reference model.

End-to-end IP connectivity can be confirmed or denied by using the `ping` or `traceroute` commands. Almost every operating system supports these commands in some form, but the syntax might be slightly different for different operating systems.

A prerequisite to using this method is that the appropriate Internet Control Message Protocol (ICMP) messages are allowed on the network and not blocked by any firewalls, including host-based firewalls on the destination host. If you cannot use ping and traceroute effectively, you might have to resort to analyzing traffic captures of the actual traffic flows to determine if packets can be sent at the network layer between the affected hosts.

Using the Correct Source Address

```
R2#ping 10.1.50.1 source Lo0

Type escape sequence to abort.
Sending 5, 100-byte ICMP Echos to 10.1.50.1, timeout is 2 seconds:
Packet sent with a source address of 10.1.202.1
!!!!!
Success rate is 100 percent (5/5), round-trip min/avg/max = 16/20/32 ms

R2#traceroute 10.1.50.1 source Lo0

Type escape sequence to abort.
Tracing the route to 10.1.50.1

  1 10.1.1.1 16 msec 16 msec 8 msec
  2 10.1.2.1 8 msec 16 msec 12 msec
  3 10.1.50.1 12 msec 12 msec 8 msec
```

Be aware that a successful ping or traceroute response is dependent on two things: the availability of a route to the destination and a route back to the source. Especially when running tests from the first-hop router in the path, make sure to specify the source address of the ping or traceroute. If you do not specify the source address, the router uses the IP address of the egress interface as the source for the packets. Using an address from a different source subnet than the client might lead you to reach wrong conclusions if the problem concerns the return path for the packets.

Sample Layer 3 Troubleshooting Flow

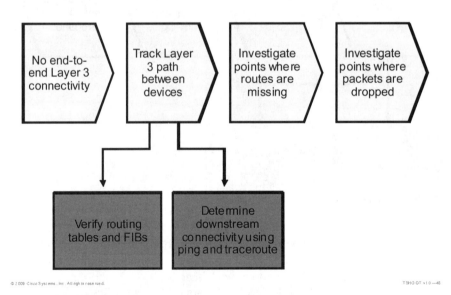

TSHOOT v1.0—48

If you have determined that there is a problem with the end-to-end IP connectivity between the affected hosts, you want to reduce the scope of the problem and isolate the points in the path between the hosts where the connectivity is lost.

A commonly used method is to track the path of the packets. You can use the following method to diagnose end-to-end IP connectivity problems:

- Determine the Layer 3 path. Based on documentation, baselines, and knowledge of your network in general, the first step is to determine the path that you would expect packets to follow between the affected hosts. Determining the expected traffic path beforehand helps in two ways. It provides a starting point for gathering information about what is happening on the network, and it makes it easier to spot abnormal behavior. The second step in determining the Layer 3 path is to follow the expected path and verify that the links on the path are up and forwarding traffic. If the actual traffic path is different from your expected path, this step might provide clues about which links or protocols are failing and the cause of these failures.

- To track the path of the packets between the hosts, first track the path that is being used according to the control plane information. Start at the client and verify the IP address, subnet mask, and default gateway. Then go to the router that is listed as the default gateway and check which route is used for the destination IP address. Determine the next-hop router based on the information in the routing table. Connect to the next-hop router and repeat this procedure until you arrive at the router that is directly connected to the destination host. Then repeat the process for the route back from the destination to the source.

- If the router has no route in the table for the destination network, you must diagnose the process that is the source of the routing information on this router, such as the routing protocol or static routes.

- If you have verified that the routing information is present on the complete path from the source to the destination and from the destination back to the source but connectivity is failing, you must track the path again, but now determine at which point packets are being dropped. The likely causes for dropped packets are Layer 1 problems, Layer 2 problems, or Layer 3 to Layer 2 mapping problems. When you have determined the point where the packets are dropped, use the specific troubleshooting methods appropriate for the Layer 2 technology that is used on the egress interface.

These steps do not necessarily have to be taken in the order presented here. Often different aspects of this generic procedure are combined, and shortcuts can be taken based on the result. For instance, determining proper packet forwarding is often done in parallel with determining the routes by using ping to verify the reachability of the next-hop derived from the route or using ping and traceroute to the final destination from intermediate routers in the path.

If you find that a ping is successful from a particular point in the path, you know that routes to the destination must be available on all the downstream routers. You can then use traceroute to determine the path to the destination, instead of connecting to each router in the path. However, this method has a hidden assumption: Packets traveling to the same destination use the same path, regardless of their source. This is not necessarily the case in a redundant network with equal-cost paths to a certain destination. The source address is typically used as part of the load-balancing algorithm that determines the path used when equal-cost paths are available. It is important to determine the exact path for the actual source and destination IP address pair that is affected, especially in cases where control plane information is available in both directions but packets are dropped.

Verify the Routing Table

```
R2#show ip route 10.1.10.1
Routing entry for 10.1.10.0/24
  Known via "eigrp 1", distance 90, metric 2172672, type internal
  Redistributing via eigrp 1
  Last update from 10.1.1.5 on Serial0/0/1, 02:05:21 ago
  Routing Descriptor Blocks:
    10.1.1.5, from 10.1.1.5, 02:05:21 ago, via Serial0/0/1
      Route metric is 2172672, traffic share count is 1
      Total delay is 20110 microseconds, minimum bandwidth is 1544 Kbit
      Reliability 255/255, minimum MTU 1500 bytes
      Loading 1/255, Hops 2
  * 10.1.1.1, from 10.1.1.1, 02:05:21 ago, via Serial0/0/0
      Route metric is 2172672, traffic share count is 1
      Total delay is 20110 microseconds, minimum bandwidth is 1544 Kbit
      Reliability 255/255, minimum MTU 1500 bytes
      Loading 1/255, Hops 2
```

When you are troubleshooting IP connectivity to a specific destination IP address, you can use the **show ip route** *ip-address* command to determine the best prefix match for the IP address, the egress interface, and, for multipoint interfaces, the next-hop IP address. If multiple equal-cost paths are present, as can be seen in the example above, each entry is listed.

The routing source is also listed, such as directly connected, static, or the routing protocol. Additional control plane parameters that are associated with the route source, such as the administrative distance, routing protocol metrics, source router, and route age, are also displayed. To interpret these parameters, more detailed knowledge of the specific routing protocol is required. More detailed information can often be gathered from that specific protocol's data structures.

This command never displays the default route 0.0.0.0/0 as a match, even if it is the longest prefix match for a packet. Therefore, if this command displays the message "% Network not in table," you cannot conclude that packets will be dropped, so you need to verify if a default route is present by using the **show ip route 0.0.0.0 0.0.0.0** command.

Verify the Cisco Express Forwarding Information Base

```
R2#show ip cef 10.1.10.1
10.1.10.0/24
  nexthop 10.1.1.1 Serial0/0/0
  nexthop 10.1.1.5 Serial0/0/1
```

To see the best match for a specific IP address in the Forwarding Information Base (FIB), use the **show ip cef** *ip-address* command. This command lists the same forwarding information as the **show ip route** command but without the associated control plane information, such as routing protocol metrics, administrative distance, and so on. This command displays the default route 0.0.0.0/0 if it is the best match for the destination IP address. If the routing table for a route contains multiple entries, these same entries will also be present in the FIB.

```
DLS1#show ip cef exact-route 10.1.10.1 10.1.202.1
10.1.10.1 -> 10.1.202.1 => IP adj out of FastEthernet0/5, addr 10.1.2.2

R2#show ip cef exact-route 10.1.202.1 10.1.50.1
10.1.202.1 -> 10.1.50.1 => IP adj out of Serial0/0/0
```

When you are tracing the packet flow between two specific hosts and the routing table and the FIB lists multiple entries (because there are multiple equal-cost paths), you must determine which entry is used to forward the packets associated with the specific source and destination IP address pair that you are troubleshooting. You can use the **show ip cef exact-route** command in these situations to determine the specific egress interface and next-hop IP address for the specific IP address pair.

On multilayer switches, instead of consulting the FIB that is stored in the main memory of the switch, you must consult the forwarding information stored in the hardware ternary content addressable memory (TCAM), because packet forwarding is handled by the TCAM, not the Cisco Express Forwarding FIB.

Although the FIB is used to compile the information that is loaded into the TCAM, the load-balancing algorithms that are used are different and do not necessarily yield the same result.

To learn more about the commands that can be used to verify the Layer 3 forwarding information contained in the TCAM, see the multilayer switching sections of the TSHOOT Student Guide and this Lab Guide.

Sample Layer 3 Troubleshooting Flow

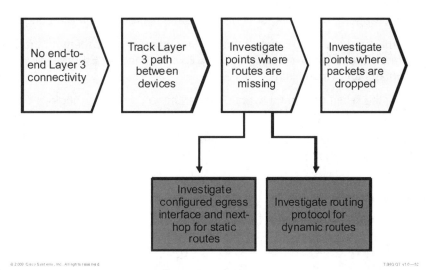

After you have found a point in the network where no route is present in the routing table for the destination IP address (or when analyzing the return path for the source IP address) of the session, you need to investigate what caused that route not to be installed in the routing table.

To correctly diagnose why a particular route is missing from the routing table, you first need to consult your documentation and baselines to find out what is the expected routing source. Is static routing or a routing protocol used on this router?

If a static route has been configured but it is not listed in the routing table, verify the status of the associated egress interface. If the egress interface for a static route is down, the route will not be installed in the routing table. If the route is not configured with an egress interface but with a next-hop IP address, the same rule applies. The router executes a recursive routing table lookup on the next hop for the static route. If no matching route and associated egress interface can be found for the configured next-hop IP address of the static route, the route is not installed in the routing table. If a match is found for the next-hop IP address, the static route is installed.

For dynamic routing protocols, you must initiate a troubleshooting process that is appropriate for that specific protocol and try to determine why the route was not learned on this router or, if it was learned, why it is not used.

Sample Layer 3 Troubleshooting Flow

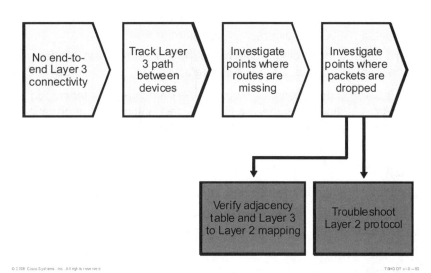

If you have verified the presence of correct routing information along the paths in both directions but you find that packets are dropped at a certain hop in the path, you must diagnose the packet-forwarding process.

If a route is present in the routing table (and the FIB if Cisco Express Forwarding is used) but packets are not forwarded correctly, verify if a correct mapping between the IP next hop and the Layer 2 protocol is used on the egress interface. If the router cannot find all the necessary Layer 2 information to construct a frame to encapsulate a packet, it is dropped, even if the routing information is present in the routing table.

The exact command to verify the Layer 3-to-Layer 2 protocol mapping is dependent on the Layer 2 technology used on the egress interface. Examples are the **show ip arp** command for Ethernet networks and the **show frame-relay map** command for Frame Relay.

For more information about the exact command syntax, research the Layer 2 technology used in the configuration guides and command references on http://www.cisco.com.

If you find incorrect mappings, or if you find the mappings to be correct but frames are not forwarded correctly, initiate a Layer 2 troubleshooting procedure for the Layer 2 technology that is being used.

Verify the Adjacency Table

```
DLS1#show adjacency fa0/5 detail
Protocol Interface                 Address
IP       FastEthernet0/5           10.1.2.2(15)
                                   0 packets, 0 bytes
                                   epoch 0
                                   sourced in sev-epoch 0
                                   Encap length 14
                                   001B530D60B100175A5BB4420800
                                   L2 destination address byte offset 0
                                   L2 destination address byte length 6
                                   Link-type after encap: ip
                                   ARP
```

Regardless of the Layer 2 technology, if Cisco Express Forwarding is used as the Layer 3 forwarding method, you can verify the availability of Layer 2 forwarding information using the **show adjacency** *int-type/#* **detail** command.

As can be seen in the example above, this command lists the Layer 2 frame header that is used to encapsulate packets transmitted via the listed adjacency. In this example, the frame header is 001B530D60B100175A5BB4420800, which is dissected as follows:

- **001B530D60B1** – This is the destination MAC address of the frame, which corresponds to the MAC address of the next hop 10.1.2.2.

- **00175A5BB442** – This is the source MAC address of the frame, which corresponds to the MAC address of interface FastEthernet 0/5.

- **0800** – This is the Ethernet type field, which indicates that the frame contains an IP packet, because Ethernet type value 0x800 is registered as the value for IP.

If you are troubleshooting a Layer 3 forwarding problem and the IP next hop and interface listed in the routing table are not present in the adjacency table, there is a problem with the Layer 3-to-Layer 2 mapping mechanisms.

If a Layer 2 frame header is listed in the adjacency table but the frames are not forwarded correctly across the Layer 2 medium, you must troubleshoot the underlying Layer 2 technology. The information contained in the header can be useful information when you start the Layer 2 troubleshooting process.

Troubleshooting EIGRP

The figure illustrates a method for diagnosing and resolving problems related to EIGRP.

Sample EIGRP Troubleshooting Flow

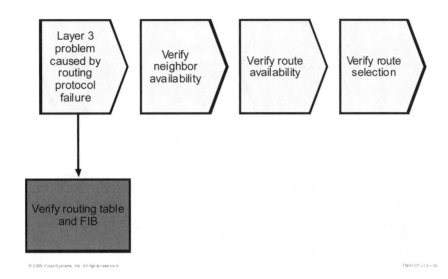

The usual trigger to start investigating routing protocol operation is when you are troubleshooting IP connectivity to a particular destination and you find that the route to the destination network is missing from the routing table of one of the routers or that a different route than expected was selected to forward the packets to that destination.

To install a route into the routing table, each router that uses a routing protocol goes through several stages:

- Discover neighbors and establish a neighbor relationship.

- Exchange routing information with neighbors and store the received information in protocol specific data structures.

- Select the best route from the available routes and install it in the routing table.

Errors during any of these stages can cause routing information to be missing or incorrect routing information to be installed in the routing table.

The exact processes that take place, the data structures that are used, and the commands to gather information about these processes and data structures are protocol-specific, but the generic troubleshooting principles are similar for all routing protocols.

The order to perform the different stages is not important as long as a structured approach is used.

Sample EIGRP Troubleshooting Flow

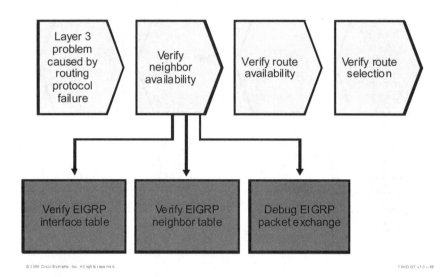

EIGRP discovers and maintains neighbor relationships by using hello packets. Neighbors that are discovered are registered in the EIGRP neighbor table and remain in the neighbor table as long as hello packets are received. A neighbor is removed from the table when its hold time expires or when the interface on which the neighbor is registered goes down. The default EIGRP hello timer is 5 seconds for these interfaces:

- High-speed multipoint interfaces, such as Ethernet interfaces

- Point-to-point interfaces, such as the following:

    — Serial interfaces running PPP or High-Level Data Link Control (HDLC)

    — Point-to-point Frame Relay subinterfaces

    — Point-to-point ATM subinterfaces

The default hold time for these interfaces is 15 seconds. Each router advertises hello and hold timers that it uses in its hellos. Although it is recommended that the timers are changed in a consistent manner on all routers if they need to be tuned, they do not need to match between two routers to allow them to become neighbors.

Verify the EIGRP Interfaces

```
R1#show ip eigrp interfaces
IP-EIGRP interfaces for process 1

                     Xmit Queue   Mean   Pacing Time   Multicast    Pending
Interface    Peers   Un/Reliable  SRTT   Un/Reliable   Flow Timer   Routes
Se0/0/0      1       0/0          19     0/15          99           0
Fa0/1        1       0/0          8      0/1           50           0
```

Neighbors can only be discovered on an interface that is operational and has been activated for EIGRP processing. An interface is activated for EIGRP packet processing if the IP address of the interface is covered by one of the network statements in the **router eigrp** configuration and the interface is not configured as a passive interface. Use the **show ip eigrp interfaces** command to display the EIGRP interfaces. An interface does not need to be operational to be listed in the output. The operational status of the interface must be verified separately using the **show interfaces**, **show interface status**, or **show ip interfaces brief** command.

If an interface is not listed in the output of the **show ip eigrp interfaces** command as expected, verify the **network** and **passive-interface** commands under the **router eigrp** configuration.

Verify the EIGRP Neighbor Table

```
R1#show ip eigrp neighbors
IP-EIGRP neighbors for process 1
H   Address               Interface       Hold Uptime    SRTT   RTO  Q   Seq
                                          (sec)          (ms)        Cnt Num
0   10.1.2.1              Fa0/1             13 04:50:36      8   200  0   12
1   10.1.1.2              Se0/0/0           10 04:07:52     19   200  0   36
```

To verify that all expected neighbor relationships are operational, display the EIGRP neighbor table using the **show ip eigrp neighbors** command.

For troubleshooting purposes, the two most relevant columns in this output are Hold, which lists the number of seconds before a neighbor expires from the table, and Uptime, which lists how long this neighbor has been operational since it was last discovered. These two items can give you a good indication of the stability of the neighbor relationship. The uptime tells you for how long the neighbor relationship has been successfully maintained, while displaying the hold time several times in a row can tell you if hellos are being received in a timely fashion. Based on the default 5 second hello and 15 second hold time, the value in this column should be between 15 and 10 seconds, because it counts down and is reset to the hold time whenever a hello is received from the neighbor.

If the uptime of a neighbor is shorter than expected, verify the console or syslog logs for interface-related events or EIGRP neighbor-related events, such as the following (these are default message – not the result of debug):

```
Nov 2 06:25:01 EST: %LINEPROTO-5-UPDOWN: Line protocol on Interface FastEthernet0/1,
changed state to down
Nov 2 06:25:02 EST: %LINK-3-UPDOWN: Interface FastEthernet0/1, changed state to down
Nov 2 06:25:02 EST: %DUAL-5-NBRCHANGE: EIGRP-IPv4:(1) 1: Neighbor 10.1.2.1
(FastEthernet0/1) is down: interface down
Nov 2 06:25:14 EST: %DUAL-5-NBRCHANGE: EIGRP-IPv4:(1) 1: Neighbor 10.1.2.1
(FastEthernet0/1) is up: new adjacency
Nov 2 06:25:16 EST: %LINK-3-UPDOWN: Interface FastEthernet0/1, changed state to up
Nov 2 06:25:17 EST: %LINEPROTO-5-UPDOWN: Line protocol on Interface FastEthernet0/1,
changed state to up
```

Specifically, the %DUAL-5-NBRCHANGE messages are very useful in troubleshooting because they indicate why the neighbor was lost. In this case, it was caused by the interface going down.

Debug EIGRP Packet Exchange

If an expected neighbor is not listed in the neighbor table on a specific interface, and you have confirmed that the interface is operational and is listed in the interface table, use the **debug eigrp packets** command to display the transmission and reception of EIGRP packets in real time. This command can potentially generate a large amount of output, so be cautious about using it.

You can limit the output by specifying the packet type (update, request, query, reply, hello, ipxsap, probe, ack, stub, siaquery, or siareply). You can also add other conditions using the **debug ip eigrp** *as-number* command, such as limiting the output to a specific neighbor or network.

To further reduce the impact of the command, disable logging to the console and log to buffers in the router instead. You can then display the contents of the log buffer using the **show logging** command. The following example shows you how to use this technique:

```
R1#configure terminal
Enter configuration commands, one per line.  End with CNTL/Z.
R1(config)#no logging console
R1(config)#logging buffered 16384
R1(config)#^Z
```

```
R1#debug eigrp packets
EIGRP Packets debugging is on
```

```
     (UPDATE, REQUEST, QUERY, REPLY, HELLO, IPXSAP, PROBE, ACK, STUB, SIAQUERY,
SIAREPLY)
```

R1#**debug ip eigrp 1 neighbor 10.1.2.1**
```
IP Neighbor target enabled on AS 1 for 10.1.2.1
IP-EIGRP Neighbor Target Events debugging is on
```

R1#**clear logging**
```
Clear logging buffer [confirm]
```

R1#**show logging**
```
Syslog logging: enabled (1 messages dropped, 108 messages rate-limited,
                0 flushes, 0 overruns, xml disabled, filtering disabled)
    Console logging: disabled
    Monitor logging: level debugging, 0 messages logged, xml disabled,
                     filtering disabled
    Buffer logging: level debugging, 13924 messages logged, xml disabled,
                    filtering disabled
    Logging Exception size (4096 bytes)
    Count and timestamp logging messages: disabled

No active filter modules.

    Trap logging: level informational, 242 message lines logged
        Logging to 10.1.50.1(global) (udp port 514, audit disabled,  link up), 242
message lines logged, xml disabled,
                filtering disabled

Log Buffer (16384 bytes):

Nov 2 07:40:38.177 PDT: EIGRP: Received HELLO on FastEthernet0/1 nbr 10.1.2.1
Nov 2 07:40:38.177 PDT:   AS 1, Flags 0x0, Seq 0/0 idbQ 0/0 iidbQ un/rely 0/0 peerQ
un/rely 0/0
Nov 2 07:40:42.517 PDT: EIGRP: Received HELLO on FastEthernet0/1 nbr 10.1.2.1
Nov 2 07:40:42.517 PDT:   AS 1, Flags 0x0, Seq 0/0 idbQ 0/0 iidbQ un/rely 0/0 peerQ
un/rely 0/0
Nov 2 07:40:47.237 PDT: EIGRP: Received HELLO on FastEthernet0/1 nbr 10.1.2.1
Nov 2 07:40:47.237 PDT:   AS 1, Flags 0x0, Seq 0/0 idbQ 0/0 iidbQ un/rely 0/0 peerQ
un/rely 0/0
```

Sample EIGRP Troubleshooting Flow

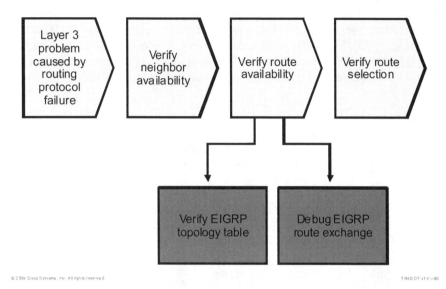

After you have verified that neighbor relationships have been established as expected, verify that the route for the destination network that you are troubleshooting has been received correctly from all appropriate neighbors. EIGRP stores all routes that it receives from its neighbors in its topology table and then selects the best route from these routes to be installed in the routing table.

By investigating the available routes to the destination network in the topology table, you can see if all options that you expected were learned and if they have the correct associated metrics.

If routes are missing from the topology table, you might need to debug the EIGRP route exchange process to see if they were not received or if they were not entered into the topology table.

Verify the EIGRP Topology Table

```
R2#show ip eigrp topology 10.1.50.0 255.255.255.0
IP-EIGRP (AS 1): Topology entry for 10.1.50.0/24
  State is Passive, Query origin flag is 1, 2 Successor(s), FD is 2172672
  Routing Descriptor Blocks:
  10.1.1.1 (Serial0/0/0), from 10.1.1.1, Send flag is 0x0
      Composite metric is (2172672/28416), Route is Internal
      Vector metric:
        Minimum bandwidth is 1544 Kbit
        Total delay is 20110 microseconds
        Reliability is 255/255
        Load is 1/255
        Minimum MTU is 1500
        Hop count is 2
  10.1.1.5 (Serial0/0/1), from 10.1.1.5, Send flag is 0x0
      Composite metric is (2172672/28416), Route is Internal
      Vector metric:
        Minimum bandwidth is 1544 Kbit
        Total delay is 20110 microseconds
        Reliability is 255/255
        Load is 1/255
        Minimum MTU is 1500
        Hop count is 2
```

The EIGRP topology table contains all routes that were received from all neighbors.

For each particular prefix, there might be the following three types of entries:

- **Successors** – These are the entries selected from the topology table as the best routes and installed in the routing table. For a router to be a successor, it must provide the lowest total metric (its advertised distance plus the metric of the link towards it) among all the routes in the topology table for that prefix. Also, the advertised distance to the prefix by that router must be strictly lower than the feasible distance (FD). Secondly, it will only be marked as a successor if it was actually installed in the routing table. If a competing route for that prefix, such as a static route, was installed in the routing table instead because it had a better administrative distance, the EIGRP route will not be marked as a successor.

- **Feasible successors** – These routers have a metric that is higher than the current lowest total metric for the prefix but still meet the feasibility condition. The feasibility condition is met if the advertised distance of the route is lower than the FD. This means that the route is considered a backup route and can be used immediately if the best route is lost, without needing to confirm its feasibility as a backup route through a query and reply process.

- **Possible successors** – These routers do not meet the feasibility condition. They are potential backup routes, but if the best route is lost, a query and reply process is necessary to confirm that they are valid and loop-free.

As an example, the content of the EIGRP topology table for network 10.1.50.0/24 is listed below and comments are interspersed with the output to help interpret the entries.

```
R2#show ip eigrp topology 10.1.50.0 255.255.255.0
IP-EIGRP (AS 1): Topology entry for 10.1.50.0/24
    State is Passive, Query origin flag is 1, 2 Successor(s), FD is 2172672
```

There are two successors for this prefix, and the FD is 2172672. This entry is the first successor, because its distance of 2172672 (the first number between the parentheses) towards the 10.1.50.0/24 network through 10.1.1.5 is also equal to the FD of 2172672.

```
Routing Descriptor Blocks:
    10.1.1.1 (Serial0/0/0), from 10.1.1.1, Send flag is 0x0
        Composite metric is (2172672/28416), Route is Internal
        Vector metric:
            Minimum bandwidth is 1544 Kbit
            Total delay is 20110 microseconds
            Reliability is 255/255
            Load is 1/255
            Minimum MTU is 1500
            Hop count is 2
```

This entry is the second successor, because its distance of 28416 is also equal to the FD of 28416.

```
    10.1.1.5 (Serial0/0/0), from 10.1.1.5, Send flag is 0x0
        Composite metric is (2172672/28416), Route is Internal
        Vector metric:
            Minimum bandwidth is 1544 Kbit
            Total delay is 20110 microseconds
            Reliability is 255/255
            Load is 1/255
            Minimum MTU is 1500
            Hop count is 2
```

Verify the EIGRP Topology Table

```
R2#debug ip eigrp
IP-EIGRP Route Events debugging is on
```

```
R2#debug ip eigrp 1 neighbor 10.1.1.1
IP Neighbor target enabled on AS 1 for 10.1.1.1
IP-EIGRP Neighbor Target Events debugging is on

R2#clear ip eigrp neighbors 10.1.1.1
R2#
Nov  2 17:18:50.945: %DUAL-5-NBRCHANGE: IP-EIGRP(0) 1: Neighbor 10.1.1.2 (Serial
0/0/0) is down: Interface Goodbye received
Nov  2 17:18:55.085: %DUAL-5-NBRCHANGE: IP-EIGRP(0) 1: Neighbor 10.1.1.2 (Serial
0/0/0) is up: new adjacency
```

If you find expected route entries to be missing from the topology table, consider using the `debug ip eigrp` command to display the processing of routing events by the router. However, this command can produce a large number of messages and, as a result, has a high risk of disrupting the router's operation. Do not use this command unless guided by the Cisco TAC or in a nonoperational network, such as a lab network that you have built to reproduce a problem.

Like the `debug eigrp packets` command, you can limit the impact of this command by logging to buffers instead of the console and by limiting the output to specific neighbors or routes. Even then, extreme care should be taken.

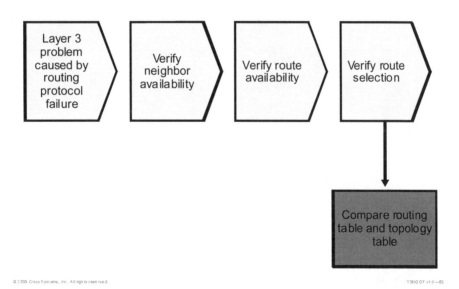

Sample EIGRP Troubleshooting Flow

If you find that an EIGRP route for a specific destination network is available in the topology table, but a different route is present in the routing table, compare the value of the administrative distance of the route in the routing table to the value of the EIGRP route (which is 90 for internal routes and 170 for external routes, by default). If the distance of the EIGRP route is higher than the distance of the competing route, it will not be installed in the routing table.

Reflection Questions

1. Which lab trouble tickets did you have the most difficulty with?

_____

_____

_____

2. For any of the trouble tickets, would you change anything about the process that you used now that you see the resolution of the problem?

_____

_____

_____

3. Which commands did you find most useful in diagnosing Layer 3 and EIGRP issues? Add these to your toolbox for future use. Which commands did you find least useful?

_____

_____

_____

References

If you need more information on the commands and their options, see the following references:

- IP Routing Protocol Command Reference

  http://www.cisco.com/cisco/web/support/index.html

- Cisco IOS IP Switching Command Reference

  http://www.cisco.com/en/US/docs/ios/ipswitch/command/reference/isw_book.html

- Enhanced Interior Gateway Routing Protocol Troubleshooting Tech Notes http://www.cisco.com/en/US/tech/tk365/tsd_technology_support_troubleshooting_technotes_list.html#anchor3

Router Interface Summary Table

Router Interface Summary				
Router Model	Ethernet Interface #1	Ethernet Interface #2	Serial Interface #1	Serial Interface #2
1700	Fast Ethernet 0 (FA0)	Fast Ethernet 1 (FA1)	Serial 0 (S0)	Serial 1 (S1)
1800	Fast Ethernet 0/0 (FA0/0)	Fast Ethernet 0/1 (FA0/1)	Serial 0/0/0 (S0/0/0)	Serial 0/0/1 (S0/0/1)
2600	Fast Ethernet 0/0 (FA0/0)	Fast Ethernet 0/1 (FA0/1)	Serial 0/0 (S0/0)	Serial 0/1 (S0/1)
2800	Fast Ethernet 0/0 (FA0/0)	Fast Ethernet 0/1 (FA0/1)	Serial 0/0/0 (S0/0/0)	Serial 0/0/1 (S0/0/1)
Note: To find out how the router is configured, look at the interfaces to identify the type of router and how many interfaces the router has. Rather than try to list all the combinations of configurations for each router class, this table includes identifiers for the possible combinations of Ethernet and serial interfaces in the device. The table does not include any other type of interface, even though a specific router might contain one. An example of this is an ISDN BRI interface. The string in parenthesis is the legal abbreviation that can be used in Cisco IOS commands to represent the interface.				

Lab 5-2, OSPF and Route Redistribution

Physical Topology (Baseline)

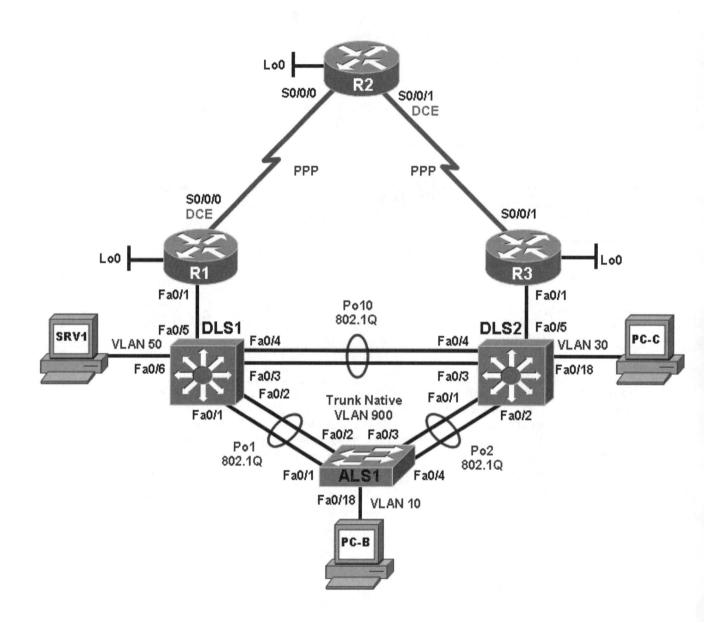

Logical Topology (Baseline)

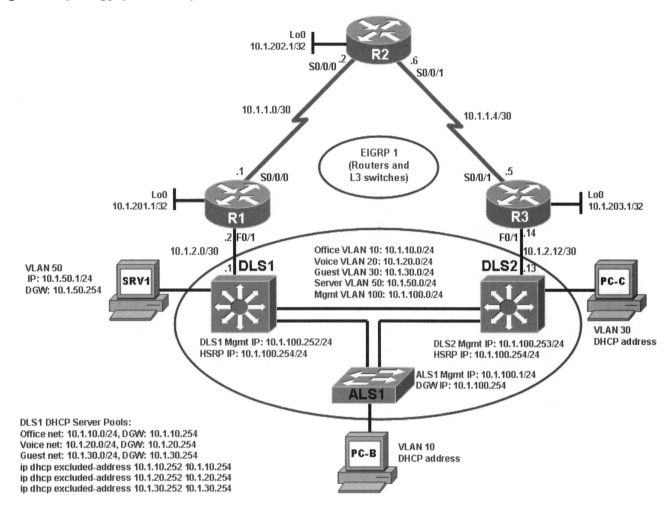

Objectives

- Load the trouble ticket device configuration files for each trouble ticket.

- Diagnose and resolve problems related to the OSPF routing protocol.

- Diagnose and resolve problems related to route redistribution.

- Document troubleshooting progress, configuration changes, and problem resolution.

Background

In this lab, you troubleshoot various problems related to the Open Shortest Path First (OSPF) routing protocol and route redistribution between routing protocols. For each task or trouble ticket, the trouble scenario and problem symptom are described. While troubleshooting, you will discover the cause of the problem, correct it, and then document the process and results.

Migrating from EIGRP to OSPF

Your company has decided to migrate from using Enhanced Interior Gateway Protocol (EIGRP) to OSPF as the routing protocol. This migration will be executed in two phases.

The engineering team planned and designed the migration, but the support team must support the new network, so they are involved in migrating the branch during Phase 2.

Phase 1—The headquarters central site campus is migrated to OSPF as well as one of the branch offices (simulated by Lo0 on R3). EIGRP is still used on the WAN toward the R2 branch office. On router R1, redistribution is configured between OSPF and EIGRP to ensure connectivity between headquarters and the branch office connected to R2.

Phase 2—The R2 branch office (simulated by Lo0 on R2) is converted from EIGRP to OSPF, and all branch offices are migrated so that OSPF is used in the entire network. Each branch site is in a separate area that is configured as totally stubby.

Today is Saturday, and the engineering team has been busy implementing OSPF and removing EIGRP at the headquarters site. Although you have not taken part in the actual implementation, some of the senior engineers in the support team are on standby to assist during the verification and troubleshooting phase. Together with the engineering team, you will have to make the decision on Sunday to either accept the implementation or, if major issues are uncovered that would threaten the stability of the network, roll back to the original configurations.

OSPF Network Design

Phases 1 and 2 of the OSPF design are depicted in the following figures. Backbone area 0 contains the FastEthernet interfaces on core Layer 3 switches DLS1 and DLS2 as well as those on routers R1 and R3. Area 0 also includes VLAN 200 and the corresponding SVI, which have been added to these two switches so that they can form an OSPF neighbor relationship and exchange routes. The headquarters campus access VLANs 10, 20, 30, and 50 and management VLAN 100 are in OSPF area 1. The R2 stub network is in area 2, and the R3 stub network is in area 3.

Phase 1 OSPF Network Design

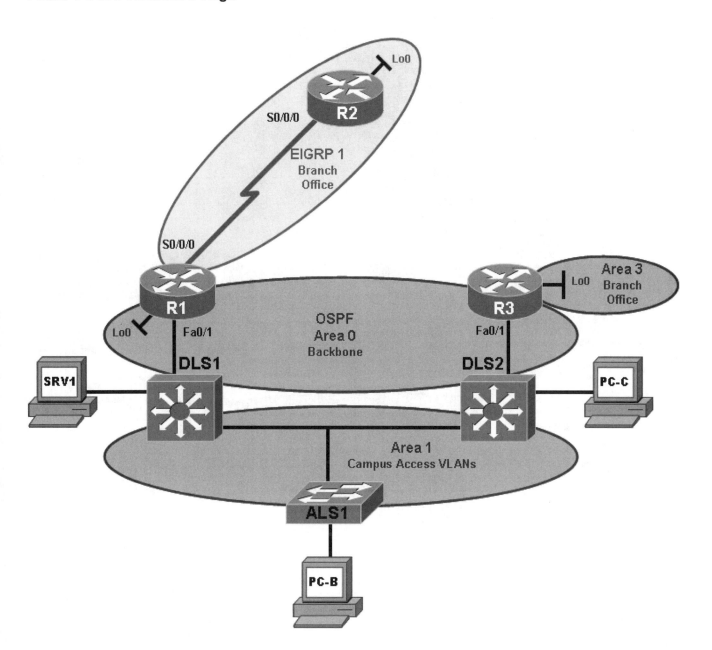

Phase 2 OSPF Network Design

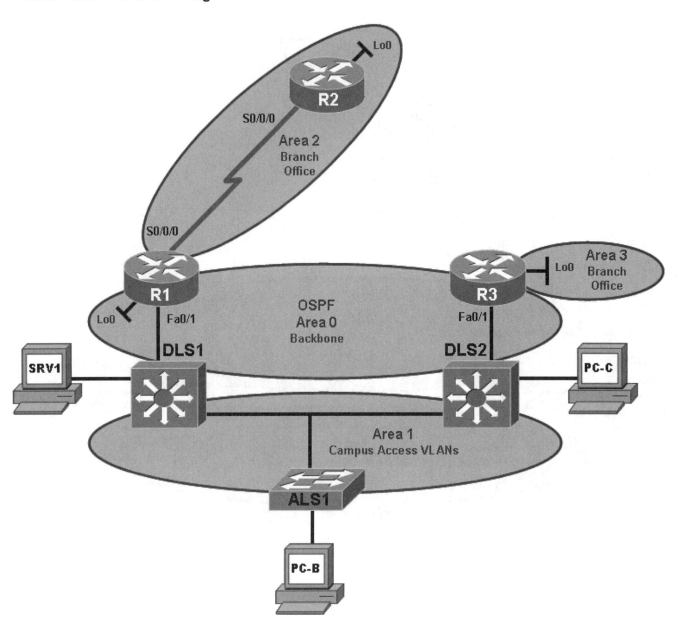

Test Plan

To test the branch connectivity using redistribution between EIGRP and OSPF and the eventual conversion to only OSPF, branch routers R2 and R3 have been specifically prepared for both of these scenarios. Router R2 functions as the default gateway for the R2 LAN, while router R3 is the default gateway for the R3 LAN. Router R2 runs EIGRP as usual. This allows testing the redistribution of EIGRP from the R2 branch office LAN (simulated by R2 Lo0) to OSPF area 0 and redistribution of OSPF into EIGRP using router R1 as an Autonomous System Border Router (ASBR). Router R3 is configured to run OSPF as an Area Border Router (ABR) between area 0 and area 3. The R3 branch office client is simulated by R3 Lo0).

At the end of Phase 1, when the network is fully converged, all OSPF routers should have EIGRP routes in their routing tables and EIGRP router R2 should have all OSPF routes in its routing table.

After the completion of Phase 2, all routers except R2 should have OSPF routes. Router R2 is totally stubby and should only have a default route to R1.

Note: Trouble ticket TT-A is related to the verification and acceptance of Phase 1 of the OSPF migration. Trouble tickets TT-B, C and D are related to the verification and acceptance of Phase 2 of the OSPF migration. Any interfaces that have been shut down on routers R2 and R3 should remain shut down for the duration of this lab exercise.

Physical and Logical Topology Diagrams

The physical and logical topologies for the existing EIGRP-based network are provided to assist the troubleshooting effort.

Lab Structure

This lab is divided into two main sections.

Section 1—Trouble Tickets and Troubleshooting Logs

This section includes multiple tasks. Each task is associated with a trouble ticket (TT) and introduces one or more errors on one or more devices. If time is a consideration, each task or trouble ticket can be performed independently.

Section 2—Troubleshooting Reference Information

This section provides OSPF and route redistribution troubleshooting information that can be applied to any trouble ticket in this lab. Sample troubleshooting flows are provided, along with examples of useful commands and output. If time permits, it is recommended that you read through Section 2 prior to starting on the trouble tickets.

This lab uses Cisco 1841 routers with Cisco IOS Release 12.4(24)T1 and the Advanced IP Services image c1841-advipservicesk9-mz.124-24.T1.bin. The switches are Cisco WS-C2960-24TT-L with the Cisco IOS image c2960-lanbasek9-mz.122-46.SE.bin and Catalyst 3560-24PS with the Cisco IOS image c3560-advipservicesk9-mz.122-46.SE.bin. Other routers (such as 2801 and 2811), switches (such as 2950 or 3550), and Cisco IOS Software versions can be used if they have comparable capabilities and features. Depending on the router or switch model and Cisco IOS Software version, the commands available and output produced might vary from what is shown in this lab.

Note: Any changes made to the baseline configurations or topology (other than errors introduced) are noted in the trouble ticket so that you are aware of them prior to beginning the troubleshooting process.

Required Resources

- 3 routers (Cisco 1841 with the Cisco IOS Release 12.4(24)T1 Advanced IP Service or comparable)
- 1 switch (Cisco 2960 with the Cisco IOS Release 12.2(46)SE C2960-LANBASEK9-M image or comparable)
- 2 switches (Cisco 3560 with the Cisco IOS Release 12.2(46)SE C3560-LANBASEK9-M image or comparable)
- SRV1 (Windows PC with static IP address) with TFTP and syslog servers plus an SSH client (PuTTY or comparable) and WireShark software
- PC-B (Windows PC - DHCP client) with PuTTY and WireShark software
- PC-C (Windows PC - DHCP client) with PuTTY and WireShark software
- Serial and Ethernet cables

Section 1—Trouble Tickets and Troubleshooting Logs

Task 1: Trouble Ticket Lab 5-2 TT-A

Step 1: Review trouble ticket Lab 5-2 TT-A.

After the completion of Phase 1—implementation of OSPF in the headquarters portion of the network and the redistribution between EIGRP and OSPF—the connectivity from the office LAN on the R2 branch router to server SRV1 at headquarters is tested. A ping from the R2 LAN client (sourced by Lo0 on R2) to server SRV1 fails.

Your task is to diagnose this problem and, if possible, resolve it. Connectivity from the R2 LAN to server SRV1 is mandatory to consider this phase of the migration successful.

Step 2: Load the device trouble ticket configuration files for TT-A.

Using the procedure described in Lab 3-1, verify that the lab configuration files are present in flash. Load the proper configuration files as indicated in the Device Configuration File table.

Note: The following device access methods are in effect after loading the configuration files:

- Console access requires no username or password.

- Telnet and SSH require username **admin** and password **adminpa55**.

- The enable password is **ciscoenpa55**.

Device Configuration File Table

Device Name	File to Load	Notes
ALS1	Lab52-ALS1-TT-A-Cfg.txt	
DLS1	Lab52-DLS1-TT-A-Cfg.txt	
DLS2	Lab52-DLS2-TT-A-Cfg.txt	
R1	Lab52-R1-TT-A-Cfg.txt	
R2	Lab52-R2-TT-A-Cfg.txt	
R3	Lab52-R3-TT-A-Cfg.txt	
SRV1	N/A	Static IP: 10.1.50.1 Default gateway: 10.1.50.254
PC-B	N/A	DHCP
PC-C	N/A	DHCP

Step 3: Configure SRV1 and start the syslog and TFTP servers.

Step 4: Release and renew the DHCP lease on PC-B.

Ensure that PC-B is configured as a DHCP client in the OFFICE VLAN.

After loading all TT-A device configuration files, issue the **ipconfig /release** and **ipconfig /renew** commands on PC-B.

Step 5: Outline the troubleshooting approach and validation steps.

Use this space to identify your troubleshooting approach and the key steps to verify that the problem is resolved. Troubleshooting approaches to select from include: follow-the-path, spot-the-differences, bottom-up, top-down, divide-and-conquer, shoot-from-the-hip, and move-the-problem.

Note: In addition to a specific approach, you can use the generic troubleshooting process described at the beginning of Section 2 of this lab.

_____

_____

_____

_____

_____

_____

Step 6: Record the troubleshooting process and configuration changes.

Note: Section 2 of this lab includes sample troubleshooting flows, useful commands, and examples of output.

Use this log to document your actions and results during the troubleshooting process. List the commands you used to gather information. As you progress, record what you think the problem might be and which actions you will take to correct the problem.

Device	Actions and Results

Step 7: Document trouble ticket debrief notes.

Use this space to make notes of the key learning points that you picked up during the discussion of this trouble ticket with your instructor. The notes can include problems encountered, solutions applied, useful commands employed, alternate solutions and methods, and procedure and communication improvements.

_____

_____

_____

_____

_____

_____

_____

Task 2: Trouble Ticket Lab 5-2 TT-B

Step 1: Review trouble ticket Lab 5-2 TT-B.

Phase 2 has been completed and all routers have been converted to OSPF. The connectivity from a branch office client on the R2 LAN (simulated by R2 Lo0) to server SRV1 at the central site is tested. A ping from the client on the R2 LAN (using source interface Lo0) to server SRV1 fails. The connectivity problem is not limited to SRV1. An attempt to connect to other headquarters servers also fails. Your task is to diagnose this problem and, if possible, resolve it. Connectivity from the branch client to server SRV1 is mandatory for this phase of the migration to be considered successful.

Note: Refer back to the implementation and test plan to review the requirements for Phase 2.

Step 2: Load the device trouble ticket configuration files for TT-B.

Using the procedure described in Lab 3-1, verify that the lab configuration files are present in flash. Load the proper configuration files as indicated in the Device Configuration File table.

Note: See Task 1, Step 2 for device access methods, usernames, and passwords after the configuration files have been loaded.

Device Configuration File Table

Device Name	File to Load	Notes
ALS1	Lab51-ALS1-TT-B-Cfg.txt	
DLS1	Lab51-DLS1-TT-B-Cfg.txt	
DLS2	Lab51-DLS2-TT-B-Cfg.txt	
R1	Lab51-R1-TT-B-Cfg.txt	
R2	Lab51-R2-TT-B-Cfg.txt	
R3	Lab51-R3-TT-B-Cfg.txt	
SRV1	N/A	Static IP: 10.1.50.1 Default gateway: 10.1.50.254
PC-B	N/A	DHCP (release and renew after loading device configurations)
PC-C	N/A	DHCP (release and renew after loading device configurations)

Step 3: Configure SRV1 and start the syslog and TFTP servers.

Step 4: Release and renew the DHCP leases on PC-B and PC-C, as described in Task 1.

Step 5: Outline the troubleshooting approach and validation steps.

Use this space to identify your troubleshooting approach and the key steps to verify that the problem is resolved. Troubleshooting approaches to select from include: follow-the-path, spot-the-differences, bottom-up, top-down, divide-and-conquer, shoot-from-the-hip, and move-the-problem.

Note: In addition to a specific approach, you can use the generic troubleshooting process described at the beginning of Section 2 of this lab.

_____

_____

_____

_____

_____

Step 6: Record the troubleshooting process and configuration changes.

Note: Section 2 of this lab includes sample troubleshooting flows, useful commands, and examples of output.

Use this log to document your actions and results during the troubleshooting process. List the commands you used to gather information. As you progress, record what you think the problem might be and which actions you will take to correct the problem.

Device	Actions and Results

Step 7: Document trouble ticket debrief notes.

Use this space to make notes of the key learning points that you picked up during the discussion of this trouble ticket with your instructor. The notes can include problems encountered, solutions applied, useful commands employed, alternate solutions and methods, and procedure and communication improvements.

_____

_____

_____

_____

_____

_____

_____

Task 3: Trouble Ticket Lab 5-2 TT-C

Step 1: Review trouble ticket Lab 5-2 TT-C.

After implementing OSPF, connectivity from the branch office on R3 (simulated by Lo0) to SRV1 is not working. A ping from PC-B to server SRV1 succeeds, but pings from R3 Lo0 to SRV1 fail.

Your task is to diagnose this problem and, if possible, resolve it. Connectivity from R3 branch office clients to server SRV1 is mandatory for this phase of the migration to be considered successful.

Step 2: Load the device trouble ticket configuration files for TT-C.

Using the procedure described in Lab 3-1, verify that the lab configuration files are present in flash. Load the proper configuration files as indicated in the Device Configuration File table.

Note: See Task 1, Step 2 for device access methods, usernames, and passwords after the configuration files have been loaded.

Device Configuration File Table

Device Name	File to Load	Notes
ALS1	Lab51-ALS1-TT-C-Cfg.txt	
DLS1	Lab51-DLS1-TT-C-Cfg.txt	
DLS2	Lab51-DLS2-TT-C-Cfg.txt	
R1	Lab51-R1-TT-C-Cfg.txt	
R2	Lab51-R2-TT-C-Cfg.txt	
R3	Lab51-R3-TT-C-Cfg.txt	

SRV1	N/A	Static IP: 10.1.50.1 Default gateway: 10.1.50.254
PC-B	N/A	DHCP (release and renew after loading device configurations)
PC-C	N/A	DHCP (release and renew after loading device configurations)

Step 3: Configure SRV1 and start the syslog and TFTP servers, as described in Task 1.

Step 4: Release and renew the DHCP leases on PC-B and PC-C, as described in Task 1.

Step 5: Outline the troubleshooting approach and validation steps.

Use this space to identify your troubleshooting approach and the key steps to verify that the problem is resolved. Troubleshooting approaches to select from include: follow-the-path, spot-the-differences, bottom-up, top-down, divide-and-conquer, shoot-from-the-hip, and move-the-problem.

Note: In addition to a specific approach, you can use the generic troubleshooting process described at the beginning of Section 2 of this lab.

_____

_____

_____

_____

_____

_____

Step 6: Record the troubleshooting process and configuration changes.

Note: Section 2 of this lab includes sample troubleshooting flows, useful commands, and examples of output.

Use this log to document your actions and results during the troubleshooting process. List the commands you used to gather information. As you progress, record what you think the problem might be and which actions you will take to correct the problem.

Device	Actions and Results

Device	Actions and Results

Step 7: Document trouble ticket debrief notes.

Use this space to make notes of the key learning points that you picked up during the discussion of this trouble ticket with your instructor. The notes can include problems encountered, solutions applied, useful commands employed, alternate solutions and methods, and procedure and communication improvements.

_____

_____

_____

_____

_____

_____

_____

_____

Task 4: Trouble Ticket Lab 5-2 TT-D

Step 1: Review trouble ticket Lab 5-2 TT-D.

A recent security audit suggested that it would be best practice to secure the OSPF implementation by using MD5 authentication between the routers. Because this could complicate the implementation, it was decided that it was too late to include this now for all areas. However, to test the concept, it was decided to enable the authentication for area 0 for two devices. If the test is successful, the authentication will be added to other areas during the second phase of the implementation. If the test is not successful, a separate project will be initiated to implement the authentication.

One of your colleagues has enabled MD5 authentication for area 0 on VLAN 200, which is the link between the core switches DLS1 and DLS2 in area 0. Unfortunately, the neighbor relationship between DLS1 and DLS2 on VLAN 200 is not established.

Your task is to diagnose this problem and, if possible, resolve it. After correcting the OSPF neighbor relationship, verify that OSPF authentication between DLS1 and DLS2 is functioning correctly. You may disable the password encryption service during authentication testing.

Step 2: Load the device trouble ticket configuration files for TT-D.

Using the procedure described in Lab 3-1, verify that the lab configuration files are present in flash. Load the proper configuration files as indicated in the Device Configuration File table.

> **Note:** See Task 1, Step 2 for device access methods, usernames, and passwords after the configuration files have been loaded.

Device Configuration File Table

Device Name	File to Load	Notes
ALS1	Lab51-ALS1-TT-D-Cfg.txt	
DLS1	Lab51-DLS1-TT-D-Cfg.txt	
DLS2	Lab51-DLS2-TT-D-Cfg.txt	
R1	Lab51-R1-TT-C-Cfg.txt	
R2	Lab51-R2-TT-C-Cfg.txt	
R3	Lab51-R3-TT-C-Cfg.txt	
SRV1	N/A	Static IP: 10.1.50.1 Default gateway: 10.1.50.254
PC-B	N/A	DHCP
PC-C	N/A	DHCP

Step 3: Configure SRV1 and start the syslog and TFTP servers, as described in Task 1.

Step 4: Release and renew the DHCP leases on PC-B and PC-C, as described in Task 1.

Step 5: Outline the troubleshooting approach and validation steps.

Use this space to identify your troubleshooting approach and the key steps to verify that the problem is resolved. Troubleshooting approaches to select from include: follow-the-path, spot-the-differences, bottom-up, top-down, divide-and-conquer, shoot-from-the-hip, and move-the-problem.

Note: In addition to a specific approach, you can use the generic troubleshooting process described at the beginning of Section 2 of this lab.

_____

_____

_____

_____

_____

_____

Step 6: Record the troubleshooting process and configuration changes.

Note: Section 2 of this lab includes sample troubleshooting flows, useful commands, and examples of output.

Use this log to document your actions and results during the troubleshooting process. List the commands you used to gather information. As you progress, record what you think the problem might be and which actions you will take to correct the problems.

Device	Actions and Results

Device	Actions and Results

Step 7: Document trouble ticket debrief notes.

Use this space to make notes of the key learning points that you picked up during the discussion of this trouble ticket with your instructor. The notes can include problems encountered, solutions applied, useful commands employed, alternate solutions and methods, and procedure and communication improvements.

_____

_____

_____

_____

_____

_____

Section 2—Troubleshooting Reference Information

General Troubleshooting Process

As a general guideline, you can use the general troubleshooting process described in the course:

1. Define the problem (symptoms).
2. Gather information.
3. Analyze the information.
4. Propose a hypothesis (possible cause).
5. Test the hypothesis.
6. Eliminate or accept the hypothesis.
7. Solve the problem.
8. Document the problem.

Commands Summary

The table lists useful commands. Sample output is shown on the following pages.

Command	Key Information Displayed
`show ip route` *ip-addr*	Displays the routing table information for a particular destination address.
`show ip ospf interface` *type/#* `show ip ospf interface brief`	Displays interfaces that are participating in the OSPF routing process. An interface does not need to be operational to be listed in the command output.
`show ip ospf neighbor`	Displays the OSPF neighbor table to verify that all expected neighbor relationships are operational.
`show ip ospf database router` *router-id*	Verifies whether the directly connected routers properly advertise the destination network. Use this command to display the router (type-1) for the connected routers.
`show ip ospf database external` *subnet*	Verifies the availability of a specific type-5 external link-state advertisement (LSA) in the OSPF database. The *subnet* option is the subnet IP address of the prefix in which you are interested.
`show ip ospf database summary` *subnet*	Verifies the availability of a specific target network in a different area. The *subnet* option is the subnet IP address of the prefix in which you are interested.
`show ip ospf database asbr-summary` *router-id*	Verifies if a type-4 summary autonomous system (AS) boundary LSA exists for the Autonomous System Boundary Router (ASBR) with the specified router ID.
`show system mtu`	Displays the switch or router Maximum Transmission Unit (MTU), normally 1500 bytes. Mismatches in MTU can cause neighbor relationships to fail.

`debug ip ospf packet`	Displays the headers of OSPF packets as they are received by the router. Transmitted packets are not displayed. Packets are only shown for interfaces that are enabled for OSPF.
`debug ip ospf adj`	Displays all the different stages of the OSPF adjacency building process. It also reveals mismatches in the basic parameters contained in the OSPF packet header, such as area ID mismatches, the source being on the wrong subnet, or authentication mismatches. It does not reveal other mismatches in hello parameters, such as hello timers, subnet masks, or flags.
`debug ip ospf events`	Displays the same information that is displayed by the `debug ip ospf adj` command. In addition, it displays the transmission and reception of hello packets and reports mismatches in the hello parameters.

Lab 5-2: Sample Troubleshooting Flows

Troubleshooting the OSPF Routing Protocol

The figure illustrates an example of a method that you could follow to diagnose and resolve problems related to the OSPF.

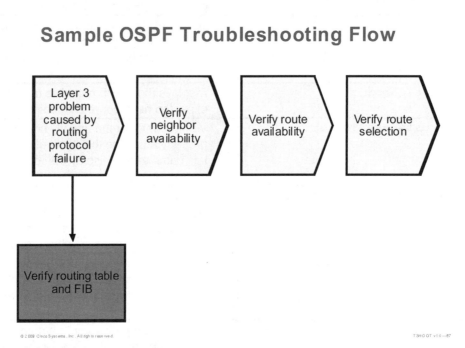

The usual trigger to start investigating routing protocol operation is when you are troubleshooting IP connectivity to a particular destination and you find that that the route to the destination network is missing from the routing table of one of the routers, or that a different route than expected was selected to forward the packets to that destination.

To install a route into the routing table, each router that uses a routing protocol goes through several stages:

- Discovers neighbors and establishes a neighbor relationship.

- Exchanges routing information with neighbors and stores the received information in protocol-specific data structures.

- Selects the best route from the available routes and installs it in the routing table.

Errors during any of these stages can cause missing routing information or wrong routing information installed in the routing table.

The exact processes that take place, the data structures that are used, and the commands to gather information about these processes and data structures are protocol-specific, but the generic troubleshooting principles are similar for all routing protocols.

The order of verification of the different process stages is not important as long as a structured approach is used.

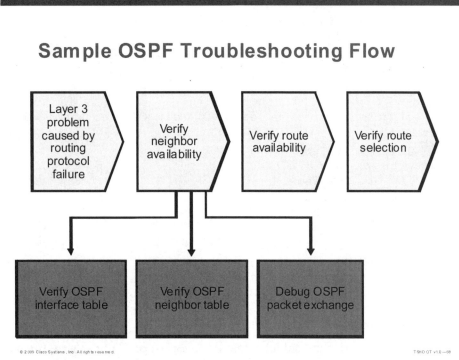

OSPF establishes and maintains neighbor relationships by using hello packets. Neighbors from which a hello packet is received are entered in the neighbor table. Subsequently, OSPF goes through the process of establishing an adjacency by transitioning through several stages in which the link-state database of the router are synchronized with its neighbor. After the completion of the database synchronization, the neighbors are considered to be fully adjacent, and both link-state updates and user traffic can be passed between the neighbors. The neighbor remains registered in the neighbor table as long as hello packets are received regularly. A neighbor is removed from the neighbor table when its dead time expires or when the interface on which the neighbor is registered goes down. The default OSPF hello timer is 10 seconds for point-to-point interfaces, such as serial interfaces running PPP or High-Level Data Link Control (HDLC), point-to-point Frame Relay or ATM subinterfaces, and broadcast-type interfaces such as Ethernet. The default dead time for these interfaces is 40 seconds. Each router advertises its hello and hold times in its hello packets, and the values must match for two routers to become neighbors.

Verify OSPF Interfaces

```
R1#show ip ospf interface brief
Interface    PID    area              IP Address/Mask    Cost   State  Nbrs F/C
Lo0          1      0                 10.1.201.1/32      1      P2P    0/0
Fa0/1        1      0                 10.1.2.2/30        1      DR     1/1
Se0/0/0      1      2                 10.1.1.1/30        64     P2P    1/1
```

Neighbors can only be discovered on an interface that has been enabled for OSPF and has not been configured as a passive interface. An interface can be enabled for OSPF in two ways. One way is if the IP address of the interface is covered by one of the **network** statements configured under the **router ospf** process, which assigns it to an area. Alternatively, an explicit **ip ospf** *process-id* **area** *area-id* command is configured on the interface, which assigns it to an area. To display a list of OSPF-enabled interfaces, use the **show ip ospf interface brief** command. This list includes interfaces that are down, which are marked as DOWN, and interfaces that have been configured as passive. However, passive interfaces are not easily recognizable in the output.

To verify whether an interface is passive, use the **show ip ospf interface** *interface-id* command. Instead of a short list, this command displays comprehensive details of the OSPF parameters and the operational state for the specified interface. This command is also useful to verify timer values, such as the hello and dead timers, which could prevent a neighbor relationship from being established.

```
R1#show ip ospf interface fastEthernet 0/1
FastEthernet0/1 is up, line protocol is up
  Internet Address 10.1.2.2/30, area 0
  Process ID 1, Router ID 10.1.201.1, Network Type BROADCAST, Cost: 1
  Transmit Delay is 1 sec, State DR, Priority 1
  Designated Router (ID) 10.1.201.1, Interface address 10.1.2.2
  No backup designated router on this network
  Timer intervals configured, hello 10, dead 40, Wait 40, Retransmit 5
    oob-resync timeout 40
    No Hellos (Passive interface)
  Supports Link-local Signaling (LLS)
  Cisco NSF helper support enabled
  IETF NSF helper support enabled
  Index 1/2, flood queue length 0
  Next 0x0(0)/0x0(0)
  Last flood scan length is 0, maximum is 0
  Last flood scan time is 0 msec, maximum is 0 msec
  Neighbor Count is 0, Adjacent neighbor count is 0
  Suppress hello for 0 neighbor(s)
```

What does this mean from a troubleshooting standpoint?

If you find that an interface is not listed in the output of the **show ip ospf interface brief** command as expected, verify the **network** commands under the **router ospf** configuration.

If you find that an interface is listed but no neighbors are registered on the interface, verify that the interface was not marked as passive by issuing the **show ip ospf interface** *interface-id* command for that interface.

Verify the OSPF Neighbor Table

```
R1#show ip ospf neighbor
```

Neighbor ID	Pri	State	dead Time	Address	Interface
10.1.211.1	1	FULL/DR	00:00:31	10.1.2.1	FastEthernet0/1
10.1.202.1	0	FULL/ -	00:00:38	10.1.1.2	Serial0/0/0

```
DLS1>show ip ospf neighbor
```

Neighbor ID	Pri	State	dead Time	Address	Interface
10.1.212.1	1	FULL/DR	00:00:35	10.1.200.253	Vlan200
10.1.201.1	1	FULL/BDR	00:00:39	10.1.2.2	FastEthernet0/5

To verify that all expected neighbor relationships are operational, you can display the OSPF neighbor table using the **show ip ospf neighbor** command.

While two routers establish an adjacency and synchronize their link-state databases, they go through the following phases: Attempt (optional), Init, 2-Way, Exstart, Exchange, Loading, and Full. The expected state for a neighbor relationship is Full. The other states are transitory states, and a neighbor should not be stuck in any of those states for an extended period of time.

The only exception to this rule is a broadcast or nonbroadcast network with more than three routers. On these types of networks, a designated router (DR) and backup designated router (BDR) are elected, and all routers establish a full adjacency with the DR and BDR. Any two routers that are both not a DR or BDR (marked "DROTHER" in the `show` commands) do not transition any further than the two-way state.

In the example output, the device has two neighbors: neighbor 10.1.212.1, which is the DR, and neighbor 10.1.201.1, which is the BDR.

Debug OSPF Packet Exchange

```
DLS1#debug ip ospf packet
OSPF packet debugging is on
DLS1#
Nov  5 15:54:32.574: OSPF: rcv. v:2 t:1 l:48 rid:10.1.212.1
     aid:0.0.0.0 chk:8B98 aut:0 auk: from Vlan200
Nov  5 15:54:38.917: OSPF: rcv. v:2 t:1 l:48 rid:10.1.201.1
     aid:0.0.0.0 chk:2394 aut:0 auk: from FastEthernet0/5


R1#debug ip ospf packet
Nov  5 15:57:21.503: OSPF: rcv. v:2 t:1 l:48 rid:10.1.211.1
     aid:0.0.0.0 chk:2394 aut:0 auk: from FastEthernet0/1
Nov  5 15:57:22.443: OSPF: rcv. v:2 t:1 l:48 rid:10.1.202.1
     aid:0.0.0.2 chk:4497 aut:0 auk: from Serial0/0/0
```

```
In this highlighted sample output for R1, router ID 10.1.202.1 is in area 2
(aid:0.0.0.2) and the hello was received on interface Serial 0/0/0.
```

When an OSPF neighbor relationship is not properly established, you can use several `debug` commands to display events related to the establishment of neighbor relationships. The most elementary command is `debug ip ospf packet`, which displays the headers of OSPF packets as they are received by the router.

This command lists only received packets. Transmitted packets are not displayed. In addition, because interfaces that are not enabled for OSPF do not listen to the OSPF multicast addresses, packets are only shown for interfaces that are enabled for OSPF.

The following fields are the most relevant in the header description of these packets:

- Type (t): Lists the type of packet. Possible packet types are:
    - Type 1: Hello packets
    - Type 2: Database description packets
    - Type 3: Link-state request packets
    - Type 4: Link-state update packets
    - Type 5: Link-state acknowledgement packets
- Router ID (rid): Lists the ID of the sending router. This is usually not the same as the source address of the packet.
- Area ID (aid): The 32-bit area ID of the sending router is represented in dotted-decimal IP address format.
- Authentication (aut): Lists the authentication type. Possible types are:
    - Type 0: No (null) authentication
    - Type 1: Cleartext authentication
    - Type 2: Message Digest 5 (MD5) authentication
- Interface (from): Lists the interface on which the packet was received.

Note: Only successfully received and accepted packets are listed in the output of the **debug ip ospf packet** command. If there is a mismatch between essential parameters in the header, such as the area ID, authentication type, or authentication data between this router and the neighbor, the packets from that neighbor are silently discarded and not listed in the output of the debug.

The usefulness of this command for troubleshooting is limited because it does not display sent packets, packets received on an interface that is not enabled for OSPF, or packets that carry mismatched header information. However, because of the relatively limited amount of generated output, it can be used to confirm the reception of correct hellos from a neighbor.

Debug OSPF Adjacencies

In the following debug outputs, DLS1 interface Fa0/5 (link to R1) is shutdown and the OSPF adjacency terminates. When the DLS1 Fa0/5 interface is reactivated, an election occurs, DLS1 becomes the DR again and builds LSAs to send to R1. DLS1 and R1 establish a neighbor relationship and exchange OSPF database information.

```
DLS1#debug ip ospf adj
OSPF adjacency events debugging is on

DLS1(config)#interface fa0/5
DLS1(config-if)#shut

Nov  5 16:04:10.619: OSPF: Interface FastEthernet0/5 going Down
Nov  5 16:04:10.619: OSPF: 10.1.211.1 address 10.1.2.1 on FastEthernet0/5 is dea
d, state DOWN
Nov  5 16:04:10.619: OSPF: Neighbor change Event on interface FastEthernet0/5
Nov  5 16:04:10.619: OSPF: DR/BDR election on FastEthernet0/5
Nov  5 16:04:10.619: OSPF: Elect BDR 10.1.201.1
Nov  5 16:04:10.619: OSPF: Elect DR 10.1.201.1
Nov  5 16:04:10.619: OSPF: Elect BDR 10.1.201.1
Nov  5 16:04:10.619: OSPF: Elect DR 10.1.201.1
Nov  5 16:04:10.619
DLS1(config-if)#:       DR: 10.1.201.1 (Id)    BDR: 10.1.201.1 (Id)
Nov  5 16:04:10.619: OSPF: Flush network LSA immediately
Nov  5 16:04:10.619: OSPF: Remember old DR 10.1.211.1 (id)
Nov  5 16:04:10.619: OSPF: 10.1.201.1 address 10.1.2.2 on FastEthernet0/5 is dea
d, state DOWN
Nov  5 16:04:10.619: %OSPF-5-ADJCHG: Process 1, Nbr 10.1.201.1 on FastEthernet0/
5 from FULL to DOWN, Neighbor Down: Interface down or detached
Nov  5 16:04:10.619: OSPF: Neighbor change Event on interface FastEthernet0/5
Nov  5 16:04:10.619: OSPF: DR/BDR election on FastEthernet0/5
Nov  5 16:04:10.619: OSPF: Elect BDR 0.0.0.0
Nov  5 16:04:10.619: OSPF: Elect DR 0.0.0.0
Nov  5 16:04:10.619:       DR: none    BDR: none
Nov  5 16:04:10.619: OSPF: Remember old DR 10.1.201.1 (id)
Nov  5 16:04:10.619: OSPF: [change notify] will poll [cnt 11] interface status f
or FastEthernet0/5
Nov  5 16:04:11.122: OSPF: We are not DR to build Net Lsa for interface FastEthe
rnet0/5
Nov  5 16:04:11.122: OSPF: Build network LSA for FastEthernet0/5, router ID 10.1
.211.1
Nov  5 16:04:11.122: OSPF: Build router LSA for area 0, router ID 10.1.211.1, se
q 0x80000012, process 1
Nov  5 16:04:12.599: %LINK-5-CHANGED: Interface FastEthernet0/5, changed state t
o administratively down
Nov  5 16:04:13.606: %LINEPROTO-5-UPDOWN: Line protocol on Interface FastEtherne
```

t0/5, changed state to down
Nov 5 16:04:20.628: OSPF: will poll [count 10] interface status for FastEtherne
t0/5
Nov 5 16:04:30.636: OSPF: will poll [count 9] interface status for FastEthernet
0/5
Nov 5 16:04:40.821: OSPF: will poll [count 8] interface status for FastEthernet
0/5
Nov 5 16:04:50.830: OSPF: will poll [count 7] interface status for FastEthernet
0/5
Nov 5 16:05:00.838: OSPF: will poll [count 6] interface status for FastEthernet
0/5
Nov 5 16:05:10.839: OSPF: will poll [count 5] interface status for FastEthernet
0/5
Nov 5 16:05:20.847: OSPF: will poll [count 4] interface status for FastEthernet
0/5
Nov 5 16:05:30.856: OSPF: will poll [count 3] interface status for FastEthernet
0/5
Nov 5 16:05:40.865: OSPF: will poll [count 2] interface status for FastEthernet
0/5
Nov 5 16:05:50.865: OSPF: will poll [count 1] interface status for FastEthernet
0/5

DLS1(config)#**interface fa0/5**
DLS1(config-if)#**no shut**

Nov 5 16:05:59.800: %LINK-3-UPDOWN: Interface FastEthernet0/5, changed state to
 up
Nov 5 16:05:59.800: OSPF: Interface FastEthernet0/5 going Up
Nov 5 16:05:59.800: OSPF: [change notify] will poll [cnt 11] interface status f
or FastEthernet0/5
Nov 5 16:06:00.303: OSPF: Build router LSA for area 0, router ID 10.1.211.1, se
q 0x80000013, process 1
Nov 5 16:06:00.807: %LINEPROTO-5-UPDOWN: Line protocol on Interface FastEtherne
t0/5, changed state to up
Nov 5 16:06:09.800: OSPF: will poll [count 10] interface status for FastEtherne
t0/5
Nov 5 16:06:09.800: OSPF: 2 Way Communication to 10.1.201.1 on FastEthernet0/5,
 state 2WAY
Nov 5 16:06:19.809: OSPF: will poll [count 9] interface status for FastEthernet
0/5
Nov 5 16:06:29.809: OSPF: will poll [count 8] interface status for FastEthernet
0/5
Nov 5 16:06:39.809: OSPF: end of Wait on interface FastEthernet0/5
Nov 5 16:06:39.809: OSPF: DR/BDR election on FastEthernet0/5
Nov 5 16:06:39.809: OSPF: Elect BDR 10.1.211.1
Nov 5 16:06:39.809: OSPF: Elect DR 10.1.211.1
Nov 5 16:06:39.809: OSPF: Elect BDR 10.1.201.1
Nov 5 16:06:39.809: OSPF: Elect DR 10.1.211.1
Nov 5 16:06:39.809:   DR: 10.1.211.1 (Id)   BDR: 10.1.201.1 (Id)
Nov 5 16:06:39.809: OSPF: Send DBD to 10.1.201.1 on FastEthernet0/5 seq 0x192E
opt 0x52 flag 0x7 len 32
Nov 5 16:06:39.818: OSPF: will poll [count 7] interface status for FastEthernet
0/5
Nov 5 16:06:40.313: OSPF: No full nbrs to build Net Lsa for interface FastEther
net0/5
Nov 5 16:06:42.209: OSPF: Rcv DBD from 10.1.201.1 on FastEthernet0/5 seq 0x8AC
opt 0x52 flag 0x7 len 32 mtu 1500 state EXSTART
Nov 5 16:06:42.209: OSPF: First DBD and we are not SLAVE

```
Nov  5 16:06:44.818: OSPF: Send DBD to 10.1.201.1 on FastEthernet0/5 seq 0x192E
opt 0x52 flag 0x7 len 32
Nov  5 16:06:44.818: OSPF: Retransmitting DBD to 10.1.201.1 on FastEthernet0/5 [
1]
Nov  5 16:06:44.818: OSPF: Rcv DBD from 10.1.201.1 on FastEthernet0/5 seq 0x192E
 opt 0x52 flag 0x2 len 432  mtu 1500 state EXSTART
Nov  5 16:06:44.818: OSPF: NBR Negotiation Done. We are the MASTER
Nov  5 16:06:44.818: OSPF: Send DBD to 10.1.201.1 on FastEthernet0/5 seq 0x192F
opt 0x52 flag 0x3 len 412
Nov  5 16:06:44.818: OSPF: Rcv DBD from 10.1.201.1 on FastEthernet0/5 seq 0x192F
 opt 0x52 flag 0x0 len 32  mtu 1500 state EXCHANGE
Nov  5 16:06:44.818: OSPF: Send DBD to 10.1.201.1 on FastEthernet0/5 seq 0x1930
opt 0x52 flag 0x1 len 32
Nov  5 16:06:44.818: OSPF: Send LS REQ to 10.1.201.1 length 24 LSA count 2
Nov  5 16:06:44.826: OSPF: Rcv LS REQ from 10.1.201.1 on FastEthernet0/5 length
36 LSA count 1
Nov  5 16:06:44.826: OSPF: Send UPD to 10.1.2.2 on FastEthernet0/5 length 64 LSA
 count 1
Nov  5 16:06:44.826: OSPF: Rcv DBD from 10.1.201.1 on FastEthernet0/5 seq 0x1930
 opt 0x52 flag 0x0 len 32  mtu 1500 state EXCHANGE
Nov  5 16:06:44.826: OSPF: Exchange Done with 10.1.201.1 on FastEthernet0/5
Nov  5 16:06:44.826: OSPF: Rcv LS UPD from 10.1.201.1 on FastEthernet0/5 length
108 LSA count 2
Nov  5 16:06:44.826: OSPF: No full nbrs to build Net Lsa for interface FastEther
net0/5
Nov  5 16:06:44.826: OSPF: Build network LSA for FastEthernet0/5, router ID 10.1
.211.1
Nov  5 16:06:44.826: OSPF: Synchronized with 10.1.201.1 on FastEthernet0/5, stat
e FULL
Nov  5 16:06:44.826: %OSPF-5-ADJCHG: Process 1, Nbr 10.1.201.1 on FastEthernet0/
5 from LOADING to FULL, Loading Done
```

The **debug ip ospf adj** command is useful for troubleshooting OSPF neighbor-related events. It displays the different stages of the OSPF adjacency-building process as two neighbors transition from the init state to the full state. This command can be helpful in diagnosing problems in which a neighbor relationship is stuck in a particular stage of the adjacency-building process.

This command also reveals mismatches in the basic parameters contained in the OSPF packet header, such as area ID mismatches, the source being on the wrong subnet, or authentication mismatches. It does not, however, reveal other mismatches in hello parameters, such as hello timers, subnet masks, or flags.

Debug OSPF Events

```
DLS2#debug ip ospf events

*Nov  5 03:03:11.043: OSPF: Send hello to 224.0.0.5 area 0 on FastEthernet0/5 fr
om 10.1.2.13
DLS2#
*Nov  5 03:03:13.551: OSPF: Send hello to 224.0.0.5 area 0 on Vlan200 from 10.1.
200.253
*Nov  5 03:03:13.845: OSPF: Rcv hello from 10.1.211.1 area 0 from Vlan200 10.1.2
00.252
*Nov  5 03:03:13.845: OSPF: End of hello processing
DLS2#
*Nov  5 03:03:16.051: OSPF: Send hello to 224.0.0.5 area 0 on FastEthernet0/5 fr
om 10.1.2.13
*Nov  5 03:03:16.286: OSPF: Rcv hello from 10.1.203.1 area 0 from FastEthernet0/
5 10.1.2.14
```

```
*Nov  5 03:03:16.286: OSPF: Mismatched hello parameters from 10.1.2.14
*Nov  5 03:03:16.286: OSPF: dead R 40 C 15, hello R 10 C 5  Mask R 255.255.255.2
52 C 255.255.255.252
DLS2#

DLS2#undebug all
All possible debugging has been turned off
DLS2#
*Nov  5 03:03:28: %OSPF-5-ADJCHG: Process 1, Nbr 10.1.203.1 on FastEthernet0/5 f
rom FULL to DOWN, Neighbor Down: dead timer expired
```

A third **debug** command that can be useful in troubleshooting the establishment of OSPF neighbor relationships is **debug ip ospf events**. This command displays the same information that is displayed by the **debug ip ospf adj** command, but it also displays the transmission and reception of hello packets and reports mismatches in the hello parameters.

Confirming the transmission of hello packets by using this command can be useful because the **debug ip ospf packet** or **debug ip ospf adj** commands do not display the transmission of hello packets.

You can also use this command to display the reception of invalid hello packets. If there is a mismatch between the neighbors in the hello parameters that prevents the neighbor relationship from forming, this command displays the type of parameter mismatch and the value of the mismatched parameters. It displays mismatches for the following parameters:

- Hello and dead timers
- Area ID
- Subnet and subnet mask
- Authentication type and authentication data
- Flags that signify the area type, such as stub or not-so-stubby area (NSSA)

Because this command displays more events, it is often better to first enable the **debug ip ospf adj** command and only use the **debug ip ospf event** command if you did not get the information you need.

Sample OSPF Troubleshooting Flow

After you have verified that neighbor relationships have been established as expected, verify that the network topology information for the destination network that you are troubleshooting has been received correctly and entered into the OSPF link-state database.

The presence or absence of specific topology information in the OSPF link-state database can help isolate the source of the problem.

Verify the OSPF Link-State Database for Intra-Area Routes

```
DLS2#show ip ospf database router 10.1.212.1

            OSPF Router with ID (10.1.212.1) (Process ID 1)

               Router Link States (area 0)

  LS age: 60
  Options: (No TOS-capability, DC)
  LS Type: Router Links
  Link State ID: 10.1.212.1
  Advertising Router: 10.1.212.1
  LS Seq Number: 80000012
  Checksum: 0x592C
  Length: 60
  area Border Router
  Number of Links: 3

    Link connected to: a Stub Network
      (Link ID) Network/subnet number: 10.1.212.1
      (Link Data) Network Mask: 255.255.255.255
       Number of TOS metrics: 0
        TOS 0 Metrics: 1

    Link connected to: a Transit Network
      (Link ID) Designated Router address: 10.1.2.13
      (Link Data) Router Interface address: 10.1.2.13
       Number of TOS metrics: 0
        TOS 0 Metrics: 1
```

To decide which information to look for in the link-state database, you first need to discern in which type of route you are interested. If the destination network that you are troubleshooting is in the same area as the router from which you are troubleshooting, you know that the path to this destination network was derived from the type-1 and type-2 LSAs in the database of that area. To begin with, you can verify whether the directly connected routers properly advertise the destination network. To do this, display the router (type-1) for the connected routers by issuing the **show ip ospf database router** *router-id* command for these routers. To troubleshoot OSPF effectively, it is necessary to know the router IDs of all routers in your network, because these are used to identify a router in many of the OSPF **show** commands.

As part of the type-1 router LSA for a specific router, all subnets corresponding to a point-to-point link, loopback interface, or nontransit broadcast network (Ethernet) are listed as stub networks. If the target network is missing in this list, this indicates that the interface on the advertising router has not been enabled for OSPF.

In the example above subnet 10.1.212.1 is advertised by router 10.1.212.1 in area 0.

For transit networks, such as an Ethernet LAN with multiple routers attached, a link to the DR for the segment is listed. This points to the type-2 network LSA that contains the full topology information for the segment.

In the example above, this router is connected to a transit network with router 10.1.2.13 as the DR. Note that this IP address is the interface IP address of the DR, not the router ID.

```
DLS1#show ip ospf database network 10.1.2.13
```

```
            OSPF Router with ID (10.1.211.1) (Process ID 1)

                Net Link States (area 0)

  Routing Bit Set on this LSA
  LS age: 695
  Options: (No TOS-capability, DC)
  LS Type: Network Links
  Link State ID: 10.1.2.13 (address of Designated Router)
  Advertising Router: 10.1.212.1
  LS Seq Number: 80000004
  Checksum: 0xDBAA
  Length: 32
  Network Mask: /30
        Attached Router: 10.1.212.1
        Attached Router: 10.1.203.1
```

To display full information about a transit LAN, issue the **show ip ospf database network** *designated-router* command, using the IP address of the DR that was listed in the type-1 router LSA for one of the routers connected to the transit LAN. In the type-2 LSA, the DR advertises the subnet mask and connected routers for the segment. The connected routers are listed by their router ID values.

In the example above, a subnet mask of /30 is advertised for the transit LAN, and two connected routers are listed.

Verify the OSPF Link-State Database for Inter-Area Routes

```
DLS1>show ip ospf database summary 10.1.203.1

            OSPF Router with ID (10.1.211.1) (Process ID 1)

                Summary Net Link States (area 0)

  LS age: 577
  Options: (No TOS-capability, DC, Upward)
  LS Type: Summary Links(Network)
  Link State ID: 10.1.203.1 (summary Network Number)
  Advertising Router: 10.1.203.1
  LS Seq Number: 8000000B
  Checksum: 0x2A58
  Length: 28
  Network Mask: /32
        TOS: 0  Metric: 1
```

If the destination network that you are troubleshooting is in a different area than the area of the router from which you are troubleshooting, the router will not learn about this network through type-1 and type-2 LSAs because these are only used for intra-area routes. OSPF inter-area routes are calculated based on type-3 LSAs that are generated by the Area Border Routers (ABRs) for the area.

To verify the availability of a specific target network in a different area, you can use the **show ip ospf database summary** *subnet* command, where *subnet* is the subnet IP address of the prefix in which you are interested.

The type-3 summary LSA contains the subnet, mask, and cost of the targeted subnet and also lists the router ID of the ABR. If multiple ABRs are advertising the same network, all entries are listed.

In the example above, subnet 10.1.203.1/32 is advertised with a cost of 1 by ABR 10.1.203.1. The cost advertised by the ABR is the cost from the advertising ABR to the target network. When executing the Shortest Path First (SPF) algorithm, the router calculates its own cost to reach the ABR within the area and adds that to the cost advertised by the ABR.

If you do not find an entry for the target network, the next step is to connect to the ABR that you expected to be advertising the route and verify if the route is available there.

Verify the OSPF Link-State Database for External Routes

DLS1#**show ip ospf database external 10.1.1.0**

```
            OSPF Router with ID (10.1.211.1) (Process ID 1)

               Type-5 AS External Link States

  Routing Bit Set on this LSA
  LS age: 1196
  Options: (No TOS-capability, DC)
  LS Type: AS External Link
  Link State ID: 10.1.1.0 (External Network Number )
  Advertising Router: 10.1.201.1
  LS Seq Number: 80000006
  Checksum: 0x6804
  Length: 36
  Network Mask: /30
        Metric Type: 2 (Larger than any link state path)
        TOS: 0
        Metric: 100
        Forward Address: 0.0.0.0
        External Route Tag: 0
```

If the destination network that you are troubleshooting did not originate in the OSPF network but was redistributed from a different source, the OSPF router learns about this network through type-5 external routes that are injected into the OSPF database by an Autonomous System Boundary Router (ASBR).

To verify the availability of a specific type-5 external LSA in the OSPF database, issue the **show ip ospf database external** *subnet* command, where *subnet* is the subnet IP address of the prefix in which you are interested.

The type-5 summary LSA contains the subnet, mask, metric type, and cost of the targeted subnet. In addition, it lists the router ID of the advertising ASBR. If multiple ASBRs are advertising the same network, all entries are listed.

In the example above, subnet 10.1.1.0/30 is advertised with a cost of 100 as a metric-type 2 external route by ASBR 10.1.201.1.

If you do not find an entry for the target network, the next step is to connect to the ASBR that you expected to be advertising the route and verify if the route is available. If the route is available but not advertised by the ASBR, troubleshoot the route redistribution process on that router.

DLS1#**show ip ospf database router 10.1.201.1**

```
            OSPF Router with ID (10.1.211.1) (Process ID 1)

               Router Link States (area 0)

  Routing Bit Set on this LSA
  LS age: 391
  Options: (No TOS-capability, DC)
  LS Type: Router Links
  Link State ID: 10.1.201.1
  Advertising Router: 10.1.201.1
  LS Seq Number: 8000000E
  Checksum: 0x1163
```

```
Length: 48
AS Boundary Router
Number of Links: 2
```

`<Output omitted>`

Instead of connecting to the ASBR, the OSPF database can also be used to verify if any form of redistribution has been configured on the router that is supposed to be an ASBR. If that router is in the same area as the router from which you are troubleshooting, you can inspect the type-1 router LSA for the ASBR and verify that it advertises itself as an ASBR.

In the example above, the router 10.1.201.1 announces its ASBR status in its type-1 LSA. If the router does not advertise its ASBR status in its type-1 LSA, this indicates that redistribution has not been configured correctly on that router.

```
DLS1#show ip ospf database asbr-summary 10.1.201.1

            OSPF Router with ID (10.1.211.1) (Process ID 1)

            Summary ASB Link States (area 1)

  LS age: 723
  Options: (No TOS-capability, DC, Upward)
  LS Type: Summary Links(AS Boundary Router)
  Link State ID: 10.1.201.1 (AS Boundary Router address)
  Advertising Router: 10.1.211.1
  LS Seq Number: 8000000D
  Checksum: 0xF583
  Length: 28
  Network Mask: /0
        TOS: 0  Metric: 1
```

If the ASBR is not in the same area as the router from which you are troubleshooting, you do not have its type-1 LSA in the database of the router. As a result, you cannot verify its ASBR status by displaying the type-1 LSA. However, if an ASBR is available in a different area, the ABRs for the area generate a type-4 summary AS Boundary (ASB) entry to announce the availability of the ASBR. The presence or absence of a type-4 entry can also yield a clue about the operation of the redistribution.

You can use the **show ip ospf database asbr-summary** *router-id* command to verify if a type-4 summary ASB LSA exists for the ASBR with the specified router ID.

In the example above, ABR 10.1.211.1 announces the availability of ASBR 10.1.201.1.

```
DLS1#show ip ospf border-routers

OSPF Process 1 internal Routing Table

Codes: i - Intra-area route, I - Inter-area route

i 10.1.212.1 [1] via 10.1.200.253, Vlan200, ABR, area 0, SPF 5
i 10.1.201.1 [1] via 10.1.2.2, FastEthernet0/5, ASBR, area 0, SPF 5
i 10.1.203.1 [2] via 10.1.200.253, Vlan200, ABR, area 0, SPF 5
```

During the execution of the SPF algorithm, a router combines the information from the various LSAs that contain information about ABR and ASBR status and calculates the shortest paths to each ABR and ASBR. You can view the result of this calculation with the **show ip ospf border-routers** command.

In the example above, area 0 has two ABRs: 10.1.212.1 and 10.1.203.1. The cost to reach ABR 10.1.212.1 is 1, as can be seen from the number in the square brackets. The cost to reach ABR 10.1.203.1 is 2. The cost to reach ASBR 10.1.201.1 is 1. This cost is important to know because it is added to the cost advertised by these routers in their type-3 LSAs to obtain the total cost to the destination network.

Sample OSPF Troubleshooting Flow

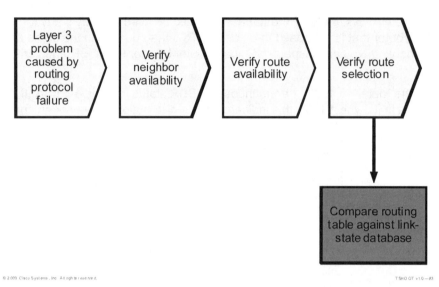

TSHOOT v1.0—83

If all appropriate entries are available in the OSPF link-state database, these should result in correct routes in the IP routing table after calculation of the SPF algorithm. Unfortunately, the results of the SPF algorithm for each individual route cannot be directly verified.

Keep in mind that OSPF competes with other routing sources to install routes in the routing table. Therefore, an OSPF route might not be installed in the routing table because a route with a better administrative distance from a different source is available.

Verify the MTU between OSPF Neighbors

Maximum Transmission Unit (MTU) mismatch between two OSPF neighbors is common when connecting together two multilayer switches of a different type (for example 3550 and 3560) or when interconnecting a multilayer switch with a router. Multilayer switches often have the system MTU set to 1504 bytes while routers typically use an MTU of 1500 bytes. An MTU mismatch usually causes two OSPF neighbors to remain stuck in EXSTART/EXCHANGE state, failing to create full adjacency.

Changes to the system MTU are made using the **system mtu** *mtu-size* command. The routing MTU can be changed using the **system mtu routing** *mtu-size* command. System MTU on a Cisco Catalyst 3560 switch can range from 1500-1998 bytes.

Note: Changes to MTU size will not take effect until the next reload is done.

MTU settings can be verified using the **show interfaces** or the **show system mtu** commands:

```
DLS2#show interfaces fastEthernet 0/5
FastEthernet0/5 is up, line protocol is up (connected)
  Hardware is Fast Ethernet, address is 0017.5a53.a3c2 (bia 0017.5a53.a3c2)
  Description: FE to R3
  Internet address is 10.1.2.13/30
  MTU 1500 bytes, BW 100000 Kbit, DLY 100 usec,
     reliability 255/255, txload 1/255, rxload 1/255

DLS2#show system mtu

System MTU size is 1500 bytes
```

```
System Jumbo MTU size is 1500 bytes
Routing MTU size is 1500 bytes
```

OSPF Neighbor status can be verified using the `show ip ospf neighbor` command. In the example shown below, the system and system routing MTU for Layer 3 switch DLS2 has been changed to 1504 bytes. The MTU of the neighbors, DLS1 (10.1.211.1) and R3 (10.1.203.1) is set to the default of 1500 bytes.

```
DLS2#show ip ospf neighbor

Neighbor ID     Pri   State          Dead Time    Address         Interface
10.1.211.1        1   EXSTART/BDR    00:00:38     10.1.200.252    Vlan200
10.1.203.1        1   EXSTART/BDR    00:00:37     10.1.2.14       FastEthernet0/5
```

Console messages:

```
DLS2#
%OSPF-5-ADJCHG: Process 1, Nbr 10.1.203.1 on FastEthernet0/5 from DOWN to
DOWN, Neighbor Down: Ignore timer expired
DLS2#
%OSPF-5-ADJCHG: Process 1, Nbr 10.1.211.1 on Vlan200 from EXSTART to DOWN,
Neighbor Down: Too many retransmissions
```

Troubleshooting Route Redistribution

The figure illustrates an example of a method that you can use to diagnose and resolve problems related to route redistribution.

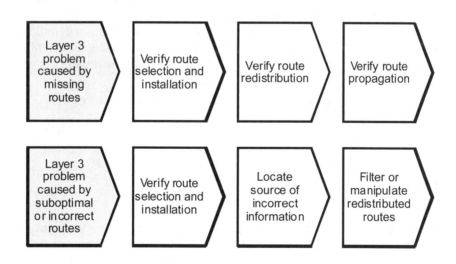

When do you start troubleshooting route redistribution?

There are two major reasons to start troubleshooting the route redistribution. The first reason is when you are experiencing IP connectivity problems in an environment in which information from a specific routing domain is redistributed into a different routing domain and the connectivity problem is caused by a route from the source routing domain that is not available on one or more of the routers participating in the destination routing domain. In this scenario, the cause of the problem is that the exchange of routing information between the source routing domain and the destination routing domain is not working correctly.

Note: In this section, the terms source and destination are used to indicate the source and destination of the routing information, not the source and destination of a traffic flow.

The second reason to start troubleshooting route redistribution is if you are experiencing IP connectivity problems caused by the use of incorrect routing information by some of the routers in a network that use route redistribution. This behavior could be caused by routing information feedback or improper route selection.

Sample troubleshooting flows for each of these scenarios are provided in this section.

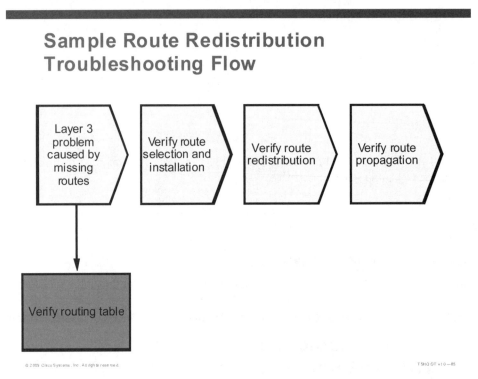

The first scenario in which you start troubleshooting route redistribution is when redistribution is configured and you are troubleshooting connectivity problems to a network in the source routing domain from a router in the destination routing domain. This type of problem is usually encountered during a generic IP connectivity troubleshooting process when a route is discovered missing from the routing table on one of the routers in the destination routing domain while the route is present in the routing tables of the routers in the source routing domain.

Troubleshooting redistribution consists of troubleshooting four generic areas:

- Source routing protocol
- Route selection and installation
- Redistribution
- Destination protocol

In this scenario, the reason to start troubleshooting the redistribution is when the route is available in the source routing domain but not in the destination routing domain. Therefore, the first step has already been taken at this point. If the route is not available everywhere in the source routing domain to begin with, there is no reason to start troubleshooting redistribution, but you should initiate a troubleshooting process for the source routing protocol first.

Therefore, we will start at the second step: troubleshooting route selection and installation.

Sample Route Redistribution Troubleshooting Flow

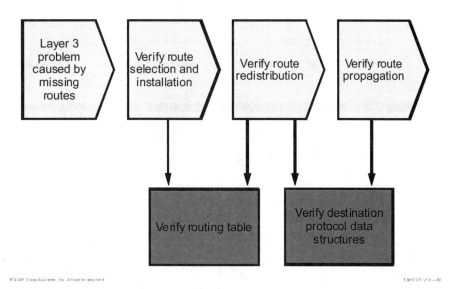

There are not many tools that are specifically targeted at troubleshooting the redistribution process. The redistribution process takes routes from the routing table after they have been installed by the source routing protocol and then injects them into the destination protocol's data structures. Therefore, the main tools that are available to track this flow of information are the commands that allow you to examine the routing table and the destination protocol data structures.

After you have verified that the routes are injected into the destination protocol's data structures, you have finished troubleshooting the actual redistribution process. If the routes are not properly propagated by the destination protocol, initiate a troubleshooting process for the destination protocol.

The `show ip route 10.1.202.1 255.255.255.255` command on R1 indicates that the route is known via EIGRP 1 and is redistributing via OSPF, but it is not being advertised by OSPF.

```
R1#show ip route 10.1.202.1 255.255.255.255
Routing entry for 10.1.202.1/32
  Known via "eigrp 1", distance 90, metric 2297856, type internal
  Redistributing via eigrp 1, ospf 1
  Last update from 10.1.1.2 on Serial0/0/0, 07:02:16 ago
  Routing Descriptor Blocks:
  * 10.1.1.2, from 10.1.1.2, 07:02:16 ago, via Serial0/0/0
      Route metric is 2297856, traffic share count is 1
      Total delay is 25000 microseconds, minimum bandwidth is 1544 Kbit
      Reliability 255/255, minimum MTU 1500 bytes
      Loading 1/255, Hops 1
```

The `show ip route 10.1.203.1 255.255.255.255` command on R1 indicates that the route is known via EIGRP 1 and is redistributing via EIGRP. It is also being advertised by EIGRP 1.

```
R1#show ip route 10.1.203.1 255.255.255.255
Routing entry for 10.1.203.1/32
  Known via "ospf 1", distance 110, metric 4, type inter area
  Redistributing via eigrp 1
  Advertised by eigrp 1 metric 1544 2000 255 1 1500
  Last update from 10.1.2.1 on FastEthernet0/1, 07:13:32 ago
```

```
Routing Descriptor Blocks:
* 10.1.2.1, from 10.1.203.1, 07:13:32 ago, via FastEthernet0/1
    Route metric is 4, traffic share count is 1
```

The best tool available in troubleshooting redistribution problems is the **show ip route** *network mask* command. Routes that are being redistributed and advertised to other routers by the destination protocol are marked with a line starting with "Advertised by" and then lists the destination protocol and any parameters configured on the redistribution statement, such as configured metrics and metric type.

What makes this command useful is that it takes into account any route maps or distribute lists that are applied to the redistribution.

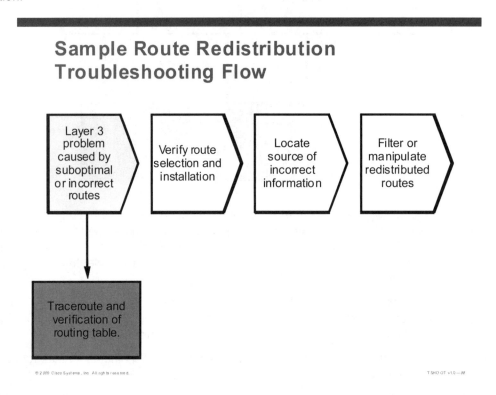

The second common scenario that might lead you to start troubleshooting route redistribution is when you discover that traffic is using unexpected suboptimal routes to reach certain destinations or that traffic enters a routing loop. This is often discovered while troubleshooting IP connectivity to a certain destination and using the **show ip route** and **traceroute** commands to track the flow of traffic. When you are redistributing routing information between routing protocols, you have to be aware that improper route selection or routing feedback can cause suboptimal paths to be used or traffic to enter a routing loop. Whenever you spot unexpected routing behavior in a network that uses redistribution, consider routing feedback or improper route selection as a possible cause.

A typical symptom of a redistribution problem is when the expected route is available on the router that you are troubleshooting, but it is not selected as the best route in the routing table. A route from a different protocol or a route of the same protocol but originated from a different source is selected as the best route and installed in the routing table.

Sample Route Redistribution Troubleshooting Flow

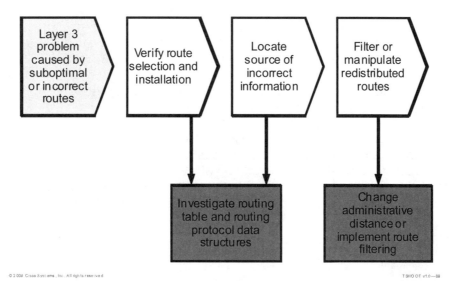

The first question to ask at this point is if the route is only improperly selected. In other words, you expected this route to be present but did not want it to be selected as the best route. If this is the case, you can manipulate the route selection process by changing the administrative distance. This can be done for all routes learned via a particular routing protocol or selectively using an access list.

If the route was not only improperly selected but should not have been present at all in the routing protocol data structures in this router, you must track the source of the route and use route-filtering techniques at the source to stop it from being advertised.

Verify the Routing Table

```
R1#show ip route
Codes: C - connected, S - static, R - RIP, M - mobile, B - BGP
       D - EIGRP, EX - EIGRP external, O - OSPF, IA - OSPF inter area
       N1 - OSPF NSSA external type 1, N2 - OSPF NSSA external type 2
       E1 - OSPF external type 1, E2 - OSPF external type 2
       i - IS-IS, su - IS-IS summary, L1 - IS-IS level-1, L2 - IS-IS level-2
       ia - IS-IS inter area, * - candidate default, U - per-user static route
       o - ODR, P - periodic downloaded static route

Gateway of last resort is not set

     10.0.0.0/8 is variably subnetted, 15 subnets, 3 masks
O IA    10.1.10.0/24 [110/2] via 10.1.2.1, 07:43:07, FastEthernet0/1
O       10.1.2.12/30 [110/3] via 10.1.2.1, 07:42:57, FastEthernet0/1
C       10.1.1.2/32 is directly connected, Serial0/0/0
C       10.1.2.0/30 is directly connected, FastEthernet0/1
C       10.1.1.0/30 is directly connected, Serial0/0/0
O IA    10.1.30.0/24 [110/2] via 10.1.2.1, 07:43:07, FastEthernet0/1
O IA    10.1.20.0/24 [110/2] via 10.1.2.1, 07:43:07, FastEthernet0/1
O IA    10.1.50.0/24 [110/2] via 10.1.2.1, 07:43:07, FastEthernet0/1
O IA    10.1.100.0/24 [110/2] via 10.1.2.1, 07:43:07, FastEthernet0/1
D       10.1.202.1/32 [90/2297856] via 10.1.1.2, 07:43:48, Serial0/0/0
O IA    10.1.203.1/32 [110/4] via 10.1.2.1, 07:42:57, FastEthernet0/1
C       10.1.201.1/32 is directly connected, Loopback0
```

```
O          10.1.200.0/24 [110/2] via 10.1.2.1, 07:43:00, FastEthernet0/1
O          10.1.211.1/32 [110/2] via 10.1.2.1, 07:43:10, FastEthernet0/1
O          10.1.212.1/32 [110/3] via 10.1.2.1, 07:43:00, FastEthernet0/1

R1#show ip route 10.1.50.0 255.255.255.0
Routing entry for 10.1.50.0/24
  Known via "ospf 1", distance 110, metric 2, type inter area
  Redistributing via eigrp 1
  Advertised by eigrp 1 metric 1544 2000 255 1 1500
  Last update from 10.1.2.1 on FastEthernet0/1, 07:42:07 ago
  Routing Descriptor Blocks:
  * 10.1.2.1, from 10.1.211.1, 07:42:07 ago, via FastEthernet0/1
      Route metric is 2, traffic share count is 1
```

The source of a route in the routing table is marked by the "from" field that follows the next-hop IP address. For distance vector protocols, the source and next-hop addresses are typically the same. For a link-state protocol, such as OSPF, this is the router that originated the LSA on which the route is based. By tracking the routing source from router to router, you can determine the point where the incorrect routing information is injected into the routing protocol's data structures, and you can apply filtering to stop it from being propagated.

Reflection Questions

1. Which lab trouble tickets did you have the most difficulty with? _____

_____

_____

_____

2. For any of the trouble tickets, would you change anything about the process that you used now that you see the resolution of the problem? _____

_____

_____

_____

3. Which commands did you find most useful in diagnosing OSPF and redistribution issues? Add these to your toolbox for future use. Which commands did you find least useful?

_____

_____

_____

4. What is required for routes to be redistributed from OSPF to EIGRP? From EIGRP to OSPF?

_____

_____

_____

References

If you need more information on the commands and their options, see the following references:

- IP Routing Protocol Command Reference

    http://www.cisco.com/cisco/web/support/index.html

- Open Shortest Path First Troubleshooting Tech Notes http://www.cisco.com/en/US/tech/tk365/
    tsd_technology_support_troubleshooting_technotes_list.html#anchor8

Router Interface Summary Table

Router Interface Summary				
Router Model	Ethernet Interface #1	Ethernet Interface #2	Serial Interface #1	Serial Interface #2
1700	Fast Ethernet 0 (FA0)	Fast Ethernet 1 (FA1)	Serial 0 (S0)	Serial 1 (S1)
1800	Fast Ethernet 0/0 (FA0/0)	Fast Ethernet 0/1 (FA0/1)	Serial 0/0/0 (S0/0/0)	Serial 0/0/1 (S0/0/1)
2600	Fast Ethernet 0/0 (FA0/0)	Fast Ethernet 0/1 (FA0/1)	Serial 0/0 (S0/0)	Serial 0/1 (S0/1)
2800	Fast Ethernet 0/0 (FA0/0)	Fast Ethernet 0/1 (FA0/1)	Serial 0/0/0 (S0/0/0)	Serial 0/0/1 (S0/0/1)
Note: To find out how the router is configured, look at the interfaces to identify the type of router and how many interfaces the router has. Rather than try to list all the combinations of configurations for each router class, this table includes identifiers for the possible combinations of Ethernet and serial interfaces in the device. The table does not include any other type of interface, even though a specific router might contain one. An example of this is an ISDN BRI interface. The string in parenthesis is the legal abbreviation that can be used in Cisco IOS commands to represent the interface.				

Lab 5-3, BGP

Physical Topology (Baseline)

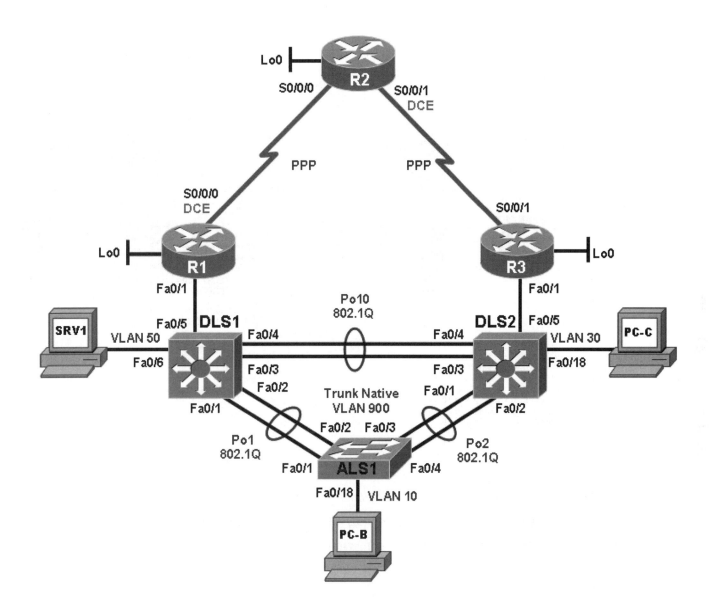

Logical Topology (Baseline)

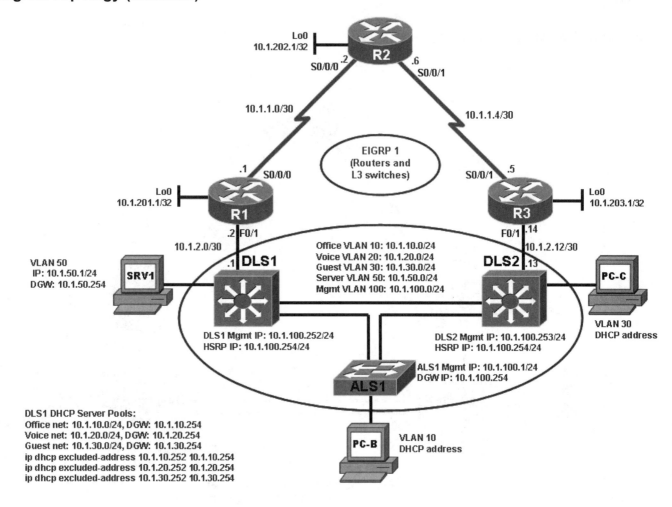

Objectives

- Load the trouble ticket device configuration files for each trouble ticket.

- Diagnose and resolve problems related to the BGP exterior routing protocol.

- Document troubleshooting progress, configuration changes, and problem resolution.

Background

Border Gateway Protocol (BGP) is the most widely used exterior routing protocol on the Internet. It is the de facto standard for route (prefix) exchange between the autonomous systems (AS) of Internet service providers (ISPs). BGP can also be used between a customer network and one or more ISPs. In this lab, you will troubleshoot various problems related to BGP. For each task or trouble ticket, the trouble scenario and problem symptom are described. While troubleshooting, you will discover the cause of the problem, correct it, and then document the process and results.

Implementing BGP

Your company has decided to implement several new Internet-based services. The current web services that the company offers are hosted at an external data center. It has been decided to build an in-house data center from which the new services will be hosted. The servers that are currently externally hosted will also be moved to the new data center.

Your company currently has a single ISP for Internet access. You have obtained a registered AS number (65501) and address block 172.30.1.0/27, which will be used for the new services. After consulting with the ISP, it has been decided to use BGP between the network edge router R1 and the ISP (R2). Upon successful completion of the BGP implementation, your company is considering adding another ISP for redundancy, but not as part of the current project.

Your support team has been working closely together with the engineering team to prepare the implementation. You have received confirmation from the ISP that they have prepared their router for the BGP implementation.

Router R1 will advertise the 172.30.1.0/27 IP address block to the ISP (R2). No other prefixes are allowed to be advertised. This ensures that only the assigned network address block will be received by the ISP. ISPs typically place filters on their edge routers to prevent customers from accidently announcing routes that do not belong to them.

The ISP router will send a default route to router R1 via BGP. The default route will be redistributed into Enhanced Interior Gateway Routing Protocol (EIGRP) by router R1. No other routes will be redistributed.

It is Friday evening, and the engineering team has just configured router R1 for BGP. To facilitate testing, a new hosted services VLAN and the corresponding subnet 172.30.1.0/27 will be created. All other devices, which have IP addresses in the 10.1.0.0/16 range, are using Network Address Translation (NAT), and their Internet access should not be affected by the BGP configuration.

You are on standby to assist in troubleshooting and testing the solution.

Implementation Plan

The implementation plan is in two phases.

Phase 1

During Phase 1, the link between edge router R1 and the existing ISP will be upgraded to a T1 leased line and converted to BGP. The remainder of the network will continue to use EIGRP. The 10.1.1.0/30 addressing on the R1-to-R2 serial WAN link will be changed to a public address (209.165.200.224/30) provided by the ISP. NAT will be used to translate the 10.1.0.0/16 internal private addresses to public address 209.165.200.225 using Port Address Translation (PAT). The loopback 0 address on R1 is also changed to 192.168.1.1.

An external BGP peering will be established between router R1 and the ISP (R2). The ISP will advertise a default route to R1 via BGP. On router R1, redistribution of the default route will be configured between BGP and EIGRP to ensure connectivity between headquarters and the ISP.

Phase 2

During Phase 2, the hosted services VLAN 130 named HSVCS and the corresponding subnet 172.30.1.0/27 will be created on switch DLS1. A test server for the hosted services subnet will be installed, simulated by switch virtual interface (SVI) VLAN 130 172.30.1.1/27 on DLS1. A static route will be provided from R1 to DLS1 VLAN 130. Some services will be migrated to the new IP address block before moving them to the newly built datacenter.

BGP Network Design

The BGP design is outlined in the following figure. BGP AS 65501 is the company's newly acquired AS number. The ISP AS is 65502.

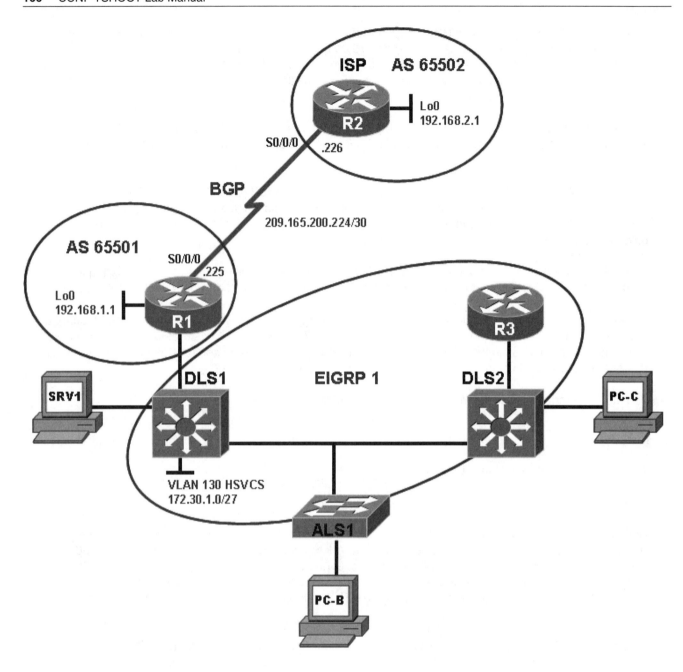

Test Plan

In Phase 1, edge router R1 must become a BGP peer with the ISP, and the internal office clients must be able to access the Internet through the ISP. In Phase 2, the Internet clients must be able to access the hosted services network.

Note: Trouble ticket A is related to the verification and acceptance of BGP Phase 1. Trouble tickets B and C are related to the second phase of BGP conversion. Any interfaces that have been shut down on routers R2 and R3 should remain shut down for the duration of this lab exercise.

Physical and Logical Topology Diagrams

The physical and logical topologies for the existing EIGRP-based network are provided in this lab to assist the troubleshooting effort.

Lab Structure

This lab is divided into two main sections.

Section 1—Trouble Tickets and Troubleshooting Logs

This section includes multiple tasks. Each task is associated with a trouble ticket (TT) and introduces one or more errors on one or more devices. If time is a consideration, each task or trouble ticket can be performed independently.

Section 2—Troubleshooting Reference Information

This section provides general BGP troubleshooting information that can be applied to any trouble ticket in this lab. Sample troubleshooting flows are provided, along with examples of useful commands and output. If time permits, it is recommended that you read Section 2 prior to starting on the trouble tickets.

Note: This lab uses Cisco 1841 routers with Cisco IOS Release 12.4(24)T1 and the Advanced IP Services image c1841-advipservicesk9-mz.124-24.T1.bin. The switches are Cisco WS-C2960-24TT-L with the Cisco IOS image c2960-lanbasek9-mz.122-46.SE.bin and Catalyst 3560-24PS with the Cisco IOS image c3560-advipservicesk9-mz.122-46.SE.bin. Other routers (such as 2801 and 2811), switches (such as 2950 or 3550), and Cisco IOS Software versions can be used if they have comparable capabilities and features. Depending on the router or switch model and Cisco IOS Software version, the commands available and output produced might vary from what is shown in this lab.

Required Resources

- 3 routers (Cisco 1841 with Cisco IOS Release 12.4(24)T1 Advanced IP Service or comparable)
- 1 switch (Cisco 2960 with the Cisco IOS Release 12.2(46)SE C2960-LANBASEK9-M image or comparable)
- 2 switches (Cisco 3560 with the Cisco IOS Release 12.2(46)SE C3560-LANBASEK9-M image or comparable)
- SRV1 (Windows PC with a static IP address) with TFTP and syslog servers, plus an SSH client (PuTTY or comparable) and WireShark software
- PC-B (Windows PC—DHCP client) with PuTTY and WireShark software
- PC-C (Windows PC—DHCP client) with PuTTY and WireShark software
- Serial and Ethernet cables

Section 1—Trouble Tickets and Troubleshooting Logs

Task 1: Trouble Ticket Lab 5-3 TT-A

Step 1: Review trouble ticket Lab 5-3 TT-A.

After your colleague finished configuring BGP on edge router R1, you tested connectivity from PC-B in VLAN 10 to the ISP router to verify the configuration and peering between R1 and R2. This test failed. When you asked your colleague, he said he did not actually test the configuration from a client PC on the internal network. He suspected there was a problem with the ISP and contacted them to find out if there was an issue at their end. They stated that everything was correctly configured on router R2.

Your task is to diagnose the problem and verify that BGP is properly configured to enable BGP peering between router R1 and the ISP.

Step 2: Load the device trouble ticket configuration files for TT-A.

Using the procedure described in Lab 3-1, verify that the lab configuration files are present in flash and load the proper configuration files as indicated in the Device Configuration File table.

Note: The following device access methods are in effect after loading the configuration files:

* Console access requires no username or password.

* Telnet and SSH require username **admin** and password **adminpa55**.

* The enable password is **ciscoenpa55**.

Device Configuration File Table

Device Name	File to Load	Notes
ALS1	Lab53-ALS1-TT-A-Cfg.txt	
DLS1	Lab53-DLS1-TT-A-Cfg.txt	
DLS2	Lab53-DLS2-TT-A-Cfg.txt	
R1	Lab53-R1-TT-A-Cfg.txt	
R2	Lab53-R2-TT-A-Cfg.txt	
R3	Lab53-R3-TT-A-Cfg.txt	
SRV1	N/A	Static IP: 10.1.50.1 Default gateway: 10.1.50.254
PC-B	N/A	DHCP
PC-C	N/A	DHCP

Step 3: Configure SRV1 and start the syslog and TFTP servers.

Step 4: Release and renew the DHCP lease on PC-B.

a. Ensure that PC-B is configured as a DHCP client in the OFFICE VLAN.

b. After loading all TT-A device configuration files, issue the **ipconfig /release** and **ipconfig /renew** commands on PC-B.

Step 5: Outline the troubleshooting approach and validation steps.

Use this space to identify your troubleshooting approach and the key steps to verify that the problem is resolved. Troubleshooting approaches to select from include the follow-the-path, spot-the-differences, bottom-up, top-down, divide-and-conquer, shoot-from-the-hip, and move-the-problem methods.

Note: In addition to a specific approach, you can use the generic troubleshooting process described at the beginning of Section 2 of this lab.

_____

_____

_____

_____

_____

_____

Step 6: Record the troubleshooting process and configuration changes.

Note: Section 2 of this lab includes sample troubleshooting flows, useful commands, and examples of output.

Use this log to document your actions and results during the troubleshooting process. List the commands you used to gather information. As you progress, record what you think the problem might be and which actions you will take to correct the problem.

Device	Actions and Results

Device	Actions and Results

Step 7: Document trouble ticket debrief notes.

Use this space to make notes of the key learning points that you picked up during the discussion of this trouble ticket with your instructor. The notes can include problems encountered, solutions applied, useful commands employed, alternate solutions and methods, and procedure and communication improvements.

_____

_____

_____

_____

_____

_____

_____

Task 2: Trouble Ticket Lab 5-3 TT-B

Step 1: Review trouble ticket Lab 5-3 TT-B.

The next step after the peering has been established is to test the new hosted services subnet, which has been created using VLAN 130. This subnet uses the 172.30.1.0/27 IP address block that was assigned to your company by the ISP. The subnet has been configured, and a test server has been installed (simulated by DLS1 SVI VLAN 130 - 172.30.1.1). Internet clients must be able to access the subnet from ISP router R2 (simulated by Lo0 192.168.2.1). Other hosts in the EIGRP 10.1.0.0/16 domain do not require access to the hosted services subnet.

Your task is to verify VLAN configuration and routing functionality. Also, verify that traffic from the Internet can be sent to the hosted network test server in VLAN 130 via R1 and that the return traffic can be received via ISP router R2.

Step 2: Load the device trouble ticket configuration files for TT-B.

Using the procedure described in Lab 3-1, verify that the lab configuration files are present in flash. Load the configuration files as indicated in the Device Configuration File table.

Note: See Task 1, Step 2 for device access methods, usernames, and passwords after the configuration files have been loaded.

Device Configuration File Table

Device Name	File to Load	Notes
ALS1	Lab53-ALS1-TT-B-Cfg.txt	
DLS1	Lab53-DLS1-TT-B-Cfg.txt	
DLS2	Lab53-DLS2-TT-B-Cfg.txt	
R1	Lab53-R1-TT-B-Cfg.txt	
R2	Lab53-R2-TT-B-Cfg.txt	
R3	Lab53-R3-TT-B-Cfg.txt	
SRV1	N/A	Static IP: 10.1.50.1 Default gateway: 10.1.50.254
PC-B	N/A	DHCP
PC-C	N/A	DHCP

Step 3: Configure SRV1 and start the syslog and TFTP servers.

Step 4: Release and renew the DHCP leases on PC-B and PC-C, as described in Task 1.

Step 5: Outline the troubleshooting approach and validation steps.

Use this space to identify your troubleshooting approach and the key steps to verify that the problem is resolved. Troubleshooting approaches to select from include the follow-the-path, spot-the-differences, bottom-up, top-down, divide-and-conquer, shoot-from-the-hip, and move-the-problem methods.

Note: In addition to a specific approach, you can use the generic troubleshooting process described at the beginning of Section 2 of this lab.

_____

_____

_____

_____

_____

Step 6: Record the troubleshooting process and configuration changes.

Note: Section 2 of this lab includes sample troubleshooting flows, useful commands, and examples of output.

Use this log to document your actions and results during the troubleshooting process. List the commands you used to gather information. As you progress, record what you think the problem might be and which actions you will take to correct the problem.

Device	Actions and Results

Step 7: Document trouble ticket debrief notes.

Use this space to make notes of the key learning points that you picked up during the discussion of this trouble ticket with your instructor. The notes can include problems encountered, solutions applied, useful commands employed, alternate solutions and methods, and procedure and communication improvements.

_____

_____

_____

_____

_____

_____

_____

Task 3: Trouble Ticket Lab 5-3 TT-C

Step 1: Review trouble ticket Lab 5-3 TT-C.

Your ISP uses prefix lists to ensure that customers do not announce routes that have not been officially assigned to them. This is critical for an ISP because if two customers were to accidently announce the same route as their own, it would create problems for both customers and the ISP. After you corrected the static route and BGP route injection issues on R1, one of your colleagues was working with the hosted services test network and made some changes. Now he can no longer ping from the hosted network test server (DLS1 VLAN 130) to the ISP. The ISP is also not receiving the advertisement for the hosted services subnet. Your task is to diagnose this problem and resolve it.

Step 2: Load the device trouble ticket configuration files for TT-C.

Using the procedure described in Lab 3-1, verify that the lab configuration files are present in flash. Load the proper configuration files as indicated in the Device Configuration File table.

Note: See Task 1, Step 2 for device access methods, usernames, and passwords after the configuration files have been loaded.

Device Configuration File Table

Device Name	File to Load	Notes
ALS1	Lab53-ALS1-TT-C-Cfg.txt	
DLS1	Lab53-DLS1-TT-C-Cfg.txt	
DLS2	Lab53-DLS2-TT-C-Cfg.txt	
R1	Lab53-R1-TT-C-Cfg.txt	
R2	Lab53-R2-TT-C-Cfg.txt	
R3	Lab53-R3-TT-C-Cfg.txt	
SRV1	N/A	Static IP: 10.1.50.1 Default gateway: 10.1.50.254
PC-B	N/A	DHCP
PC-C	N/A	DHCP

Step 3: Configure SRV1 and start the syslog and TFTP servers, as described in Task 1.

Step 4: Release and renew the DHCP leases on PC-B and PC-C, as described in Task 1.

Step 5: Outline the troubleshooting approach and validation steps.

Use this space to identify your troubleshooting approach and the key steps to verify that the problem is resolved. Troubleshooting approaches to select from include the follow-the-path, spot-the-differences, bottom-up, top-down, divide-and-conquer, shoot-from-the-hip, and move-the-problem methods.

Note: In addition to a specific approach, you can use the generic troubleshooting process described at the beginning of Section 2 of this lab.

_____

_____

_____

_____

_____

_____

Step 6: Record the troubleshooting process and configuration changes.

Note: Section 2 of this lab includes sample troubleshooting flows, useful commands, and examples of output.

Use this log to document your actions and results during the troubleshooting process. List the commands you used to gather information. As you progress, record what you think the problem might be and which actions you will take to correct the problem.

Device	Actions and Results

Step 7: Document trouble ticket debrief notes.

Use this space to make notes of the key learning points that you picked up during the discussion of this trouble ticket with your instructor. The notes can include problems encountered, solutions applied, useful commands employed, alternate solutions and methods, and procedure and communication improvements.

_____

_____

_____

_____

_____

_____

_____

Section 2—Troubleshooting Reference Information

General Troubleshooting Process

As a general guideline, you can use the following general troubleshooting process described in the course.

1. Define the problem (symptoms).
2. Gather information.
3. Analyze the information.
4. Propose a hypothesis (possible cause).
5. Test the hypothesis.
6. Eliminate or accept the hypothesis.
7. Solve the problem.
8. Document the problem.

Command Summary

The table lists useful commands. Sample output is shown on the following pages.

Command	Key Information Displayed

`show ip route`
or
`show ip route ip-addr`
	Displays the entire routing table or information for a particular destination address.

`show ip bgp`	Displays local and learned network entries in the BGP table with next hop, metric, local preference, weight, and AS path.
`show ip bgp summary`	Displays a summary of the BGP neighbor table. This command lists important BGP parameters, such as the AS number and router ID, statistics about the memory consumption of the various BGP data structures, and a brief overview of the configured neighbors and their state.

`show ip bgp neighbors`
or
`show ip bgp neighbor ip-address`
	Displays parameters and extensive statistics about the peering session for all neighbors or for a particular neighbor address.

`show ip bgp network mask`	Displays the contents of the BGP table for a specific prefix. The information is organized in the following manner: The entry for each available path in the table starts with the AS path attribute of the path, using the word "Local" to represent the empty AS path string.
`debug ip tcp transactions`	Displays TCP connection activity between peers. Can be used to investigate whether the TCP session is refused, established, and subsequently torn down again, or no response is received at all from the neighbor.
`debug ip bgp`	Displays the successive state transitions during the establishment of the BGP peering. If one of the peers decides to close the session because of a parameter problem, such as a mismatched AS number or an invalid router ID, the debug also displays information about the cause.

`clear ip bgp *`	Clears the contents of the BGP table.
`show ip bgp` *network mask* `longer prefixes`	Displays more specific prefixes present in the BGP table (including the prefix itself) that are contained in the prefix specified by the *network* and *mask* options.
`show ip bgp neighbor` *ip-address* `routes`	Displays all routes in the BGP table that were received from the neighbor specified by the *ip-address* option.
`show ip bgp neighbor` *ip-address* `advertised-routes`	Displays all routes in the BGP table that will be advertised to the neighbor specified by the *ip-address* option.
`show ip bgp regexp` *regular-expression*	Displays all routes from the BGP table that have an AS path string that is matched by the specified regular expression.

Lab 5-3: Sample Troubleshooting Flows

The figure illustrates an example of a method that you could follow to diagnose and resolve problems related to BGP.

Sample BGP Troubleshooting Flow

Layer 3 problem caused by routing protocol failure → Verify neighbor availability → Verify route availability → Verify route selection

Verify routing table and FIB

© 2009 Cisco Systems, Inc. All rights reserved.   TSHOOT v1.0 —93

The typical trigger to start investigating BGP operation is when you are using BGP as an exterior gateway protocol to connect to other autonomous systems and you are troubleshooting IP connectivity to a destination in a different AS. Some reasons to start investigating BGP are if a route to the destination network is missing from the routing table of one of the routers, a different route than expected was selected to forward the packets to that destination, or return traffic from the other AS is not making it back to the source.

Troubleshooting problems with missing return traffic usually requires coordination with those responsible for the routing in the destination AS and possibly even intermediate autonomous systems. The only thing you can verify from within your own AS is if your routing information is correctly passed to the neighbor AS. Propagation of your routes beyond your direct peers cannot be verified without access to routers in other autonomous systems.

Therefore, this flow focuses mainly on troubleshooting traffic to a destination network in a different AS. However, commands that are helpful in troubleshooting route advertisement to a different AS are also highlighted, if appropriate.

To install a route into the routing table, each router that uses BGP goes through several stages:

1. Establish neighbor relationships with its configured neighbors.

2. Exchange routing information with neighbors and store the received information in the BGP table.

3. Select the best route from the available routes and install it in the routing table.

Errors during any of these stages can cause routing information to be missed or incorrect routing information to be installed in the routing table.

The order in which the different stages are verified is not important, as long as a structured approach is used.

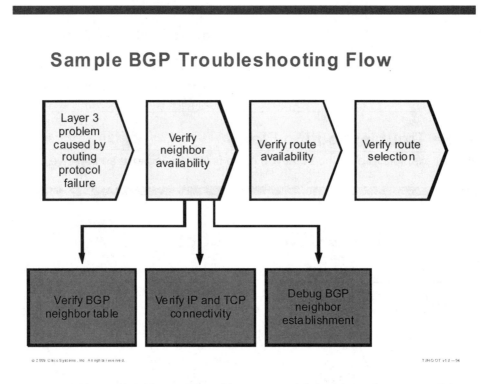

Sample BGP Troubleshooting Flow

BGP does not discover neighbors. Neighbor relationships are established based on an explicit configuration on both routers that participate in the peering session.

BGP uses TCP as a transport protocol. Establishing a peering relationship always starts with the establishment of a TCP session on port 179 between the configured neighbor IP addresses. By default, both neighbors attempt to initiate the TCP session to the configured IP address of the neighbor. When a router receives an incoming session request, it compares the source IP address of the session to its list of configured neighbors. It only accepts the session if the source IP address matches one of the IP addresses of its configured neighbors. Therefore, it is important that a router always sources the BGP packets that it sends to a specific neighbor from the IP address that has been configured as the neighbor IP address on the peer router. For neighbors that are directly connected on an interface, the correct source address is automatically used. For neighbors that are not directly connected, the appropriate source IP address for the session to a neighbor might need to be selected with the **neighbor** *ip-address* **update-source** *interface-id* command.

Verify the BGP Neighbor Table

```
R1#show ip bgp
BGP table version is 2, local router ID is 192.168.1.1
Status codes: s suppressed, d damped, h history, * valid, > best, i - internal,
              r RIB-failure, S Stale
Origin codes: i - IGP, e - EGP, ? - incomplete

   Network          Next Hop            Metric LocPrf Weight Path
*> 0.0.0.0          192.168.2.1              0             0 65502 i

R1#show ip bgp summary
```

```
BGP router identifier 192.168.1.1, local AS number 65501
BGP table version is 3, main routing table version 3
2 network entries using 264 bytes of memory
2 path entries using 104 bytes of memory
3/2 BGP path/bestpath attribute entries using 504 bytes of memory
1 BGP AS-PATH entries using 24 bytes of memory
0 BGP route-map cache entries using 0 bytes of memory
0 BGP filter-list cache entries using 0 bytes of memory
Bitfield cache entries: current 1 (at peak 1) using 32 bytes of memory
BGP using 928 total bytes of memory
BGP activity 2/0 prefixes, 2/0 paths, scan interval 60 secs

Neighbor        V     AS MsgRcvd MsgSent   TblVer  InQ OutQ Up/Down  State/PfxRcd
192.168.2.1     4  65502      36      36        3    0    0 00:33:01           1
```

To verify that all expected neighbor relationships are operational, you can display a summary of the BGP neighbor table using the **show ip bgp summary** command. This command lists important BGP parameters, such as the AS number and router ID, statistics about the memory consumption of the various BGP data structures, and a brief overview of the configured neighbors and their state.

For each neighbor, the configured IP address and AS of the neighbor are listed. The Up/Down column lists the time that has elapsed since the last state change. For a neighbor that is currently up, it lists the time elapsed since the session was established. For a neighbor that is down, it lists the time elapsed since the session was lost.

The most important column to verify the operational state of the neighbor is State/PfxRcd. This column can display the following values:

- **Idle** – Indicates that there is no session with the peer, and the router is not currently attempting to establish a session with the peer. The router is ready to accept incoming sessions.

- **Idle (Admin)** – Indicates that the session has been administratively shut down with the **neighbor** *ip-address* **shutdown** command.

- **Active** – The router is actively trying to open a TCP session with the neighbor. If it does not succeed in establishing the session, the router toggles between the Idle and Active states

- **Open Sent** – An Open message has been sent to the neighboring router containing the router ID, AS number, BGP version, hold timer, and capabilities.

- **Open Confirm** – An Open message from the neighbor has been received, the parameters in the message have been processed and accepted, and a hello message has been sent to acknowledge the acceptance of the neighbor's Open message.

- **Number of received prefixes** – After an acknowledgment from the neighbor confirming the reception of this router's Open message, the state of the session moves to the Established state. At this point, the State/PfxRcd column does not list the state. It shows the number of prefixes that have been received from that neighbor and installed in the BGP table. The desired result is to see a number listed in this column, because that indicates that the session with the peer has been successfully established.

The Open Sent and Open Confirm states are transitory states. When the state for a neighbor toggles between Active and Idle, this indicates that the router is not successful in establishing a session with the neighbor.

You can use the **show ip bgp neighbor** *ip-address* command to display additional parameters and extensive statistics about the peering session. For more information about these parameters and statistics, see the BGP command references on www.cisco.com.

Verify IP and TCP Connectivity

```
R1#debug ip tcp transactions
TCP special event debugging is on
```

```
R1#conf t
Enter configuration commands, one per line.  End with CNTL/Z.
R1(config)#no router bgp 65501
R1(config)#
*Nov 16 17:21:35.102: %BGP-5-ADJCHANGE: neighbor 192.168.2.1 Down BGP protocol i
nitialization
R1(config)#
*Nov 16 17:21:35.102: TCP0: state was ESTAB -> FINWAIT1 [179 -> 192.168.2.1(1188
9)]
*Nov 16 17:21:35.102: TCP0: sending FIN
*Nov 16 17:21:35.126: Released port 179 in Transport Port Agent for TCP IP type
0 delay 240000
*Nov 16 17:21:35.126: TCP0: state was LISTEN -> CLOSED [179 -> 192.168.2.1(0)]
*Nov 16 17:21:35.126: TCB 0x66EE8F34 destroyed
*Nov 16 17:21:35.138: TCP0: state was FINWAIT1 -> FINWAIT2 [179 -> 192.168.2.1(1
1889)]
*Nov 16 17:21:35.138: TCP0: FIN processed
*Nov 16 17:21:35.138: TCP0: state was FINWAIT2 -> TIMEWAIT [179 -> 192.168.2.1(1
1889)]
R1(config)#
*Nov 16 17:21:50.286: Reserved port 0 in Transport Port Agent for TCP IP type 0
*Nov 16 17:21:50.286: TCP: sending RST, seq 0, ack 2752306274
*Nov 16 17:21:50.286: TCP: sent RST to 192.168.2.1:41738 from 192.168.1.1:179
*Nov 16 17:21:50.290: Released port 0 in Transport Port Agent for TCP IP type 0
delay 240000
*Nov 16 17:21:50.290: TCP0: state was LISTEN -> CLOSED [0 -> UNKNOWN(0)]
*Nov 16 17:21:50.290: TCB 0x66F17E40 destroyed
R1(config)#
*Nov 16 17:21:55.006: Reserved port 0 in Transport Port Agent for TCP IP type 0
*Nov 16 17:21:55.006: TCP: sending RST, seq 0, ack 3974493125
*Nov 16 17:21:55.006: TCP: sent RST to 192.168.2.1:47416 from 192.168.1.1:179
*Nov 16 17:21:55.006: Released port 0 in Transport Port Agent for TCP IP type 0
delay 240000


R1(config)#router bgp 65501
R1(config-router)#no synchronization
R1(config-router)#bgp log-neighbor-changes
R1(config-router)#neighbor 192.168.2.1 remote-as 65502
R1(config-router)#neighbor 192.168.2.1 ebgp-multihop 2
R1(config-router)#neighbor 192.168.2.1 update-source Loopback0
*Nov 16 17:28:46.549: TCB65950C34 created
*Nov 16 17:28:46.549: TCB65950C34 setting property TCP_PMTU (38) 66A7C214
*Nov 16 17:28:46.549: TCB65950C34 setting property TCP_TOS (11) 66A7C220
*Nov 16 17:28:46.549: TCB65950C34 setting property TCP_VRFTABLEID (20) 66F233F8
*Nov 16 17:28:46.549: TCB65950C34 setting property TCP_IN_TTL (29) 66A7C200
*Nov 16 17:28:46.553: TCB65950C34 setting property TCP_OUT_TTL (30) 66A7C200
*Nov 16 17:28:46.553: TCB65950C34 setting property TCP_OUT_TTL (30) 66F2359A
*Nov 16 17:28:46.553: TCB65950C34 bound to UNKNOWN.179
*Nov 16 17:28:46.553: TCB65950C34 setting property TCP_ACCESS_CHECK (5) 60B47108

*Nov 16 17:28:46.553: TCB65950C34 setting property TCP_MD5KEY (4) 0
*Nov 16 17:28:46.553: Reserved port 179 in Transport Port Agent for TCP IP type
0
*Nov 16 17:28:46.553: TCB65950C34 listening with queue 1
*Nov 16 17:28:46.585: TCB65950C34 setting property TCP_IN_TTL (29) 66A7C278
*Nov 16 17:28:46.585: TCB65950C34 setting property TCP_OUT_TTL (30) 66A7C278
*Nov 16 17:28:46.585: TCB65950C34 setting property TCP_OUT_TTL (30) 66F2359A
```

```
R1(config-router)#
*Nov 16 17:28:50.581: TCB67096718 created
*Nov 16 17:28:50.581: TCB67096718 setting property TCP_VRFTABLEID (20) 66F233F8
*Nov 16 17:28:50.581: TCB67096718 setting property TCP_MD5KEY (4) 0
*Nov 16 17:28:50.581: TCB67096718 setting property TCP_ACK_RATE (32) 66F1B4D4
*Nov 16 17:28:50.581: TCB67096718 setting property TCP_TOS (11) 66F1B4C0
*Nov 16 17:28:50.581: TCB67096718 setting property TCP_PMTU (38) 66F1B48C
*Nov 16 17:28:50.581: TCB67096718 setting property TCP_IN_TTL (29) 66F1B478
*Nov 16 17:28:50.581: TCB67096718 setting property TCP_OUT_TTL (30) 66F1B478
*Nov 16 17:28:50.581: TCB67096718 setting property TCP_OUT_TTL (30) 66F2359A
*Nov 16 17:28:50.581: TCP: Random local port generated 30517, network 1
*Nov 16 17:28:50.581: TCB67096718 bound to 192.168.1.1.30517
*Nov 16 17:28:50.581: TCB67096718 setting property TCP_RTRANSTMO (31) 66F1B4D8
*Nov 16 17:28:50.581: Reserved port 30517 in Transport Port Agent for TCP IP typ
e 1
*Nov 16 17:28:50.581: TCP: sending SYN, seq 3632881552, ack 0
*Nov 16 17:28:50.581: TCP0: Connection to 192.168.2.1:179, advertising MSS 536
*Nov 16 17:28:50.585: TCP0: state was CLOSED -> SYNSENT [30517 -> 192.168.2.1(17
9)]
*Nov 16 17:28:50.593: TCP0: state was SYNSENT -> ESTAB [30517 -> 192.168.2.1(179
)]
*Nov 16 17:28:50.593: TCP: tcb 67096718 connection to 192.168.2.1:179, peer MSS
536, MSS is 536
*Nov 16 17:28:50.593: TCB67096718 connected to 192.168.2.1.179
*Nov 16 17:28:50.593: TCB67096718 setting property TCP_NO_DELAY (0) 66F1B4D8
*Nov 16 17:28:50.593: TCB67096718 setting property TCP_RTRANSTMO (31) 66F1B4D8
*Nov 16 17:28:50.621: %BGP-5-ADJCHANGE: neighbor 192.168.2.1 Up
R1(config-router)#
*Nov 16 17:28:50.821: TCP0: ACK timeout timer expired
R1(config-router)#do u all
All possible debugging has been turned off
```

If a session to one of the neighbors is not established correctly, you can take several steps to diagnose the issue. The first step is to test IP connectivity to the IP address of the neighbor by using the `ping` command. Make sure that you specify the same source interface that is used as the source interface for the BGP session. If the ping fails, initiate a troubleshooting process to first restore IP connectivity to the neighbor.

If the ping is successful, the next step is to determine whether the TCP session with the neighbor is established and successively torn down again, or if the TCP session is never established.

You can use the `debug ip tcp transactions` command to investigate whether the TCP session is refused (indicated by the reception of a TCP RST), established and subsequently torn down again (indicated by the normal TCP initiation and termination handshakes), or no response is received at all from the neighbor.

In the example output above, you can see that the TCP session to IP address 192.168.2.1 and TCP port 179 is refused by the peer, as indicated by the reception of the TCP RST from the peer. Clues like these can help eliminate possible problem causes. For instance, in this particular example, the output rules out an access list as the cause of the problem, because a TCP RST has been successfully received from the neighbor in response to the transmitted TCP SYN. In general, the fact that the peer refuses the session indicates that it does not recognize the session as coming from one of its configured neighbors. Possible causes are a missing neighbor statement or a mismatch between the configured IP address on the neighbor and the source IP address used by this router. Note that the source IP address and TCP port of the session are also displayed in the output of the debug as "bound to 192.168.1.1.30517." You must work together with the party that manages the peer router to determine the exact cause of the problem.

Debug BGP Neighbor Establishment

```
R1#debug ip bgp
BGP debugging is on for address family: IPv4 Unicast
```

```
R1#conf t
Enter configuration commands, one per line.  End with CNTL/Z.
R1(config)#interface s0/0/0
R1(config-if)#shutdown
R1(config-if)#
*Nov 16 17:38:51.181: %LINK-5-CHANGED: Interface Serial0/0/0, changed state to a
dministratively down
*Nov 16 17:38:52.181: %LINEPROTO-5-UPDOWN: Line protocol on Interface Serial0/0/
0, changed state to down

R1(config-if)#do clear ip bgp 192.168.2.1
R1(config-if)#
*Nov 16 17:40:21.093: BGPNSF state: 192.168.2.1 went from nsf_not_active to nsf_
not_active
*Nov 16 17:40:21.093: BGP: 192.168.2.1 went from Established to Idle
*Nov 16 17:40:21.093: %BGP-5-ADJCHANGE: neighbor 192.168.2.1 Down User reset
R1(config-if)#
*Nov 16 17:40:21.093: BGP: 192.168.2.1 closing
R1(config-if)#
*Nov 16 17:40:22.973: BGP: 192.168.2.1 went from Idle to Active
*Nov 16 17:40:22.973: BGP: 192.168.2.1 active open failed - route to peer is inv
alid, open active delayed 26762ms (35000ms max, 60% jitter)


R1(config-if)#interface s0/0/0
R1(config-if)#no shutdown
R1(config-if)#
*Nov 16 17:40:51.041: %LINK-3-UPDOWN: Interface Serial0/0/0, changed state to up

R1(config-if)#
*Nov 16 17:40:52.045: %LINEPROTO-5-UPDOWN: Line protocol on Interface Serial0/0/
0, changed state to up
R1(config-if)#
*Nov 16 17:41:11.365: BGP: 192.168.2.1 open active, local address 192.168.1.1
*Nov 16 17:41:11.373: BGP: 192.168.2.1 read request no-op
*Nov 16 17:41:11.377: BGP: 192.168.2.1 went from Active to OpenSent
*Nov 16 17:41:11.377: BGP: 192.168.2.1 sending OPEN, version 4, my as: 65501, ho
ldtime 180 seconds
*Nov 16 17:41:11.377: BGP: 192.168.2.1 send message type 1, length (incl. header
) 53
*Nov 16 17:41:11.397: BGP: 192.168.2.1 rcv message type 1, length (excl. header)
 34
*Nov 16 17:41:11.397: BGP: 192.168.2.1 rcv OPEN, version 4, holdtime 180 seconds

*Nov 16 17:41:11.397: BGP: 192.168.2.1 rcv OPEN w/ OPTION parameter len: 24
*Nov 16 17:41:11.397: BGP: 192.168.2.1 rcvd OPEN w/ optional parameter type 2 (C
apability) len 6
*Nov 16 17:41:11.397: BGP: 192.168.2.1 OPEN has CAPABILITY code: 1, length 4
*Nov 16 17:41:11.397: BGP: 192.168.2.1 OPEN has MP_EXT CAP for afi/safi: 1/1
*Nov 16 17:41:11.397: BGP: 192.168.2.1 rcvd OPEN w/ optional parameter type 2 (C
apability) len 2
*Nov 16 17:41:11.397: BGP: 192.168.2.1 OPEN has CAPABILITY code: 128, length 0
*Nov 16 17:41:11.397: BGP: 192.168.2.1 OPEN has ROUTE-REFRESH capability(old) fo
r all address-families
*Nov 16 17:41:11.397: BGP: 192.168.2.1 rcvd OPEN w/ optional parameter type 2 (C
apability) len 2
*Nov 16 17:41:11.397: BGP: 192.168.2.1 OPEN has CAPABILITY code: 2, length 0
*Nov 16 17:41:11.397: BGP: 192.168.2.1 OPEN has ROUTE-REFRESH capability(new) fo
```

```
r all address-families
*Nov 16 17:41:11.397: BGP: 192.168.2.1 rcvd OPEN w/ optional parameter type 2 (C
apability) len 6
*Nov 16 17:41:11.397: BGP: 192.168.2.1 OPEN has CAPABILITY code: 65, length 4
*Nov 16 17:41:11.397: BGP: 192.168.2.1 OPEN has 4-byte ASN CAP for: 65502
BGP: 192.168.2.1 rcvd OPEN w/ remote AS 65502, 4-byte remote AS 65502
*Nov 16 17:41:11.401: BGP: 192.168.2.1 went from OpenSent to OpenConfirm
*Nov 16 17:41:11.405: BGP: 192.168.2.1 went from OpenConfirm to Established
*Nov 16 17:41:11.405: %BGP-5-ADJCHANGE: neighbor 192.168.2.1 Up
R1(config-if)#
*Nov 16 17:41:11.433: BGP_Router: unhandled major event code 128, minor 0
R1(config-if)#do u all
All possible debugging has been turned off
```

If the TCP session is successfully established but consecutively torn down again, the likely cause is that one of the BGP peers is rejecting one of the parameters in the received Open message from the peer. The **debug ip bgp** command displays the successive state transitions during the establishment of the BGP peering. If one of the peers decides to close the session because of a parameter problem, such as a mismatched AS number or invalid router ID, the debug output displays information about the exact cause.

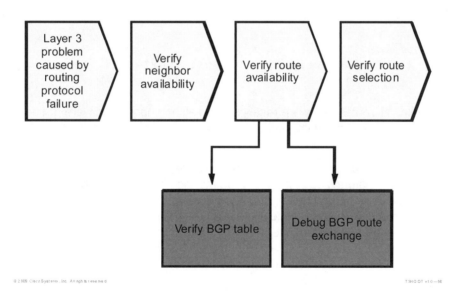

Sample BGP Troubleshooting Flow

After you have verified that neighbor relationships have been established as expected, verify that the route for the destination network that you are troubleshooting has been received correctly from all appropriate neighbors. BGP stores all routes that it receives from its neighbors in the BGP table and then selects the best route for each prefix to be installed in the routing table and advertised to other neighbors.

By investigating all available paths to the destination network in the BGP table, you can see if all the paths you expected to find are available. If multiple paths to the same prefix are listed, you can see which one was selected. In addition, you can see all the associated BGP attributes for the route, which can be useful to verify the path selection process and the results of the possible attribute manipulation by route maps that are used.

If routes are missing from the BGP table, you might need to debug the BGP route exchange process to see if they were not received or not entered into the BGP table.

Debug BGP Neighbor Establishment

```
R1#show ip bgp 0.0.0.0 0.0.0.0
BGP routing table entry for 0.0.0.0/0, version 4
Paths: (1 available, best #1, table Default-IP-Routing-Table)
  Not advertised to any peer
  65502
    192.168.2.1 from 192.168.2.1 (192.168.2.1)
      Origin IGP, metric 0, localpref 100, valid, external, best
```

In the output above, the prefix is 0.0.0.0/0, the AS path is 65502, and the next hop is 192.168.2.1.

```
R1#show ip bgp 172.30.1.0 255.255.255.224
BGP routing table entry for 172.30.1.0/27, version 5
Paths: (1 available, best #1, table Default-IP-Routing-Table)
Flag: 0x820
  Advertised to update-groups:
        1
  Loc   10.1.2.1 from 0.0.0.0 (192.168.1.1)
      Origin IGP, metric 0, localpref 100, weight 32768, valid, sourced, local,
```

```
R2>sh ip bgp 172.30.1.0/27
BGP routing table entry for 172.30.1.0/27, version 5
Paths: (1 available, best #1, table Default-IP-Routing-Table)
Flag: 0x820
  Not advertised to any peer
  65501
    192.168.1.1 from 192.168.1.1 (192.168.1.1)
      Origin IGP, metric 0, localpref 100, valid, external, best
```

The BGP table contains all routes that were received from all neighbors and were not denied by an incoming access list, prefix list, or route map. In the output for R2 above, the prefix is 172.30.1.0/27, the AS path is 65501 to the network, and the next hop is 192.168.1.1.

When you issue the **show ip bgp** *network mask* command to display the content of the BGP table for a specific prefix, the information is organized in the following manner. The entry for each available path in the table starts with the AS path attribute of the path (using the word "Local" to represent the empty AS path string). On the following lines, the other BGP attributes of the route, such as the next hop, origin code, and local preference, are listed. In addition, other information associated with the route is displayed. For example, the route is marked as internal if it was received from a BGP neighbor in the same AS. It is marked as external if it was received from a neighbor in a different AS. The path that was selected as the best path by the BGP path selection algorithm is marked as "best."

Note: The following section uses some sample output not produced from the equipment in this lab to demonstrate how to interpret the output of this command. This output is interspersed with comments that explain the important fields and their interpretation.

```
IRO1#show ip bgp 172.34.224.0 255.255.224.0
BGP routing table entry for 172.34.224.0/19, version 98
Paths: (2 available, best #1, table Default-IP-Routing-Table)
```

Two paths are available to reach prefix 172.34.224.0/19. The first path listed has been selected as the best path.

```
Advertised to update-groups:
        2
```

The best path is advertised to all neighbors in update group 2. Use the **show ip bgp update-group** command to view the neighbors that are members of a specific update group.

```
65525 65486
```

The first path has 65525 65486 as its AS path attribute, which indicates that the route has originated in AS 65486 and then passed to AS 65525, which subsequently passed it to this AS.

```
192.168.224.254 from 192.168.224.254 (192.168.100.1)
```

The BGP next hop for this route is 192.168.224.254. The route was received from neighbor 192.168.224.254. The router ID of that neighbor is 192.168.100.1.

```
Origin IGP, localpref 100, valid, external, best
```

The origin attribute for this route is IGP, and the local preference attribute has a value of 100. This route is a valid route received from an external BGP peer, and it has been selected as the best path.

```
64566 65486
```

The second path has 64566 65486 as its AS path attribute, which indicates that the route has originated in AS 65486 and then passed to AS 64566, which subsequently passed it to this AS.

```
172.24.244.86 (metric 30720) from 10.1.220.4 (10.1.220.4)
```

The BGP next hop for this route is 172.24.244.86, and the IGP metric to reach this next-hop IP address is 30720 (which is the EIGRP metric listed in the routing table to reach 172.24.244.86). The route was received from neighbor 10.1.220.4, and the router ID of that neighbor is also 10.1.220.4.

```
Origin IGP, metric 0, localpref 100, valid, internal
```

The origin attribute for this route is IGP, the multi-exit discriminator (MED) attribute has a value of 0, and the local preference attribute has a value of 100. The route is a valid route received from an internal BGP peer.

For troubleshooting purposes, the AS path, next hop, and best path indicator are the most important fields in the output of this command. For a full description of all possible fields, see the BGP command references on www. cisco.com.

Instead of viewing a specific entry in the BGP table, it can also be useful to select a set of routes from the BGP table based on certain criteria. The Cisco IOS BGP command toolkit includes the following options to select specific routes from the BGP table:

- **show ip bgp** *network mask* **longer-prefixes** – Lists more specific prefixes present in the BGP table (including the prefix itself) that are contained in the *network* and *mask* options.

- **show ip bgp neighbor** *ip-address* **routes** – Lists all routes in the BGP table that were received from the neighbor specified by the *ip-address* option.

- **show ip bgp neighbor** *ip-address* **advertised-routes** – Lists all routes in the BGP table that will be advertised to the neighbor specified by the *ip-address* option.

- **show ip bgp regexp** *regular-expression* – Selects all routes from the BGP table that have an AS path string that is matched by the specified regular expression.

For more information about how to match specific AS paths using regular expressions, see the "Understanding Regular Expressions" section in the *Cisco IOS Configuration Fundamentals Configuration Guide* at

http://www.cisco.com/en/US/docs/ios/fundamentals/configuration/guide/cf_cli-basics_ps6350_TSD_Products_Configuration_Guide_Chapter.html#wp1002051

Debug BGP Route Exchange

```
R1#debug ip bgp update
BGP updates debugging is on for address family: IPv4 Unicast

R1#clear ip bgp *
R1#
*Nov 16 18:14:11.508: %BGP-5-ADJCHANGE: neighbor 192.168.2.1 Down User reset
R1#
*Nov 16 18:14:13.844: %BGP-5-ADJCHANGE: neighbor 192.168.2.1 Up
R1#
*Nov 16 18:14:13.860: BGP(0): 192.168.2.1 rcvd UPDATE w/ attr: nexthop 192.168.2
.1, origin i, metric 0, merged path 65502, AS_PATH
*Nov 16 18:14:13.860: BGP(0): 192.168.2.1 rcvd 0.0.0.0/0
*Nov 16 18:14:14.832: BGP(0): Revise route installing 1 of 1 routes for 0.0.0.0/
0 -> 192.168.2.1(main) to main IP table
R1#
*Nov 16 18:14:47.264: BGP(0): nettable_walker 172.30.1.0/27 route sourced locall
y
*Nov 16 18:14:47.268: BGP(0): 192.168.2.1 send UPDATE (format) 172.30.1.0/27, ne
xt 192.168.1.1, metric 0
```

If you find expected route entries to be missing from the BGP table, or you doubt whether the router is sending specific routes to a neighbor, consider using the `debug ip bgp updates` command to display the processing of BGP updates by the router. However, this command can generate a large number of messages, especially if your BGP table carries many routes. Consequently, it has a high risk of disrupting the router's operation. In production networks, you should take extreme care when using this command, and you should use command options to limit the output to the prefixes and neighbor that you are troubleshooting.

Note: The following section uses sample output not produced from the equipment in this lab to demonstrate how to limit the output of the `debug ip bgp updates` command by specifying a neighbor and using an access list to select only certain prefixes.

The commands are interspersed with comments that explain the procedure and output.

```
IRO1#configure terminal
Enter configuration commands, one per line.  End with CNTL/Z.
IRO1(config)#access-list 37 permit 172.17.76.0 0.0.3.255
IRO1(config)#^Z
IRO1#
```

An access list with number 37 is created. When used to filter BGP routes, this access list matches any prefix in the 172.17.76.0–172.17.79.0 IP range.

```
IRO1#debug ip bgp 192.168.224.254 updates 37
BGP updates debugging is on for access list 37 for neighbor 192.168.224.254
for address family: IPv4 Unicast
```

The debug is enabled for neighbor 192.168.224.254 and access list 37. Only update messages transmitted to or received from neighbor 192.168.224.254 that are permitted by access list 37 will be displayed.

```
IRO1#clear ip bgp 192.168.224.254 soft
```

A "soft" clear of BGP neighbor 192.168.224.254 is issued. As opposed to a "hard" clear, a soft clear does not tear down and restart the session completely. It just forces the routes between this router and the neighbor to be retransmitted.

```
IRO1#

Apr 29 06:36:57.549 PDT: BGP(0): 192.168.224.254 send UPDATE (format)
172.17.76.0/22, next 192.168.224.241, metric 0, path Local
```

An update about prefix 172.17.76.0/22 is transmitted to neighbor 192.168.224.254. Note that both the neighbor and the prefix match the imposed restrictions.

```
Apr 29 06:36:57.553 PDT: BGP(0): 192.168.224.254 rcv UPDATE w/ attr: nexthop
192.168.224.254, origin i, originator 0.0.0.0, path 65525 64568, community ,
extended community

Apr 29 06:36:57.553 PDT: BGP(0): 192.168.224.254 rcv UPDATE about
172.17.76.0/22 -- DENIED due to: AS-PATH contains our own AS;
```

An update about prefix 172.17.76.0/22 is received but denied, because the AS path attribute contains this router's autonomous system (AS 64568).

Many more updates were sent between this router and its neighbor, but only updates that match the imposed restrictions were displayed, limiting the impact of the command.

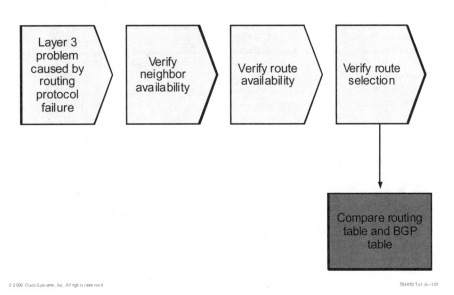

Sample BGP Troubleshooting Flow

If you find that a route is available in the BGP table but not in the routing table, there are two possible explanations. Either BGP has not been able to select any of the paths as the best path, or it has selected a best path, but a competing route from a different source with a better administrative distance is present and has been installed in the routing table.

If none of the paths has been selected as the best path, this will be clearly visible in the BGP table, and clues about the cause of the best path selection failure can be gathered from the BGP table. For example, if none of the paths has a next hop that can be resolved in the IP routing table, "Inaccessible" is displayed instead of the IGP metric to reach the next hop. If the BGP synchronization rule is causing a route not to be installed in the routing table, "not synchronized" is displayed behind the route.

If a best path has been selected for the prefix but not installed in the routing table due to the presence of a competing route with a better administrative presence, the route is marked as a "RIB-failure" in the BGP table. To list all BGP routes that have not been installed in the routing table due to a RIB failure, use the `show ip bgp rib-failure` command.

Reflection Questions

1. Which lab trouble tickets did you have the most difficulty with? _____

_____

_____

_____

2. Would you change anything about the process that you used for any of the trouble tickets now that you see the resolution of the problem? _____

_____

_____

_____

3. Which commands did you find most useful in diagnosing BGP issues? Add these to your toolbox for future use. Which commands did you find least useful?

_____

_____

_____

References

If you need more information on the commands and their options, see the following references:

- IP Routing Protocol Command Reference

    http://www.cisco.com/cisco/web/support/index.html

- Border Gateway Protocol Troubleshooting Tech Notes http://www.cisco.com/en/US/tech/tk365/tsd_technology_support_troubleshooting_technotes_list.html#anchor1

Router Interface Summary Table

Router Interface Summary				
Router Model	Ethernet Interface #1	Ethernet Interface #2	Serial Interface #1	Serial Interface #2
1700	Fast Ethernet 0 (FA0)	Fast Ethernet 1 (FA1)	Serial 0 (S0)	Serial 1 (S1)
1800	Fast Ethernet 0/0 (FA0/0)	Fast Ethernet 0/1 (FA0/1)	Serial 0/0/0 (S0/0/0)	Serial 0/0/1 (S0/0/1)
2600	Fast Ethernet 0/0 (FA0/0)	Fast Ethernet 0/1 (FA0/1)	Serial 0/0 (S0/0)	Serial 0/1 (S0/1)
2800	Fast Ethernet 0/0 (FA0/0)	Fast Ethernet 0/1 (FA0/1)	Serial 0/0/0 (S0/0/0)	Serial 0/0/1 (S0/0/1)
Note: To find out how the router is configured, look at the interfaces to identify the type of router and how many interfaces the router has. Rather than try to list all the combinations of configurations for each router class, this table includes identifiers for the possible combinations of Ethernet and serial interfaces in the device. The table does not include any other type of interface, even though a specific router might contain one. An example of this is an ISDN BRI interface. The string in parenthesis is the legal abbreviation that can be used in Cisco IOS commands to represent the interface.				

Chapter 6 Troubleshooting Addressing Service

Lab 6-1, IP Addressing—NAT and DHCP

Physical Topology (Baseline)

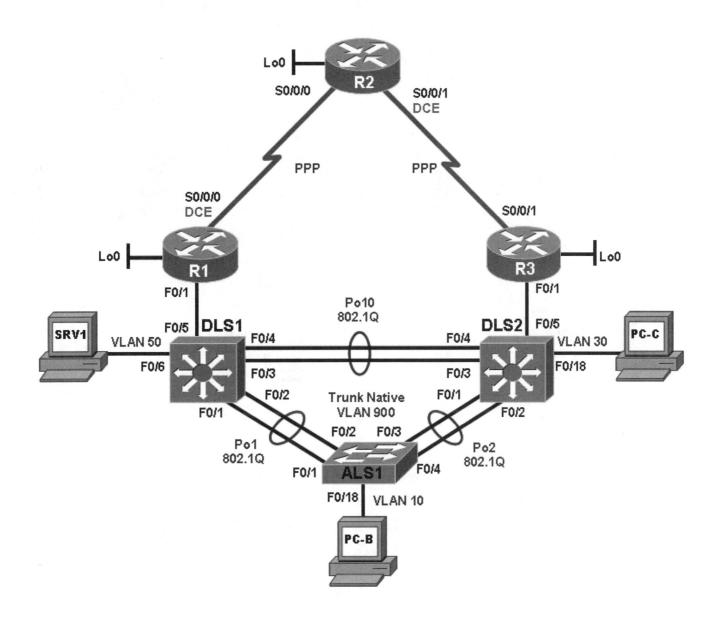

Logical Topology (Baseline)

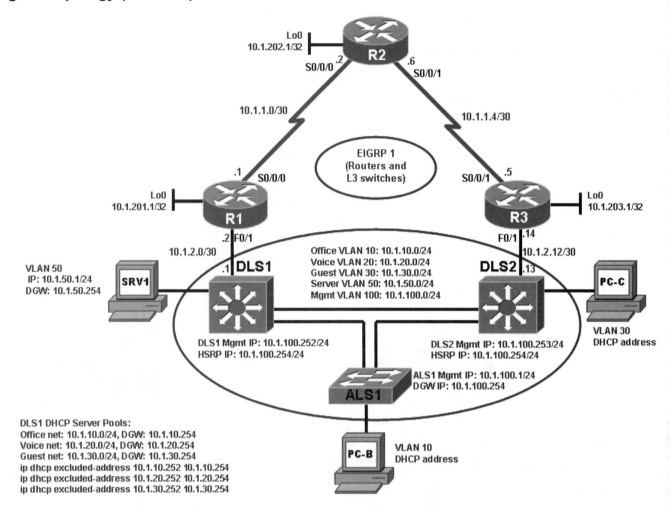

Objectives

- Load the device configuration files for each trouble ticket.

- Diagnose and resolve problems related to IP addressing and NAT.

- Diagnose and resolve problems related to IP addressing and DHCP.

- Document the troubleshooting progress, configuration changes, and problem resolution.

Background

Network Address Translation (NAT) is routinely employed in small and large networks. NAT preserves the public IPv4 address space and can provide a measure of security by using private addresses internally. Network layer connectivity issues associated with NAT can include address pool definition, pool depletion, address configuration, interface boundaries, and the type of NAT employed: static, dynamic, or Port Address Translation (PAT).

DHCP is the most common method of assigning IP addressing information to end-user clients. Network layer connectivity issues associated with DHCP include address pool definition, pool depletion, address and default gateway configuration, and server accessibility. In this lab, you will troubleshoot various problems related to NAT and DHCP.

For each task or trouble ticket, the trouble scenario and problem symptom are described. While troubleshooting, you will discover the cause of the problem, correct it, and then document the process and results.

NAT and DHCP Configuration

Your company has decided not to implement a hosted services data center because of cost considerations. Because you will not be advertising a hosted services network, it was decided to discontinue the use of Border Gateway Protocol (BGP) in favor of a simple default static configuration.

Phase 1 (TT-A and TT-B): Dynamic NAT will be used for internal users accessing the Internet. Static NAT will give teleworkers access to some of the key internal servers. Your Internet service provider (ISP) has assigned a block of public addresses using prefix 198.133.219.0/27. These addresses will be used for dynamic NAT with the internal 10.1.0.0/16 network, as well as static NAT to specific servers. Server SRV1 will act as a test server that provides access to an internal web-based application for remote workers. Router R1 will have a default route to the ISP (R2) and will redistribute that route into Enhanced Interior Gateway Routing Protocol (EIGRP). The ISP will use a static route to the NAT public address pool on R1.

Phase 2 (TT-C): A second DHCP server will be added in TT-C to support the branch office router R3 LAN. Switch DLS2 will be configured to provide DHCP addresses to the R3 LAN clients. The following diagram provides information on the NAT (Phase 1) and DHCP (Phase 2) implementation.

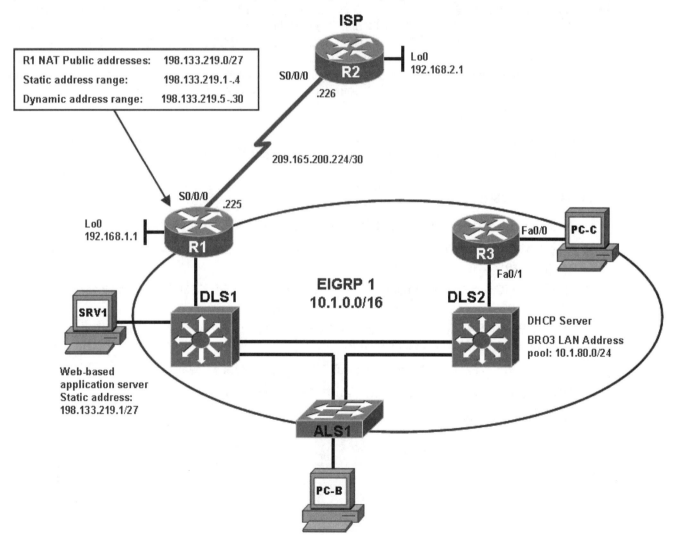

Physical and Logical Topology Diagrams

The baseline physical and logical topologies for the existing EIGRP-based network are provided in this lab to assist the troubleshooting effort.

Lab Structure

This lab is divided into two main sections.

Section 1—Trouble Tickets and Troubleshooting Logs

This section includes multiple tasks. Each task is associated with a trouble ticket (TT) and introduces one or more errors on one or more devices. If time is a consideration, each task or trouble ticket can be performed independently.

Section 2—Troubleshooting Reference Information

This section provides general troubleshooting information that can be applied to any of the trouble tickets in this lab. Examples of useful commands and output are provided. If time permits, it is recommended that you read through Section 2 prior to starting on the trouble tickets.

Note: This lab uses Cisco 1841 routers with Cisco IOS Release 12.4(24)T1 and the Advanced IP Services image c1841-advipservicesk9-mz.124-24.T1.bin. The switches are Cisco WS-C2960-24TT-L with the Cisco IOS image c2960-lanbasek9-mz.122-46.SE.bin and Catalyst 3560-24PS with the Cisco IOS image c3560-advipservicesk9-mz.122-46.SE.bin. Other routers (such as 2801 and 2811), switches (such as 2950 or 3550), and Cisco IOS Software versions can be used if they have comparable capabilities and features. Depending on the router or switch model and Cisco IOS Software version, the commands available and output produced might vary from what is shown in this lab.

Any changes made to configurations or topology (other than errors introduced) are noted in the lab and trouble tickets so that you are aware of them prior to beginning the troubleshooting process.

Required Resources

- 3 routers (Cisco 1841 with Cisco IOS Release 12.4(24)T1 Advanced IP Service or comparable)
- 1 switch (Cisco 2960 with the Cisco IOS Release 12.2(46)SE C2960-LANBASEK9-M image or comparable)
- 2 switches (Cisco 3560 with the Cisco IOS Release 12.2(46)SE C3560-advipservicesk9-mz image or comparable)
- SRV1 (Windows PC with static IP address) with TFTP and syslog servers, plus an SSH client (PuTTY or comparable) and WireShark software
- PC-B (Windows PC DHCP client) with PuTTY and WireShark software
- PC-C (Windows PC DHCP client) with PuTTY and WireShark software
- Serial and Ethernet cables

Section 1—Trouble Tickets and Troubleshooting Logs

Task 1: Trouble Ticket Lab 6-1 TT-A

Step 1: Review trouble ticket Lab 6-1 TT-A.

Your colleague has configured NAT on the edge router (R1), and the external users (simulated by R2 Lo0) can access the test server on the internal private network. However, host PC-B on the internal network cannot access the Internet. Your task is to diagnose the problem and verify that NAT is properly configured. In addition to external users accessing SRV1, internal users must also be able to access the Internet.

Step 2: Load the device trouble ticket configuration files for TT-A.

Using the procedure described in Lab 3-1, verify that the lab configuration files are present in flash. Load the proper configuration files as indicated in the Device Configuration File table.

Note: The following device access methods are in effect after loading the configuration files:

- Console access requires no username or password.

- Telnet and SSH require username **admin** and password **adminpa55**.

- The enable password is **ciscoenpa55**.

Device Configuration File Table

Device Name	File to Load	Notes
ALS1	Lab61-ALS1-TT-A-Cfg.txt	
DLS1	Lab61-DLS1-TT-A-Cfg.txt	
DLS2	Lab61-DLS2-TT-A-Cfg.txt	
R1	Lab61-R1-TT-A-Cfg.txt	
R2	Lab61-R2-TT-A-Cfg.txt	
R3	Lab61-R3-TT-A-Cfg.txt	
SRV1	N/A	Static IP: 10.1.50.1 Default gateway: 10.1.50.254
PC-B	N/A	DHCP
PC-C	N/A	DHCP

Step 3: Configure SRV1 and start the syslog and TFTP servers.

Step 4: Release and renew the DHCP leases.

a. Ensure that PC-B and PC-C are configured as a DHCP clients.

b. After loading all TT-A device configuration files, issue the `ipconfig /release` and `ipconfig /renew` commands on both PCs.

Note: This trouble ticket assumes that PC-C is in its standard location (connected to Fa0/18 on DLS2).

Step 5: Outline the troubleshooting approach and validation steps.

Use this space to identify your troubleshooting approach and the key steps to verify the problem is resolved. Troubleshooting approaches to select from include the follow-the-path, spot-the-differences, bottom-up, top-down, divide-and-conquer, shoot-from-the-hip, and move-the-problem methods.

Note: In addition to a specific approach, you can use the generic troubleshooting process described at the beginning of Section 2 of this lab.

_____

_____

_____

_____

_____

Step 6: Record the troubleshooting process and configuration changes.

Note: Section 2 of this lab includes useful commands and examples of output.

Use this log to document your actions and results during the troubleshooting process. List the commands you used to gather information. As you progress, record what you think the problem might be and the actions you take to correct the problem.

Device	Actions and Results

Step 7: Document trouble ticket debrief notes.

Use this space to make notes of the key learning points that you picked up during the discussion of this trouble ticket with your instructor. The notes can include problems encountered, solutions applied, useful commands employed, alternate solutions, methods, and processes, and procedure and communication improvements.

_____

_____

_____

_____

_____

_____

_____

Task 2: Trouble Ticket Lab 6-1 TT-B

Step 1: Review trouble ticket Lab 6-1 TT-B.

The NAT configuration has been corrected, and dynamic NAT is now functioning between internal hosts and the ISP. However, some users have called the help desk stating that Internet access is inconsistent. Sometimes it works, and other times it does not. Your task is to diagnose the problem and correct it. At a minimum, propose a possible solution to the problem so that internal users can consistently access the Internet.

Step 2: Load the device trouble ticket configuration files for TT-B.

Using the procedure described in Lab 3-1, verify that the lab configuration files are present in flash. Load the proper configuration files as indicated in the Device Configuration File table.

Note: See Task 1, Step 2 for device access methods, usernames, and passwords after the configuration files have been loaded.

Device Configuration File Table

Device Name	File to Load	Notes
ALS1	Lab61-ALS1-TT-B-Cfg.txt	
DLS1	Lab61-DLS1-TT-B-Cfg.txt	
DLS2	Lab61-DLS2-TT-B-Cfg.txt	
R1	Lab61-R1-TT-B-Cfg.txt	
R2	Lab61-R2-TT-B-Cfg.txt	
R3	Lab61-R3-TT-B-Cfg.txt	
SRV1	N/A	Static IP: 10.1.50.1 Default gateway: 10.1.50.254
PC-B	N/A	DHCP
PC-C	N/A	DHCP

Step 3: Configure SRV1 and start the syslog and TFTP servers.

Step 4: Release and renew the DHCP leases.

a.   Ensure that PC-B and PC-C are configured as a DHCP clients.

b.   After loading all TT-A device configuration files, issue the **ipconfig /release** and ipconfig /renew commands on both PCs.

Note: This trouble ticket assumes that PC-C is in its standard location (connected to Fa0/18 on DLS2).

Step 5: Outline the troubleshooting approach and validation steps.

Use this space to identify your troubleshooting approach and the key steps to verify that the problem is resolved. Troubleshooting approaches to select from include the follow-the-path, spot-the-differences, bottom-up, top-down, divide-and-conquer, shoot-from-the-hip, and move-the-problem methods.

Note: In addition to a specific approach, you can use the generic troubleshooting process described at the beginning of Section 2 of this lab.

_____

_____

_____

_____

_____

_____

Step 6: Record the troubleshooting process and configuration changes.

Note: Section 2 of this lab includes sample troubleshooting flows, useful commands, and examples of output.

Use this log to document your actions and results during the troubleshooting process. List the commands you used to gather information. As you progress, record what you think the problem might be and the actions you take to correct the problem.

Device	Actions and Results

Device	Actions and Results

Step 7: Document trouble ticket debrief notes.

Use this space to make notes of the key learning points that you picked up during the discussion of this trouble ticket with your instructor. The notes can include problems encountered, solutions applied, useful commands employed, alternate solutions, methods, and processes, and procedure and communication improvements.

_____

_____

_____

_____

_____

_____

_____

Task 3: Trouble Ticket Lab 6-1 TT-C

Step 1: Review trouble ticket Lab 6-1 TT-C.

The company is expanding and opening a new branch office LAN that will be connected to router R3. It has been decided that switch DLS2 will provide DHCP services to this remote office. The branch office is represented by test host PC-C, which will be configured as a DHCP client. Your colleague says he has configured DHCP on DLS2 with a corresponding subnet and DHCP pool. However, test client PC-C has not been able to access server SRV1. The first address in the pool should be excluded because it is reserved for the R3 default gateway Fa0/0.

Your task is to verify VLAN configuration and DHCP services and that PC-C can access internal server SRV1.

Step 2: Load the device trouble ticket configuration files for TT-C.

Using the procedure described in Lab 3-1, verify that the lab configuration files are present in flash. Load the proper configuration files as indicated in the Device Configuration File table.

Note: See Task 1, Step 2 for device access methods, usernames, and passwords after the configuration files have been loaded.

Device Configuration File Table

Device Name	File to Load	Notes
ALS1	Lab61-ALS1-TT-C-Cfg.txt	
DLS1	Lab61-DLS1-TT-C-Cfg.txt	
DLS2	Lab61-DLS2-TT-C-Cfg.txt	
R1	Lab61-R1-TT-C-Cfg.txt	
R2	Lab61-R2-TT-C-Cfg.txt	
R3	Lab61-R3-TT-C-Cfg.txt	
SRV1	N/A	Static IP: 10.1.50.1 Default gateway: 10.1.50.254
PC-B	N/A	DHCP (release and renew after loading the device configurations)
PC-C	N/A	DHCP (release and renew after loading the device configurations)

Step 3: Configure SRV1 and start the syslog and TFTP servers.

Step 4: Release and renew the DHCP lease on PC-C.

a. Ensure that PC-C is configured as a DHCP client.

b. Connect PC-C to R3.

c. After loading all TT-C device configuration files, issue the `ipconfig /release` and `ipconfig /renew` commands on PC-C.

Step 5: Outline the troubleshooting approach and validation steps.

Use this space to identify your troubleshooting approach and the key steps to take to verify that the problem is resolved. Troubleshooting approaches to select from include the follow-the-path, spot-the-differences, bottom-up, top-down, divide-and-conquer, shoot-from-the-hip, and move-the-problem methods.

Note: In addition to a specific approach, you can use the generic troubleshooting process described at the beginning of Section 2 of this lab.

_____

_____

_____

_____

_____

Step 6: Record the troubleshooting process and configuration changes.

Note: Section 2 of this lab includes sample troubleshooting flows, useful commands, and examples of output.

Use this log to document your actions and results during the troubleshooting process. List the commands that you used to gather information. As you progress, record what you think the problem might be and the actions you take to correct the problem.

Device	Actions and Results

Step 7: Document trouble ticket debrief notes.

Use this space to make notes of the key learning points that you picked up during the discussion of this trouble ticket with your instructor. The notes include problems encountered, solutions applied, useful commands employed, alternate solutions and methods, and procedure and communication improvements.

_____

_____

_____

_____

_____

_____

_____

Section 2 Troubleshooting Reference Information

NAT command examples include verification of NAT boundaries, the type of NAT configured, NAT statistics, NAT translations, and debugging NAT translations.

DHCP examples include verification of the DHCP server configuration, address pools, DHCP server statistics, client configuration, and debugging DHCP activity.

General Troubleshooting Process

As a general guideline, you can use the following general troubleshooting process described in the course.

1. Define the problem (symptoms).

2. Gather information.

3. Analyze the information.

4. Propose a hypothesis (possible cause).

5. Test the hypothesis.

6. Eliminate or accept the hypothesis.

7. Solve the problem.

8. Document the problem.

Command Summary

The table lists useful commands for this lab. The sample output is shown on following pages

Command	Key Information Displayed
`show ip nat statistics`	Displays the NAT pool configuration information, boundaries (inside and outside interfaces), translation pool size, and usage statistics.
`show ip nat translations`	Displays all current translations (static and dynamic), including the initiating protocol as well as inside global, inside local, outside local, and outside global addresses.
`debug ip icmp`	Displays real-time information related to ping (echo request and echo reply) and other protocols that make use of ICMP.
`debug ip nat`	Displays real-time information related to NAT translation activity (static and dynamic).
`clear ip nat translations *`	Clears all dynamic translations.
`clear ip nat statistics *`	Clears NAT counters.
`show ip dhcp server statistics`	Displays DHCP pool activity from hosts requesting IP addressing.
`show ip dhcp pool`	Displays DHCP pool information, including the address range, number of excluded addresses, and lease activity.
`show ip dhcp conflicts`	Displays conflicts resulting from assigning addresses that are already assigned to a device interface in the same subnet or network.
`show ip dhcp binding`	Displays the IP address, hardware (MAC) address, and lease expiration for a DHCP address assignment.
`debug dhcp detail`	Displays real-time information on a Cisco IOS DHCP client (router or switch).

`debug ip dhcp server events`	Displays real-time information for DHCP server process messages.
`clear ip dhcp server statistics`	Clears DHCP server statistics.
`clear ip dhcp conflict *`	Clears conflicted addresses.
`show ip sockets`	Displays the current connections for this server, including which services are running.

Sample Troubleshooting Output

NAT-related Commands

The following commands and output are samples from the devices in this lab.

```
R1#show ip nat translations
Pro Inside global       Inside local        Outside local       Outside global
icmp 198.133.219.7:512  10.1.10.1:512       192.168.2.1:512     192.168.2.1:512
--- 198.133.219.7       10.1.10.1           ---                 ---
--- 198.133.219.1       10.1.50.1           ---                 ---
udp 198.133.219.6:123   10.1.100.1:123      192.168.2.1:123     192.168.2.1:123
tcp 198.133.219.6:38711 10.1.100.1:38711    192.168.2.1:23      192.168.2.1:23
--- 198.133.219.6       10.1.100.1          ---                 ---
udp 198.133.219.4:123   10.1.100.252:123    192.168.2.1:123     192.168.2.1:123
--- 198.133.219.4       10.1.100.252        ---                 ---
tcp 198.133.219.3:1121  10.1.10.1:1121      192.168.2.1:80      192.168.2.1:80
--- 198.133.219.3       10.1.10.1           ---                 ---
udp 198.133.219.5:123   10.1.100.253:123    192.168.2.1:123     192.168.2.1:123
--- 198.133.219.5       10.1.100.253        ---                 ---
```

In the above example, the connections resulted from pings (ICMP port 512), NTP (UDP port 123), Telnet (TCP port 23), and HTTP (TCP port 80).

```
R1#show ip nat statistics
Total active translations: 7 (1 static, 6 dynamic; 2 extended)
Peak translations: 9, occurred 00:45:03 ago
Outside interfaces:
  Serial0/0/0
Inside interfaces:
  FastEthernet0/1
Hits: 2442  Misses: 0
CEF Translated packets: 2439, CEF Punted packets: 11
Expired translations: 15
Dynamic mappings:
-- Inside Source
[Id: 8] access-list 1 pool public-addrs refcount 6
 pool public-addrs: netmask 255.255.255.248
       start 198.133.219.3 end 198.133.219.6
       type generic, total addresses 4, allocated 4 (100%), misses 8
Appl doors: 0
Normal doors: 0
Queued Packets: 0
```

The above output shows NAT pool configuration information, boundaries (inside and outside interfaces), translation pool size, and usage statistics.

```
R1#debug ip nat
IP NAT debugging is on
```

```
R1#terminal monitor
R1#
Nov 18 16:52:09.304: NAT*: s=10.1.10.1->198.133.219.6, d=192.168.2.1 [108]
Nov 18 16:52:09.316: NAT*: s=192.168.2.1, d=198.133.219.6->10.1.10.1 [108]
Nov 18 16:52:10.300: NAT*: s=10.1.10.1->198.133.219.6, d=192.168.2.1 [109]
Nov 18 16:52:10.308: NAT*: s=192.168.2.1, d=198.133.219.6->10.1.10.1 [109]
Nov 18 16:52:11.300: NAT*: s=10.1.10.1->198.133.219.6, d=192.168.2.1 [110]
Nov 18 16:52:11.308: NAT*: s=192.168.2.1, d=198.133.219.6->10.1.10.1 [110]
Nov 18 16:52:12.300: NAT*: s=10.1.10.1->198.133.219.6, d=192.168.2.1 [111]
Nov 18 16:52:12.312: NAT*: s=192.168.2.1, d=198.133.219.6->10.1.10.1 [111]
Nov 18 16:52:59.356: NAT*: s=10.1.100.252->198.133.219.4, d=192.168.2.1 [0]
Nov 18 16:52:59.368: NAT*: s=192.168.2.1, d=198.133.219.4->10.1.100.252 [0]
Nov 18 16:53:12.772: NAT: expiring 198.133.219.6 (10.1.10.1) icmp 512 (512)
Nov 18 16:53:47.140: NAT*: s=10.1.100.1->198.133.219.5, d=192.168.2.1 [0]
Nov 18 16:53:47.152: NAT*: s=192.168.2.1, d=198.133.219.5->10.1.100.1 [0]
Nov 18 16:53:53.992: NAT*: s=10.1.100.253->198.133.219.3, d=192.168.2.1 [0]
Nov 18 16:53:54.004: NAT*: s=192.168.2.1, d=198.133.219.3->10.1.100.253 [0]
```

This first output example of NAT debug shows dynamic NAT translation of test pings from internal host PC-B to simulated ISP R2, Lo0. Note that translations are aged out (expired) if the source host does not refresh the address assignment. The **terminal monitor** command was issued on R1 so that the debug output could be viewed from a Telnet connection.

```
R1#debug ip nat
IP NAT debugging is on
R1#
Nov 18 19:31:36.112: NAT: translation failed (A), dropping packet s=10.1.10.1 d=
192.168.2.1
Nov 18 19:31:37.108: NAT: translation failed (A), dropping packet s=10.1.10.1 d=
192.168.2.1
R1#
Nov 18 19:31:38.112: NAT: translation failed (A), dropping packet s=10.1.10.1 d=
192.168.2.1
R1#
Nov 18 19:31:39.112: NAT: translation failed (A), dropping packet s=10.1.10.1 d=
192.168.2.1
```

The above output example shows error messages reported on the NAT router because of pool depletion and the inability to assign a public source address to the packet being routed.

```
R1#debug ip icmp
ICMP packet debugging is on

Nov 18 19:50:50.879: ICMP: dst (192.168.2.1) host unreachable sent to 10.1.10.1
Nov 18 19:50:51.875: ICMP: dst (192.168.2.1) host unreachable sent to 10.1.10.1
R1#
Nov 18 19:50:52.879: ICMP: dst (192.168.2.1) host unreachable sent to 10.1.10.1
R1#
Nov 18 19:50:53.879: ICMP: dst (192.168.2.1) host unreachable sent to 10.1.10.1
```

The **debug ip icmp** output shows R1 responding to host PC-B with an error during a ping to the ISP because of the lack of NAT translation.

```
R2#debug ip icmp
Nov 18 18:29:31.381: ICMP: echo reply sent, src 192.168.2.1, dst 10.1.10.1
Nov 18 18:29:36.737: ICMP: echo reply sent, src 192.168.2.1, dst 10.1.10.1
Nov 18 18:29:41.745: ICMP: echo reply sent, src 192.168.2.1, dst 10.1.10.1
Nov 18 18:29:46.753: ICMP: echo reply sent, src 192.168.2.1, dst 10.1.10.1
```

The above output shows R2 sending replies to PC-B at the internal private address because of the lack of NAT translation.

DHCP-Related Commands

```
DLS2#show ip dhcp server statistics
Memory usage            15668
Address pools           1
Database agents         0
Automatic bindings      1
Manual bindings         0
Expired bindings        0
Malformed messages      0
Secure arp entries      0
Renew messages          2

Message                 Received
BOOTREQUEST             0
DHCPDISCOVER            4
DHCPREQUEST             4
DHCPDECLINE             0
DHCPRELEASE             1
DHCPINFORM              0

Message                 Sent
BOOTREPLY               0
DHCPOFFER               2
DHCPACK                 4
DHCPNAK                 0
```

The above output displays DHCP pool activity from hosts requesting IP addressing.

```
DLS2#show ip dhcp pool
Pool BRO3 :
 Utilization mark (high/low)    : 100 / 0
 Subnet size (first/next)       : 0 / 0
 Total addresses                : 254
 Leased addresses               : 1
 Excluded addresses             : 3
 Pending event                  : none
 1 subnet is currently in the pool :
 Current index        IP address range                       Leased/Excluded/Total
 10.1.80.1            10.1.80.1        - 10.1.80.254          1      / 3      / 254
```

The above output displays DHCP pool information, including the address range, number of excluded addresses, and lease activity.

```
DLS2#show ip dhcp conflict
IP address         Detection method   Detection time          VRF
10.1.80.1          Gratuitous ARP     Nov 20 2009 06:09 PM
```

The above output displays an address conflict resulting from the attempted assignment of the 10.1.80.1 address. The server sends a ping for an address before it attempts to assign that address from the pool. Also, after the client is assigned an IP address by the DHCP server, it sends a Gratuitous ARP or test ARP for that address. If the address is already assigned to a device interface, the device to which it is assigned responds, and the DHCP server marks it as a conflicted address. Conflicted addresses can be cleared with the **clear ip dhcp conflict *** command.

```
DLS2#show ip dhcp binding
Bindings from all pools not associated with VRF:
IP address              Client-ID/                Lease expiration        Type
                        Hardware address/
                        User name
10.1.80.2               0100.0bdb.04a5.cd         Nov 21 2009 02:50 PM    Automatic
```

The above output displays the IP address, hardware (MAC) address, and lease expiration for a DHCP address assignment.

```
DLS2#debug ip dhcp server events
DHCP server event debugging is on.
DLS2#
Nov 20 15:20:31.653: DHCPD: Sending notification of TERMINATION:
Nov 20 15:20:31.653: DHCPD: address 10.1.80.2 mask 255.255.255.0
Nov 20 15:20:31.653: DHCPD: reason flags: RELEASE
Nov 20 15:20:31.653: DHCPD: htype 1 chaddr 000b.db04.a5cd
Nov 20 15:20:31.653: DHCPD: lease time remaining (secs) = 86356
Nov 20 15:20:31.653: DHCPD: interface = FastEthernet0/5
Nov 20 15:20:31.653: DHCPD: returned 10.1.80.2 to address pool BRO3.
DLS2#
Nov 20 15:20:46.226: DHCPD: Sending notification of DISCOVER:
Nov 20 15:20:46.226: DHCPD: htype 1 chaddr 000b.db04.a5cd
Nov 20 15:20:46.226:    DHCPD: giaddr = 10.1.80.1
Nov 20 15:20:46.226:    DHCPD: interface = FastEthernet0/5
Nov 20 15:20:46.226:    DHCPD: class id 4d53465420352e30
Nov 20 15:20:46.226:    DHCPD: Sending notification of DISCOVER:
Nov 20 15:20:46.226:    DHCPD: htype 1 chaddr 000b.db04.a5cd
Nov 20 15:20:46.226:    DHCPD: giaddr = 10.1.80.1
Nov 20 15:20:46.226:    DHCPD: interface = FastEthernet0/5
Nov 20 15:20:46.226:    DHCPD: class id 4d53465420352e30
Nov 20 15:20:48.239:    DHCPD: client requests 10.1.80.2.
Nov 20 15:20:48.239:    DHCPD: Adding binding to radix tree (10.1.80.2)
Nov 20 15:20:48.239:    DHCPD: Adding binding to hash tree
Nov 20 15:20:48.239:    DHCPD: assigned IP address 10.1.80.2 to client
0100.0bdb.04a5.cd. (471 0)
Nov 20 15:20:48.239:    DHCPD: Sending notification of ASSIGNMENT:
Nov 20 15:20:48.239:    DHCPD: address 10.1.80.2 mask 255.255.255.0
Nov 20 15:20:48.239:    DHCPD: htype 1 chaddr 000b.db04.a5cd
Nov 20 15:20:48.239:    DHCPD: lease time remaining (secs) = 86400
Nov 20 15:20:48.239:    DHCPD: interface = FastEthernet0/5

Nov 20 15:21:49.307: DHCPD: checking for expired leases.
```

The above output shows the process that the DHCP server goes through when a client issues the **ipconfig / release** and **ipconfig /renew** commands.

```
R3#debug ip udp
UDP packet debugging is on
R3#conf t
Enter configuration commands, one per line.  End with CNTL/Z.
R3(config)#int f0/0
R3(config-if)#no ip helper-address 10.1.2.13
R3(config-if)#
*Nov 20 15:53:29.606: UDP: rcvd src=0.0.0.0(68), dst=255.255.255.255(67), length
```

```
=308
*Nov 20 15:53:32.606: UDP: rcvd src=0.0.0.0(68), dst=255.255.255.255(67), length
=308
*Nov 20 15:53:41.610: UDP: rcvd src=0.0.0.0(68), dst=255.255.255.255(67), length
=308
*Nov 20 15:53:57.614: UDP: rcvd src=0.0.0.0(68), dst=255.255.255.255(67), length
=308
R3#
```

The above output shows the DHCP relay agent (R3) messages when a helper address is not configured. The UDP packets received are from the DHCP client (the source address is 0.0.0.0 port 68) searching for a DHCP server (the destination broadcast address is 255.255.255.255 port 67). There are no sent messages to the client because the broadcast is not forwarded to the DHCP server.

```
R3(config)#int f0/0
R3(config-if)#ip helper-address 10.1.2.13
R3(config-if)#
*Nov 20 15:54:19.547: Reserved port 67 in Transport Port Agent for UDP IP type 1
*Nov 20 15:54:34.035: UDP: rcvd src=0.0.0.0(68), dst=255.255.255.255(67), length
=308
*Nov 20 15:54:34.035: UDP: sent src=10.1.80.1(67), dst=10.1.2.13(67), length=308
*Nov 20 15:54:36.043: UDP: rcvd src=10.1.2.13(67), dst=10.1.80.1(67), length=308
*Nov 20 15:54:36.047: UDP: sent src=0.0.0.0(67), dst=255.255.255.255(68), length
=308
*Nov 20 15:54:36.047: UDP: rcvd src=0.0.0.0(68), dst=255.255.255.255(67), length
=324
*Nov 20 15:54:36.047: UDP: sent src=10.1.80.1(67), dst=10.1.2.13(67), length=324
*Nov 20 15:54:36.051: UDP: rcvd src=10.1.2.13(67), dst=10.1.80.1(67), length=308
*Nov 20 15:54:36.051: UDP: sent src=0.0.0.0(67), dst=255.255.255.255(68), length
=308
```

The above output shows the DHCP relay agent (R3) messages when a helper address is configured. The DHCP exchange between the server and the client are captured.

```
DLS2#show ip sockets
Proto     Remote       Port     Local         Port  In  Out  Stat  TTY OutputIF
  17    --listen--            10.1.200.253     1985   0    0  1001    0
  17  10.1.50.1        162  10.1.100.253     62682   0    0     0    0
  17    --listen--            10.1.200.253     1975   0    0    11    0
  17  10.1.80.1         67  10.1.200.253       67    0    0  2211    0
  17  0.0.0.0            0  10.1.200.253     2228    0    0   211    0
  17    --listen--            10.1.200.253      161   0    0     1    0
  17    --listen--            10.1.200.253      162   0    0    11    0
  17    --listen--            10.1.200.253    55485   0    0     1    0
  17    --listen--            --any--           161   0    0 20001    0
  17    --listen--            --any--           162   0    0 20011    0
  17    --listen--            --any--         61812   0    0 20001    0
  17    --listen--            10.1.200.253      123   0    0     1    0
  17  10.1.50.1        514  10.1.100.253     58346   0    0 400201    0
```

The above output displays the current connections for this server. The remote connection with R3 Fa0/0 (10.1.80.1) shows that the DHCP server is running on DLS2 and listening for requests on port 67 (DHCP server).

Reflection Questions

1. Which lab trouble tickets did you have the most difficulty with? _____

_____

_____

_____

2. Would you change anything about the process that you used for any of the trouble tickets now that you see the resolution of the problem? _____

_____

_____

_____

3. Which commands did you find most useful in diagnosing NAT and DHCP issues? Add these to your toolbox for future use. Which commands did you find least useful?

_____

_____

_____

References

If you need more information on the commands and their options, see the following references:

- IP Routing Protocol Command Reference
  http://www.cisco.com/cisco/web/support/index.html

- Cisco IOS IP Switching Reference http://www.cisco.com/en/US/docs/ios/ipswitch/command/reference/isw_book.html

- Configuring Network Address Translation
  http://www.cisco.com/en/US/tech/tk648/tk361/technologies_tech_note09186a0080094e77.shtml

- Configuring a Cisco IOS DHCP Server http://www.cisco.com/en/US/docs/ios/12_2/ip/configuration/guide/1cfdhcp.html

Router Interface Summary Table

Router Interface Summary				
Router Model	Ethernet Interface #1	Ethernet Interface #2	Serial Interface #1	Serial Interface #2
1700	Fast Ethernet 0 (FA0)	Fast Ethernet 1 (FA1)	Serial 0 (S0)	Serial 1 (S1)
1800	Fast Ethernet 0/0 (FA0/0)	Fast Ethernet 0/1 (FA0/1)	Serial 0/0/0 (S0/0/0)	Serial 0/0/1 (S0/0/1)
2600	Fast Ethernet 0/0 (FA0/0)	Fast Ethernet 0/1 (FA0/1)	Serial 0/0 (S0/0)	Serial 0/1 (S0/1)
2800	Fast Ethernet 0/0 (FA0/0)	Fast Ethernet 0/1 (FA0/1)	Serial 0/0/0 (S0/0/0)	Serial 0/0/1 (S0/0/1)
Note: To find out how the router is configured, look at the interfaces to identify the type of router and how many interfaces the router has. Rather than try to list all the combinations of configurations for each router class, this table includes identifiers for the possible combinations of Ethernet and serial interfaces in the device. The table does not include any other type of interface, even though a specific router might contain one. An example of this is an ISDN BRI interface. The string in parenthesis is the legal abbreviation that can be used in Cisco IOS commands to represent the interface.				

Chapter 7 Troubleshooting Network Performance Issues

Lab 7-1, Router Performance

Lab Topology

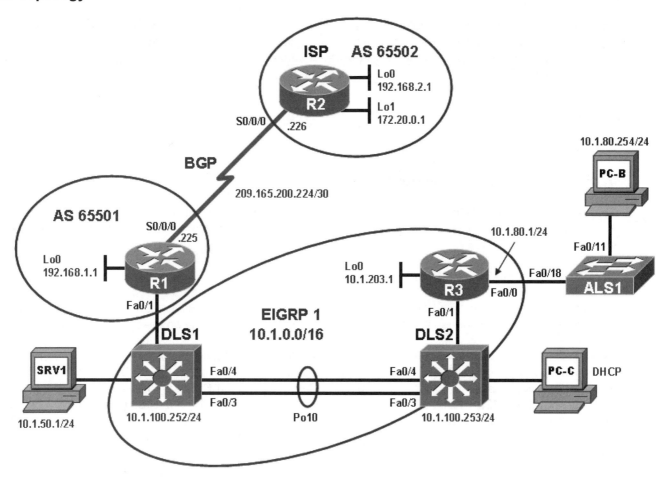

Note: The topology for this lab moves access switch ALS1 to R3 and disconnects it from switches DLS1 and DLS2. This allows a load to be placed on R3 using ALS1 and DLS2. PC-B is moved to switch ALS1 port Fa0/11. Performance testing is done using Cisco IOS commands on R3 and pings from PC-B. Even though ALS1 is no longer attached to DSL1 and DLS2, VLAN 10 still exists. The interfaces for port channel 1 on DLS1 and port channel 2 on DLS2 are temporarily shutdown.

Objectives

- Load the trouble ticket device configuration files for each trouble ticket.

- Diagnose and resolve problems related to router performance, such as excessive CPU and memory utilization.

- Document troubleshooting progress, configuration changes, and problem resolution.

Background

A number of factors can affect router performance. In addition to heavy traffic loads, these can include suboptimal configurations for interfaces, WAN links, access lists, and routing protocols. In this activity, you troubleshoot various problems related to router performance and use Cisco IOS utilities to help diagnose the issues. For each task or trouble ticket, the trouble scenario and problem symptom is described. While troubleshooting, you will discover the cause of the problem, correct it, and then document the process and results.

Note: The focus of this lab is on the tools available to diagnose performance issues. The problems induced are intended to create symptoms in a lab environment and are not necessarily real-world examples. In addition to the information provided in Section 2, command examples and assistance are provided inline with the trouble tickets.

Lab Structure

This lab is divided into two main sections.

Section 1—Trouble Tickets and Troubleshooting Logs

This section includes multiple tasks. Each task is associated with a trouble ticket (TT) and introduces one or more errors on one or more devices. If time is a consideration, each task or trouble ticket can be performed independently.

Section 2—Troubleshooting Reference Information

This section provides a generic troubleshooting process and examples of useful commands and output. If time permits, it is recommended you read through Section 2 prior to starting on the trouble tickets.

Note: This lab uses Cisco 1841 routers with Cisco IOS Release 12.4(24)T1 and the Advanced IP Services image c1841-advipservicesk9-mz.124-24.T1.bin. The switches are Cisco WS-C2960-24TT-L with the Cisco IOS image c2960-lanbasek9-mz.122-46.SE.bin and Catalyst 3560-24PS with the Cisco IOS image c3560-advipservicesk9-mz.122-46.SE.bin. Other routers (such as 2801 and 2811), switches (such as 2950 or 3550), and Cisco IOS Software versions can be used if they have comparable capabilities and features. Depending on the router or switch model and Cisco IOS Software version, the commands available and output produced might vary from what is shown in this lab.

Required Resources

- 3 routers (Cisco 1841 with the Cisco IOS Release 12.4(24)T1 Advanced IP Service or comparable)
- 1 switch (Cisco 2960 with the Cisco IOS Release 12.2(46)SE C2960-LANBASEK9-M image or comparable)
- 2 switches (Cisco 3560 with the Cisco IOS Release 12.2(46)SE C3560- advipservicesk9-mz image or comparable)
- SRV1 (Windows PC with static IP address) with TFTP and syslog servers plus an SSH client (PuTTY or comparable) and WireShark software
- PC-B (Windows PC DHCP client) with PuTTY and WireShark software
- PC-C (Windows PC DHCP client) with PuTTY and WireShark software
- Serial and Ethernet cables

Section 1—Trouble Tickets and Troubleshooting Logs

Task 1: Trouble Ticket Lab 7-1 TT-A

In this lab, the Cisco IOS command `ttcp` is used to simulate a heavy traffic load between switches ALS1 and DLS2. The TTCP utility is a hidden, unsupported Cisco IOS command. This lab provides step-by-step assistance for using Cisco IOS performance diagnostic commands and the TTCP utility.

Note: Appendix A contains additional information on how to set up a PC as a client end device for TTCP.

A recommended approach to this lab is to follow a troubleshooting process that includes the following high-level tasks:

- Generate test traffic using the `ping` or `ttcp` command, as described in this task.
- Use `ping` to measure the performance between the headquarters and branch office. For example, ping from client PC-B to server SRV1.
- Examine the key performance indicators, such as interfaces, CPU, and memory on the routers, and look for symptoms associated with performance problems.
- Examine the routers for features and configurations that deviate from the baseline configurations and attempt to find the root cause of the problems.
- Address the issues causing the performance problems and test to verify that the performance has improved.

Step 1: Review trouble ticket Lab 7-1 TT-A.

It is Monday morning and as soon as you enter your office at headquarters, you receive a call from your colleague from the branch office (R3 LAN). She tells you that client (PC-B) applications report errors while connecting to the corporate server (SRV1) for large file transfers (simulated by TTCP). Your colleague suspects that there is performance degradation on the R3 router and has run some tests to verify this. She also has the baseline performance tests to compare with.

Another colleague who works the night shift has full access to the branch office devices. You suspect he might have made some configuration changes.

Your task is to diagnose the branch office problems and correct them.

Step 2: Load the device trouble ticket configuration files for TT-A.

Using the procedure described in Lab 3-1, verify that the lab configuration files are present in flash. Load the proper configuration files as indicated in the Device Configuration File Table.

Note: The following device access methods are in effect after loading the configuration files:

- Console access requires no username or password.
- Telnet and SSH require username **admin** and password **adminpa55**.
- The enable password is **ciscoenpa55**.

Device Configuration File Table

Device Name	File to Load	Notes
ALS1	Lab71-ALS1-TT-A-Cfg.txt	
DLS1	Lab71-DLS1-TT-A-Cfg.txt	
DLS2	Lab71-DLS2-TT-A-Cfg.txt	
R1	Lab71-R1-TT-A-Cfg.txt	
R2	Lab71-R2-TT-A-Cfg.txt	
R3	Lab71-R3-TT-A-Cfg.txt	
SRV1	N/A	Static IP: 10.1.50.1/24 Default gateway: 10.1.50.254
PC-B	N/A	Static IP: 10.1.80.254/24 Default gateway: 10.1.80.1
PC-C	N/A	DHCP

Step 3: Configure PC-B.

Configure PC-B with static IP address 10.1.80.254/24 and default gateway 10.1.80.1.

Step 4: Test R3 performance without the TTCP load generator.

Use Cisco IOS commands and pings to record the router performance figures simulating a condition where no large file transfers are currently being transmitted from PC-B to SRV1. These results can be compared to the baseline output (selected baseline information is shown) and the output obtained when using the TTCP utility.

Note: Sample output is provided. Depending on your timing and the devices in use, the output and results may vary.

a. Ping from PC-B to SRV1 (10.1.50.1) and record the results here. Include minimum, maximum, and average round-trip times. _____

_____

_____

```
C:\>ping 10.1.50.1

Pinging 10.1.50.1 with 32 bytes of data:
Reply from 10.1.50.1: bytes=32 time=3ms TTL=64
Reply from 10.1.50.1: bytes=32 time=1ms TTL=64
Reply from 10.1.50.1: bytes=32 time=1ms TTL=64
Reply from 10.1.50.1: bytes=32 time=1ms TTL=64

Ping statistics for 10.1.50.1:
    Packets: Sent = 4, Received = 4, Lost = 0 (0% loss),
Approximate round trip times in milli-seconds:
    Minimum = 1ms, Maximum = 3ms, Average = 1ms
```

b. Issue the **show interfaces fa0/0** command and note the transmit and receive loads (txload and rxload). _____

```
R3#show interfaces fa0/0
FastEthernet0/0 is up, line protocol is up
   Hardware is Gt96k FE, address is 001b.530d.6028 (bia 001b.530d.6028)
   Internet address is 10.1.80.1/24
   MTU 1500 bytes, BW 100000 Kbit/sec, DLY 100 usec,
      reliability 255/255, txload 1/255, rxload 1/255
```

c. Issue the **show interfaces fa0/0 stats** command. Record the switching path and the packets in and out for processor and route cache. _____

_____

_____

```
R3#show interfaces fa0/0 stats

FastEthernet0/0
          Switching path    Pkts In   Chars In   Pkts Out   Chars Out
                 Processor        50      16309        176       18457
               Route cache         1        159          0           0
                     Total        51      16468        176       18457

                     Total    116557   66924378     115034     6384079
```

d. Issue the **show interfaces fa0/0 summary** command for Fa0/0 and note the transmit (tx) and receive (rx) rates in bits per second and packets per second. With no load, there might be very little activity. _____

_____

```
R3#show interfaces fa0/0 summary

 *: interface is up
 IHQ: pkts in input hold queue       IQD: pkts dropped from input queue
 OHQ: pkts in output hold queue      OQD: pkts dropped from output queue
 RXBS: rx rate (bits/sec)            RXPS: rx rate (pkts/sec)
 TXBS: tx rate (bits/sec)            TXPS: tx rate (pkts/sec)
 TRTL: throttle count

  Interface          IHQ   IQD   OHQ    OQD   RXBS  RXPS   TXBS  TXPS  TRTL
 -------------------------------------------------------------------------
 * FastEthernet0/0     0     0     0      0      0     1      0     0     0
```

e. Issue the **show processes cpu sorted** command on R3 and note the CPU utilization for five seconds, one minute, and five minutes. Also note that the processes running are sorted by highest CPU utilization.

_____

_____

```
R3#show processes cpu sorted
CPU utilization for five seconds: 0%/0%; one minute: 0%; five minutes: 0%
 PID Runtime(ms)    Invoked  uSecs    5Sec   1Min   5Min TTY Process
 153           4   1366369      0   0.15%  0.12%  0.10%   0 HQF Shaper Backg
```

```
   2              0       7658        0  0.07%  0.02%  0.02%    0 Load Meter

   5              4          3     1333  0.00%  0.00%  0.00%    0 Pool Manager
<output omitted>
```

f. Generate some traffic by pinging from switch ALS1 to SRV1. From privileged EXEC mode on ALS1, issue the **ping 10.1.50.1 repeat 1000 size 1000** command. What are the minimum, maximum, and average round-trip times?

_____

_____

```
    Success rate is 100 percent (1000/1000), round-trip min/avg/max = 1/4/9 ms
```

g. Quickly issue the **show processes cpu sorted** command on R3 again and note the CPU utilization for five seconds, one minute, and five minutes.

_____

_____

```
R3#show processes cpu sorted
CPU utilization for five seconds: 17%/5%; one minute: 3%; five minutes: 1%
 PID Runtime(ms)    Invoked  uSecs   5Sec   1Min   5Min TTY Process
  91        2308       4797    481 11.19%  2.10%  0.52%    0 IP Input

   3       13308       2477   5372  0.87%  0.18%  0.05%    0 Exec

 124          12        265     45  0.15%  0.03%  0.00%    0 TCP Timer

 153          20      93423      0  0.15%  0.12%  0.10%    0 HQF Shaper Backg

 265        1280      11572    110  0.07%  0.01%  0.00%    0 IP-EIGRP: HELLO
<output omitted>
```

h. Issue the **show processes cpu history** command on R3 to see CPU utilization history in graph format. Note the CPU utilization for the last 60 seconds, last 60 minutes, and last 72 hours.

_____

_____

```
R3#show processes cpu history

R3    06:04:05 PM Monday Nov 30 2009 UTC


        1              11111                        11111
   100
    90
    80
    70
    60
    50
    40
```

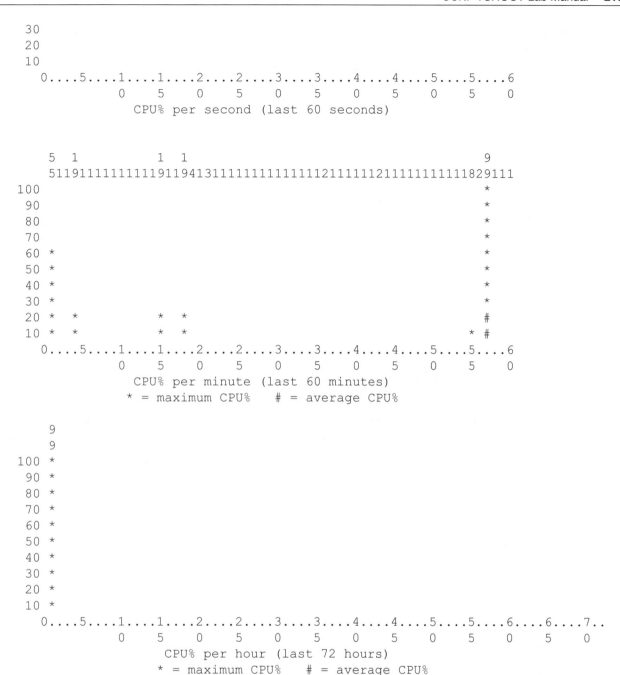

```
30
20
10
 0....5....1....1....2....2....3....3....4....4....5....5....6
      0    5    0    5    0    5    0    5    0    5    0
          CPU% per second (last 60 seconds)


        5  1           1  1                                    9
        51191111111111911941311111111111111112111111121111111111111829111
 100                                                          *
  90                                                          *
  80                                                          *
  70                                                          *
  60 *                                                        *
  50 *                                                        *
  40 *                                                        *
  30 *                                                        *
  20 *    *           *    *                                  #
  10 *    *           *    *                             *    #
     0....5....1....1....2....2....3....3....4....4....5....5....6
          0    5    0    5    0    5    0    5    0    5    0
          CPU% per minute (last 60 minutes)
          * = maximum CPU%   # = average CPU%


        9
        9
 100 *
  90 *
  80 *
  70 *
  60 *
  50 *
  40 *
  30 *
  20 *
  10 *
     0....5....1....1....2....2....3....3....4....4....5....5....6....6....7..
          0    5    0    5    0    5    0    5    0    5    0    5    0
          CPU% per hour (last 72 hours)
          * = maximum CPU%   # = average CPU%
```

Step 5: Generate loads on R3 using the TTCP utility.

For this trouble ticket, you can use the Cisco IOS command `ttcp` to simulate a heavy traffic load instead of performing large file transfers between the client (PC-B) and server SRV1 for testing. The TTCP utility consists of a client side and server side. Because this lab revolves around router performance, you can use the switches as test points.

> **Note:** The `ttcp` command is a hidden, unsupported, privileged mode command, and it is not available for all Cisco IOS Software releases. For instance, some platforms require the Cisco IOS Enterprise feature set to perform this activity. For more information about TTCP, see the URL references provided at the end of the lab and in Appendix A.

To initiate a TTCP connection and generate test traffic from switch ALS1 at the branch office to switch DLS2 at headquarters, use the following procedure.

a. On DLS2, the device that will perform the receiving (server) side of the connection, issue the `ttcp` command. You are prompted for information about this connection. You can accept the default values or enter new values. You can also use the command line to enter all the parameters as one command. The command generated is shown after the last entry prompt.

As TTCP waits for the transmitting (client) side to make a connection, the console screen freezes.

```
DLS2#ttcp
transmit or receive [receive]:
receive packets asynchronously [n]:
perform tcp half close [n]:
receive buflen [32768]:
bufalign [16384]:
bufoffset [0]:
port [5001]:
sinkmode [y]:
rcvwndsize [32768]:
ack frequency [0]:
delayed ACK [y]:
show tcp information at end [n]:

ttcp-r: buflen=32768, align=16384/0, port=5001
rcvwndsize=32768, delayedack=yes  tcp
```

b. On ALS1, the device that will perform the client side of the connection, you must specify that this side is the transmitting side because the default is to run in receive mode. You must also specify the IP address of the receiving side (DLS2) to initiate the connection.

```
ALS1#ttcp
transmit or receive [receive]: transmit
Target IP address: 10.1.100.253
calculate checksum during buffer write [y]:
perform tcp half close [n]:
send buflen [32768]:
send nbuf [2048]:
bufalign [16384]:
bufoffset [0]:
port [5001]:
sinkmode [y]:
buffering on writes [y]:
show tcp information at end [n]:

ttcp-t: buflen=32768, nbuf=2048, align=16384/0, port=5001  tcp  ->
10.1.100.253
ttcp-t: connect
ttcp-t: 67108864 bytes in 106812 ms (106.812 real seconds) (~613 kB/s) +++
ttcp-t: 2048 I/O calls
ttcp-t: 0 sleeps (0 ms total) (0 ms average)
```

The DLS2 (receive) side of the connection shows the following information when the transfer completes:

```
ttcp-r: accept from 10.1.80.251
ttcp-r: 67108864 bytes in 106837 ms (106.837 real seconds) (~613 kB/s) +++
ttcp-r: 43182 I/O calls
ttcp-r: 0 sleeps (0 ms total) (0 ms average)
```

Referring to the above results, the TTCP utility transmitted over 67 million bytes in approximately 106 seconds or about 613 Kilobytes per second (kB/s). As a comparison, the baseline configuration without the errors in this trouble ticket took approximately 70 seconds to transmit the same amount of data but at a rate of about 898 kB/s. Different devices and network links produce different results.

Note: You cannot issue any commands on the console of either device until the transfer finishes. The transmission can be interrupted at any point in time from the transmitting side using the key combination Ctrl-Shift-6.

Caution: This utility can overload a router with test traffic. It is not recommended to use it on production devices. Read the TTCP documentation before using the TTCP utility.

Step 6: Test R3 with load applied.

Note: For this lab, TTCP utility creates a load that lasts 60–120 seconds. The actual length of time depends on the capabilities of the devices and links being used.

On R3, use Cisco IOS commands and pings to record the router performance figures simulating a condition where large file transfers are being transmitted. These results can be compared to the baseline output (selected baseline information is shown) and the output obtained when using the TTCP utility.

Try to issue the following Cisco IOS commands on R3 while TTCP is generating traffic between ALS1 and DSL2. If it stops, restart the transmit-receive process between switches ALS1 and DLS2. You can also increase the length of time traffic runs by increasing the **send buflen** parameter, which defaults to 32768 (for example, you can increase it 65536 or higher).

a.   While TTCP is running, ping from PC-B to SRV1 and record the minimum, maximum, and average round-trip results.

The times should be 10 times or more higher than without the TTCP load on R3.

```
C:\>ping 10.1.50.1

Pinging 10.1.50.1 with 32 bytes of data:
Reply from 10.1.50.1: bytes=32 time=39ms TTL=64
Reply from 10.1.50.1: bytes=32 time=38ms TTL=64
Reply from 10.1.50.1: bytes=32 time=38ms TTL=64
Reply from 10.1.50.1: bytes=32 time=38ms TTL=64

Ping statistics for 10.1.50.1:
    Packets: Sent = 4, Received = 4, Lost = 0 (0% loss),
Approximate round trip times in milli-seconds:
    Minimum = 38ms, Maximum = 39ms, Average = 38ms
```

b   On Fa0/0, change the period over which the loads are computed to 30 seconds.

```
interface fa0/0
    load-interval 30
```

c.   Issue the **show interfaces fa0/0** command and note the values for txload and rxload. _____

```
R3#show interfaces fa0/0
FastEthernet0/0 is up, line protocol is up
   Hardware is Gt96k FE, address is 001b.530d.6028 (bia 001b.530d.6028)
   Internet address is 10.1.80.1/24
   MTU 1500 bytes, BW 100000 Kbit/sec, DLY 100 usec,
      reliability 255/255, txload 0/255, rxload 4/255
```

d. Issue the **show interfaces fa0/0 stats** command and record the switching path and the packets in and out for processor and route cache. _____

_____

_____

```
R3#show interfaces f0/0 stats
FastEthernet0/0
          Switching path    Pkts In   Chars In   Pkts Out   Chars Out
              Processor      134289    77529720     129782    10884700
            Route cache           1         159          0           0
                  Total      134290    77529879     129782    10884700
```

e. Issue the **show interfaces summary** command for Fa0/0 and record the transmit (tx) and receive (rx) rates in bits per second and packets per second. How do they compare to the rates when TTCP is not running? _____

_____

```
R3#show interfaces f0/0 summary

 *: interface is up
 IHQ: pkts in input hold queue      IQD: pkts dropped from input queue
 OHQ: pkts in output hold queue     OQD: pkts dropped from output queue
 RXBS: rx rate (bits/sec)           RXPS: rx rate (pkts/sec)
 TXBS: tx rate (bits/sec)           TXPS: tx rate (pkts/sec)
 TRTL: throttle count

  Interface              IHQ   IQD   OHQ    OQD  RXBS RXPS   TXBS TXPS TRTL
 -------------------------------------------------------------------------
 * FastEthernet0/0         0     0     0      0 969000  204  94000  201    0
```

f. While TTCP is transferring data, issue the **show processes cpu sorted** command on R3 and note the CPU utilization for five seconds, one minute, and five minutes. How do they compare with utilization when TTCP is not running?

_____

```
R3#show processes cpu sorted
CPU utilization for five seconds: 99%/29%; one minute: 77%; five minutes: 26%
 PID Runtime(ms)      Invoked      uSecs   5Sec   1Min   5Min TTY Process
  91      201824        20441       9873 69.50% 54.19% 18.26%   0 IP Input

<output omitted>
```

g. After the TTCP transfer process ends, issue the **show processes cpu history** command on R3 to see the CPU utilization history in graph format. Note the CPU utilization for the last 60 seconds, 60 minutes, and 72 hours. What is the maximum utilization shown?

_____

```
R3#show processes cpu history

R3   07:54:09 PM Monday Nov 30 2009 UTC


    999988888
    99999999922222                        11111
100 ****
 90 ********
 80 ********
 70 ********
 60 ********
 50 ********
 40 ********
 30 ********
 20 ********
 10 ********
    0....5....1....1....2....2....3....3....4....4....5....5....6
         0    5    0    5    0    5    0    5    0    5    0
            CPU% per second (last 60 seconds)


         992                                          3
    1111111199811112111111112111111111121111112111111131111111111
100        *#
 90        *#
 80        ##
 70        ##
 60        ##
 50        ##
 40        ##
 30        ##*                             *
 20        ##*                             *
 10        ##*                             *
    0....5....1....1....2....2....3....3....4....4....5....5....6
         0    5    0    5    0    5    0    5    0    5    0
            CPU% per minute (last 60 minutes)
          * = maximum CPU%   # = average CPU%


    99
    99
100 **
 90 **
 80 **
 70 **
 60 **
 50 **
 40 **
 30 **
 20 **
 10 **
    0....5....1....1....2....2....3....3....4....4....5....5....6....6....7..
         0    5    0    5    0    5    0    5    0    5    0    5    0
            CPU% per hour (last 72 hours)
          * = maximum CPU%   # = average CPU%
```

h. Issue the `show memory statistics` command and note the free memory and the amount used. Is there an issue with memory usage with this router?

_____

_____

```
R3#show memory statistics
                Head      Total(b)    Used(b)     Free(b)     Lowest(b)    Largest(b)

Processor    64E822C0    101178688    24016328    77162360    75584536    75588172

     I/O     EAF00000     17825792     5421744    12404048    12363136     1238780
```

Step 7: Outline the troubleshooting approach and validation steps.

The following approach is recommended as a troubleshooting process:

1. Generate test traffic using the `ping` and `ttcp` commands, as described in this task.

2. Use `ping` to measure the performance between the headquarters and branch office. For example, ping from client PC-B to server SRV1.

3. Examine the key performance indicators, such as the interfaces, CPU and memory on the routers, and watch for symptoms associated with performance problems.

4. Examine the routers for features and configurations that deviate from the baseline configurations and attempt to find the root cause of the problems.

5. Address the issues causing the performance problems and test to verify that the performance has improved.

Step 8: Record the troubleshooting process and configuration changes.

Document your actions and results during the troubleshooting process. List the commands you used to gather information. As you progress, record what you think the problem might be and which actions you will take to correct the problem.

Device	Actions and Results

Step 9: Document trouble ticket debrief notes.

Use this space to make notes of the key learning points that you picked up during the discussion of this trouble ticket with your instructor. This can include problems encountered, solutions applied, useful commands, alternate solutions, methods, and processes, and procedure and communication improvements.

_____

_____

_____

_____

_____

_____

_____

Task 2: Trouble Ticket Lab 7-1 TT-B

Step 1: Review trouble ticket Lab 7-1 TT-B.

After the Internet service provider (ISP) reconfigured Border Gateway Protocol (BGP) on router R2, you received complaints from branch office users on the R3 LAN about it being slow or having no connection at all to the partner servers outside the corporate network residing in the IP address block 172.20.0.0/16 (simulated by R2 Lo1).

You have access to the R1 and R2 routers. Your task is to diagnose the problem and verify that BGP is properly configured to minimize the impact on internal routing performance for devices such as R3, DLS1, and DLS2.

Step 2: Load the device trouble ticket configuration files for TT-B.

Using the procedure described in Lab 3-1, verify that the lab configuration files are present in flash. Load the proper configuration files as indicated in the Device Configuration File table.

Note: See Task 1, Step 2 for device access methods, usernames, and passwords after the configuration files have been loaded.

Device Configuration File Table

Device Name	File to Load	Notes
ALS1	Lab71-ALS1-TT-B-Cfg.txt	
DLS1	Lab71-DLS1-TT-B-Cfg.txt	
DLS2	Lab71-DLS2-TT-B-Cfg.txt	
R1	Lab71-R1-TT-B-Cfg.txt	
R2	Lab71-R2-TT-B-Cfg.txt	

R3	Lab71-R3-TT-B-Cfg.txt	
SRV1	N/A	Static IP: 10.1.50.1 Default gateway: 10.1.50.254
PC-B	N/A	Static IP: 10.1.80.254/24 Default gateway: 10.1.80.1
PC-C	N/A	DHCP

Step 3: Test R3 performance without the TTCP load generator.

Use Cisco IOS commands and pings to record the router performance figures simulating a condition in which no large file transfers are currently being transmitted. These results can be compared to the baseline output (selected baseline information is shown) and the output obtained when using the TTCP utility.

a. Ping from PC-B to R2 Lo1 (simulated remote server) and record the minimum, maximum, and average round-trip times.

```
C:\>ping 172.20.0.1

Pinging 172.20.0.1 with 32 bytes of data:
Reply from 172.20.0.1 : bytes=32 time=11ms TTL=64
Reply from 172.20.0.1 : bytes=32 time=10ms TTL=64
Reply from 172.20.0.1 : bytes=32 time=10ms TTL=64
Reply from 172.20.0.1 : bytes=32 time=10ms TTL=64

Ping statistics for 172.20.0.1 :
    Packets: Sent = 4, Received = 4, Lost = 0 (0% loss),
Approximate round trip times in milli-seconds:
    Minimum = 10ms, Maximum = 11ms, Average = 10ms
```

b. Issue the **show interfaces fa0/0** command and note the txload and rxload information.

```
R3#show interfaces fa0/0
FastEthernet0/0 is up, line protocol is up
  Hardware is Gt96k FE, address is 001b.530d.6028 (bia 001b.530d.6028)
  Internet address is 10.1.80.1/24
  MTU 1500 bytes, BW 100000 Kbit/sec, DLY 100 usec,
     reliability 255/255, txload 1/255, rxload 1/255
<output omitted>
```

c. Issue the **show interfaces fa0/0 stats** command and record the switching path and the packets in and out for the processor and route cache.

```
R3#show interfaces fa0/0 stats
FastEthernet0/0
          Switching path    Pkts In    Chars In    Pkts Out    Chars Out
               Processor        831      356623        4075       408723
```

```
        Route cache      381399   221941950      375270   20282949
              Total      382230   222298573      379345   20691672
```

d. Issue the **show processes cpu sorted** command on R3 and note the CPU utilization for five seconds, one minute, and five minutes.

_____

```
R3#show processes cpu sorted
CPU utilization for five seconds: 0%/0%; one minute: 0%; five minutes: 0%
```

e. Generate some traffic by pinging from switch ALS1 to R2 Lo1. From privileged EXEC mode on ALS1, issue the **ping 172.20.0.1 repeat 100 size 1000** command. What are the round-trip minimum, average, and maximum times?

_____

Success rate is 100% (100/100), round-trip min/avg/max = 125/129/135 ms

f. While the ping is running, issue the **show processes cpu sorted** command on R3 again and note the CPU utilization for five seconds, one minute, and five minutes. Was there an increase? _____

```
R3#show processes cpu sorted
CPU utilization for five seconds: 11%/11%; one minute: 6%; five minutes: 2%
<output omitted>
```

g. Issue the **show processes cpu history** command on R3 to see the CPU history in graph format. Note the CPU utilization for the last 60 seconds, 60 minutes, and 72 hours. Does the CPU appear to be heavily loaded? _____

```
R3#show processes cpu history


R3   04:08:25 PM Tuesday Dec 1 2009 UTC



                         11111     11111
100
 90
 80
 70
 60
 50
 40
 30
 20
 10
   0....5....1....1....2....2....3....3....4....4....5....5....6
          0    5    0    5    0    5    0    5    0    5    0
          CPU% per second (last 60 seconds)
```

```
            2111211111111111111111112111111111111111111111111311151111111
        100
         90
         80
         70
         60                                                              *
         50                                                              *
         40                                                              *
         30                                                              *
         20                                                              *
         10                                                              *
            0....5....1....1....2....2....3....3....4....4....5....5....6
                 0    5    0    5    0    5    0    5    0    5    0
                      CPU% per minute (last 60 minutes)
                   * = maximum CPU%    # = average CPU%


            344351
            251910
        100
         90
         80
         70
         60
         50     *   *
         40     ****
         30     *****
         20     *****
         10     ******
            0....5....1....1....2....2....3....3....4....4....5....5....6....6....7..
                 0    5    0    5    0    5    0    5    0    5    0    5    0
                      CPU% per hour (last 72 hours)
                   * = maximum CPU%    # = average CPU%
```

h. Issue the **show processes memory sorted** command on R3. Note the processes running and the holding amount of memory. The holding amount is the memory the process is currently using. The entries go from highest holding memory to lowest.

```
R3#show processes memory sorted
Processor Pool Total:  101178688 Used:     24024572 Free:     77154116
        I/O Pool Total:   17825792 Used:      5421728 Free:     12404064

  PID TTY  Allocated       Freed      Holding     Getbufs     Retbufs Process
    0   0   64042304    36231984     23552016           0           0 *Init*

   55   0     659620        1328       640292           0           0 USB Startup

    1   0     474960           0       482164           0           0 Chunk Manager

  219   0     469096       18304       436816           0           0 VLAN Manager

   25   0     260308           0       270512       99792           0 EEM ED Syslog

  170   0     218420         504       215916           0           0 Crypto HW Proc

  221   0     196192           0       203396           0           0 EEM Server
```

183	0	114340	532	123012	0	0	Crypto WUI
167	0	76476	252	83428	0	0	HTTP Process

i. Issue the **show memory statistics** command on R3. Note the amount of used and free memory for the processor for later comparison. By comparing the amount of memory used to the baseline (shown below), you can determine how much is used when the trouble ticket issues are introduced. You can also compare this to the memory when running the TTCP utility. The baseline memory amounts and after the TT was loaded are provided here for comparison.

Note: As can be seen below, the trouble ticket issues cause an increase of nearly 70 KB of memory over the baseline. This is not enough to cause serious memory depletion issues with the router but serves to illustrate the type of problem that can occur in a lab environment. Actual results might be very different in a production environment.

Baseline

```
R3#show memory statistics
              Head      Total(b)    Used(b)     Free(b)     Lowest(b)   Largest(b)

Processor  64E822C0   101178688   24016328    77162360    75584536    75588172

     I/O   EAF00000    17825792    5421744    12404048    12363136     1238780
```

After TT Issues Are Introduced

```
R3#show memory statistics
              Head      Total(b)    Used(b)     Free(b)     Lowest(b)   Largest(b)

Processor  64E822C0   101178688   24085092    77093596    75584536    75579176

     I/O   EAF00000    17825792    5421744    12404048    12363136     1238780
```

Step 4: Generate loads on R3 using the TTCP utility.

To initiate a TTCP connection and generate test traffic from switch ALS1 at the branch office to switch DLS2 at headquarters, use the following procedure.

a. On switch DLS2 (receiver), enter the command sequence.

```
DLS2#ttcp
transmit or receive [receive]:
receive packets asynchronously [n]:
perform tcp half close [n]:
receive buflen [32768]:
bufalign [16384]:
bufoffset [0]:
port [5001]:
sinkmode [y]:
rcvwndsize [32768]:
ack frequency [0]:
delayed ACK [y]:
show tcp information at end [n]:

ttcp-r: buflen=32768, align=16384/0, port=5001
rcvwndsize=32768, delayedack=yes   tcp
```

b. On switch ALS1 (transmitter), enter the command sequence:

```
ALS1#ttcp
transmit or receive [receive]: transmit
Target IP address: 10.1.100.253
calculate checksum during buffer write [y]:
perform tcp half close [n]:
send buflen [32768]:
send nbuf [2048]:
bufalign [16384]:
bufoffset [0]:
port [5001]:
sinkmode [y]:
buffering on writes [y]:
show tcp information at end [n]:

ttcp-t: buflen=32768, nbuf=2048, align=16384/0, port=5001  tcp  ->
10.1.100.253
ttcp-t: connect

ttcp-t: 67108864 bytes in 68434 ms (68.434 real seconds) (~957 kB/s) +++
ttcp-t: 2048 I/O calls
ttcp-t: 0 sleeps (0 ms total) (0 ms average)
```

c. Record the time required to complete the TTCP data transfer.

_____

Note: Referring to the above results, the TTCP utility transmitted over 67 million bytes in approximately 68 seconds. This is comparable to the baseline performance, which indicates that this router is not significantly loaded. Different devices and network links will produce different results.

Step 5: Test R3 with load applied.

Note: In this lab, the TCP utility creates a load that lasts for about 60–120 seconds. The actual length of time depends on the capabilities of the devices and links in use.

Use Cisco IOS commands and pings to record the router performance figures simulating a condition in which large file transfers are currently being transmitted. These results can be compared to the baseline output (selected baseline information is shown) and the output obtained when using the TTCP utility.

a. Ping from PC-B to R2 Lo1 and record the results.

_____

Include the minimum, maximum, and average round-trip times. The times should be about the same as without the TTCP load on R3.

```
C:\>ping 172.20.0.1

Pinging 172.20.0.1 with 32 bytes of data:
Reply from 172.20.0.1 : bytes=32 time=12ms TTL=64
Reply from 172.20.0.1 : bytes=32 time=11ms TTL=64
Reply from 172.20.0.1 : bytes=32 time=11ms TTL=64
Reply from 172.20.0.1 : bytes=32 time=11ms TTL=64
```

```
Ping statistics for 172.20.0.1 :
    Packets: Sent = 4, Received = 4, Lost = 0 (0% loss),
Approximate round trip times in milli-seconds:
    Minimum = 11ms, Maximum = 12ms, Average = 11ms
```

b. While TTCP is transferring data, issue the **show processes cpu sorted** command on R3 and note the CPU utilization for five seconds, one minute, and five minutes

---

```
R3#show processes cpu sorted
CPU utilization for five seconds: 10%/9%; one minute: 2%; five minutes: 1%
 PID Runtime(ms)      Invoked      uSecs    5Sec   1Min   5Min TTY Process

<output omitted>
```

Based on the output above, you can see that R3 is not CPU bound.

c. Issue the **show processes cpu history** command on R3 to see the CPU history in graph format. Note the CPU utilization for the last 60 minutes and 72 hours.

```
R3#show processes cpu history

R3   05:46:25 PM Tuesday Dec 1 2009 UTC

<Output omitted>
                                         4           11
    111111111111111111111111111111119111111111110111111111111111111
100
 90
 80
 70
 60
 50                                   *
 40                                   *
 30                                   *
 20                                   *
 10                                   *           *#
   0....5....1....1....2....2....3....3....4....4....5....5....6
            0    5    0    5    0    5    0    5    0    5    0
            CPU% per minute (last 60 minutes)
           * = maximum CPU%   # = average CPU%


    35344351
    15251910
100
 90
 80
 70
 60  *
 50  *  *   *
 40  * ****
 30 *******
```

```
20 *******
10 ********
 0....5....1....1....2....2....3....3....4....4....5....5....6....6....7..
      0    5    0    5    0    5    0    5    0    5    0    5    0
           CPU% per hour (last 72 hours)
           * = maximum CPU%   # = average CPU%
```

As with the output for the **show processes cpu sorted** command, you can see that R3 is not CPU bound.

d. Issue the **show memory statistics** command on R3. Note the amount of used and free memory for the processor. By comparing the amount of memory used to the baseline and the TT issues, you can determine how much is used when running the TTCP utility. The memory amounts for the baseline after the TT was loaded and while TTCP was running are shown here for comparison.

Note: The trouble ticket issues cause an increase of nearly 70 KB of memory over the baseline. This is not enough to cause real memory depletion issues with the router but serves to illustrate the type of problem that can occur in a production environment. Running the TTCP load utility caused an increase of about 7 KB over the TT issues.

Baseline

```
R3#show memory statistics
           Head     Total(b)    Used(b)     Free(b)     Lowest(b)   Largest(b)

Processor  64E822C0  101178688  24016328    77162360    75584536    75588172

     I/O   EAF00000  17825792   5421744     12404048    12363136    1238780
```

After TT Issues Are Introduced

```
R3#show memory statistics
           Head     Total(b)    Used(b)     Free(b)     Lowest(b)   Largest(b)

Processor  64E822C0  101178688  24085092    77093596    75584536    75579176

     I/O   EAF00000  17825792   5421744     12404048    12363136    1238780
```

While Running TTCP

```
R3#show memory statistics
           Head     Total(b)    Used(b)     Free(b)     Lowest(b)   Largest(b)

Processor  64E822C0  101178688  24092388    77086300    75584536    75579176

     I/O   EAF00000  17825792   5424292     12401500    12363136    1238780
```

Step 6: Outline the troubleshooting approach and validation steps.

The following approach is recommended as a troubleshooting process:

1. Generate test traffic using the **ping** and **ttcp** commands, as described in this task.

2. Use **ping** to measure the performance between the headquarters and Internet or network servers. For example, ping from client PC-B to server SRV1, R1 or R2.

3. Examine the key performance indicators, such as the interfaces, CPU, and memory, on the routers and watch for symptoms associated with performance problems.

4. Examine the routers for features and configurations that deviate from the baseline configurations and attempt to find the root cause of the problems.

5. Address the issues causing the performance problems and test to verify that performance has improved.

Step 7: Record the troubleshooting process and configuration changes.

Use this log to document your actions and results during the troubleshooting process. List the commands you used to gather information. As you progress, record what you think the problem might be and which actions you will take to correct the problem.

Device	Actions and Results

Step 8: Document trouble ticket debrief notes.

Use this space to make notes of the key learning points that you picked up during the discussion of this trouble ticket with your instructor. This can include problems encountered, solutions applied, useful commands employed, alternate solutions, methods, and processes, and procedure and communication improvements.

_____

_____

_____

_____

_____

_____

_____

Section 2—Troubleshooting Reference Information

General Troubleshooting Process

As a general guideline, you can use the following general troubleshooting process described in the course.

1. Define the problem (symptoms).

2. Gather information.

3. Analyze the information.

4. Propose a hypothesis (possible cause).

5. Test the hypothesis.

6. Eliminate or accept the hypothesis.

7. Solve the problem.

8. Document the problem.

Command Summary

The table lists useful commands for this lab. The sample output is shown on following pages.

Command	Key Information Displayed
`show interfaces` *type/#*	Displays the interface IP address, subnet mask, MAC address, and load statistics.
`show interfaces` *type/# summary*	Displays a summary of input and output queues and packet transmit and receive rates.
`show interfaces` *type/#* `stats`	Displays the switching path and the number of characters or packets in and out for the processor and route cache (Cisco Express Forwarding).
`show ip interface` *type/#*	Displays primarily IP-related information for the interface, such as the helper address, multicast groups, and route cache processing status.
`clear counters` *type/#*	Clears the interface counters on an interface.
`show processes cpu sorted`	Displays short-term CPU utilization (five seconds, one minute, and five minutes). It also lists the currently running processes, sorted by the most CPU utilization to the least.
`show processes cpu history`	Displays long-term CPU utilization in a graph format for the last 60 seconds, 60 minutes, and 72 hours. Useful for analyzing CPU load over time.
`show processes memory sorted`	Displays memory CPU utilization (used and free) for the processor and I/O memory pools. The entries are sorted by the highest amount of holding memory used.
`show memory statistics`	Displays a summary of memory utilization (total, used, and free) for the processor and I/O memory pools. The lowest is the smallest amount of free memory since the last boot. The largest is the size of the largest available free block.
`show ip cef`	Displays all known prefix entries in the Cisco Express Forwarding Forwarding Information Base (FIB). The prefix, next-hop IP address, and the exit interface are shown. If Cisco Express Forwarding is not enabled, the output states this.

Display Interface Load, Statistics, and Forwarding Information

```
R3#show interfaces fastethernet 0/0
FastEthernet0/0 is up, line protocol is up
  Hardware is Gt96k FE, address is 001b.530d.6028 (bia 001b.530d.6028)
  Internet address is 10.1.80.1/24
  MTU 1500 bytes, BW 100000 Kbit/sec, DLY 100 usec,
     reliability 255/255, txload 1/255, rxload 2/255
  Encapsulation ARPA, loopback not set
  Keepalive set (10 sec)
  Full-duplex, 100Mb/s, 100BaseTX/FX
  ARP type: ARPA, ARP Timeout 04:00:00
  Last input 00:00:00, output 00:00:00, output hang never
  Last clearing of "show interface" counters never
  Input queue: 0/75/0/0 (size/max/drops/flushes); Total output drops: 0
  Queueing strategy: fifo
  Output queue: 0/40 (size/max)
  5 minute input rate 913000 bits/sec, 179 packets/sec
  5 minute output rate 62000 bits/sec, 175 packets/sec
     381659 packets input, 222009886 bytes
     Received 257 broadcasts, 0 runts, 0 giants, 0 throttles
     0 input errors, 0 CRC, 0 frame, 0 overrun, 0 ignored
     0 watchdog
     0 input packets with dribble condition detected
     377267 packets output, 20429223 bytes, 0 underruns
     0 output errors, 0 collisions, 3 interface resets
     0 unknown protocol drops
     0 babbles, 0 late collision, 0 deferred
     0 lost carrier, 0 no carrier
     0 output buffer failures, 0 output buffers swapped out
```

The output of the **show interfaces fastethernet 0/0** command above shows the IP address and mask, hardware (MAC) address, as well as the reliability, transmit (txload), receive (rxload), and details on packet input and output rates. The **summary** option shown below provides a quick view of input and output queues and bit per packet transmit and receive rates. As can be seen, there are no packets in the input and output queues.

```
R3#show interfaces fa0/0 summary

 *: interface is up
 IHQ: pkts in input hold queue     IQD: pkts dropped from input queue
 OHQ: pkts in output hold queue    OQD: pkts dropped from output queue
 RXBS: rx rate (bits/sec)          RXPS: rx rate (pkts/sec)
 TXBS: tx rate (bits/sec)          TXPS: tx rate (pkts/sec)
 TRTL: throttle count

  Interface          IHQ   IQD   OHQ   OQD  RXBS RXPS  TXBS TXPS TRTL
  -------------------------------------------------------------------
 * FastEthernet0/0     0     0     0     0  969000  204 94000  201    0
```

```
R3#show interfaces fa0/0 stats
      FastEthernet0/0
              Switching path   Pkts In   Chars In   Pkts Out   Chars Out
                    Processor       831     356623       4075      408723
```

```
          Route cache     381399  221941950     375270   20282949
              Total       382230  222298573     379345   20691672
```

The **stats** option shown above displays the switching path and the number of characters and packets in and out for processor and route cache (Cisco Express Forwarding). As can be seen, only a few packets have been process-switched and a very large number have been switched via the route cache (with Cisco Express Forwarding enabled).

```
R3#show ip interface fastethernet 0/0
FastEthernet0/0 is up, line protocol is up
  Internet address is 10.1.80.1/24
  Broadcast address is 255.255.255.255
  Address determined by non-volatile memory
  MTU is 1500 bytes
  Helper address is 10.1.2.13
  Directed broadcast forwarding is disabled
  Multicast reserved groups joined: 224.0.0.10
  Outgoing access list is not set
  Inbound  access list is not set
  Proxy ARP is enabled
  Local Proxy ARP is disabled
  Security level is default
  Split horizon is enabled
  ICMP redirects are always sent
  ICMP unreachables are always sent
  ICMP mask replies are never sent
  IP fast switching is enabled
  IP fast switching on the same interface is disabled
  IP Flow switching is disabled
  IP CEF switching is enabled
  IP CEF switching turbo vector
  IP multicast fast switching is enabled
  IP multicast distributed fast switching is disabled
  IP route-cache flags are Fast, CEF
  Router Discovery is disabled
  IP output packet accounting is disabled
  IP access violation accounting is disabled
  TCP/IP header compression is disabled
  RTP/IP header compression is disabled
  Policy routing is disabled
  Network address translation is disabled
  BGP Policy Mapping is disabled
  Input features: Ingress-NetFlow, MCI Check
  Output features: Post-Ingress-NetFlow
  WCCP Redirect outbound is disabled
  WCCP Redirect inbound is disabled
  WCCP Redirect exclude is disabled
```

The output from the **show ip interface fastethernet** 0/0 command above shows primarily IP-related information for the interface. Note the helper address pointing to the switch DLS2 DHCP server IP address. This router interface has joined multicast group 224.0.0.10 for communication between EIGRP routers. Also note that Cisco Express Forwarding is enabled.

```
R1#show ip cef
Prefix               Next Hop             Interface
0.0.0.0/0            209.165.200.226      Serial0/0/0
```

```
0.0.0.0/8              drop
0.0.0.0/32             receive
10.1.2.0/30            attached          FastEthernet0/1
10.1.2.0/32            receive           FastEthernet0/1
10.1.2.1/32            attached          FastEthernet0/1
10.1.2.2/32            receive           FastEthernet0/1
10.1.2.3/32            receive           FastEthernet0/1
10.1.2.12/30           10.1.2.1          FastEthernet0/1
10.1.10.0/24           10.1.2.1          FastEthernet0/1
10.1.20.0/24           10.1.2.1          FastEthernet0/1
10.1.30.0/24           10.1.2.1          FastEthernet0/1
10.1.50.0/24           10.1.2.1          FastEthernet0/1
10.1.80.0/24           10.1.2.1          FastEthernet0/1
10.1.100.0/24          10.1.2.1          FastEthernet0/1
10.1.200.0/24          10.1.2.1          FastEthernet0/1
10.1.203.1/32          10.1.2.1          FastEthernet0/1
127.0.0.0/8            drop
172.20.0.0/21          209.165.200.226   Serial0/0/0
192.168.1.0/24         attached          Loopback0
192.168.1.0/32         receive           Loopback0
Prefix                 Next Hop          Interface
192.168.1.1/32         receive           Loopback0
192.168.1.255/32       receive           Loopback0
192.168.2.1/32         209.165.200.226   Serial0/0/0
209.165.200.224/30     attached          Serial0/0/0
209.165.200.224/32     receive           Serial0/0/0
209.165.200.225/32     receive           Serial0/0/0
209.165.200.226/32     attached          Serial0/0/0
209.165.200.227/32     receive           Serial0/0/0
224.0.0.0/4            drop
224.0.0.0/24           receive
240.0.0.0/4            drop
255.255.255.255/32     receive
```

The output from the **show ip cef** command above shows all the known prefix entries in the Cisco Express Forwarding FIB. The prefix, next-hop IP address, and the exit interface are shown. If Cisco Express Forwarding is not enabled, the output states this.

Display CPU Load and Process Statistics

```
R3#show processes cpu sorted
CPU utilization for five seconds: 17%/5%; one minute: 3%; five minutes: 1%
 PID Runtime(ms)   Invoked  uSecs    5Sec    1Min   5Min TTY Process
  91       2308      4797    481  11.19%   2.10%  0.52%   0 IP Input

   3      13308      2477   5372   0.87%   0.18%  0.05%   0 Exec

 124         12       265     45   0.15%   0.03%  0.00%   0 TCP Timer

 153         20     93423      0   0.15%   0.12%  0.10%   0 HQF Shaper Backg

 265       1280     11572    110   0.07%   0.01%  0.00%   0 IP-EIGRP: HELLO
<output omitted>
```

The output from the **show processes cpu sorted** command above shows short-term CPU utilization for the last five seconds, one minute, and five minutes. It also lists the currently running processes, sorted by the most

CPU utilization to the least. This router CPU is not heavily loaded at this time (not CPU bound).

R3#**show processes cpu history**

R3   07:54:09 PM Monday Nov 30 2009 UTC


```
      999988888
      99999999922222                        11111
100  ****
 90  ********
 80  ********
 70  ********
 60  ********
 50  ********
 40  ********
 30  ********
 20  ********
 10  ********
     0....5....1....1....2....2....3....3....4....4....5....5....6
              0    5    0    5    0    5    0    5    0    5    0
              CPU% per second (last 60 seconds)


          992                                  3
     11111111199811111211111111211111111111121111112111111113111111111
100           *#
 90           *#
 80           ##
 70           ##
 60           ##
 50           ##
 40           ##
 30           ##*                          *
 20           ##*                          *
 10           ##*                          *
     0....5....1....1....2....2....3....3....4....4....5....5....6
              0    5    0    5    0    5    0    5    0    5    0
              CPU% per minute (last 60 minutes)
               *  = maximum CPU%    #  = average CPU%


      99
      99
100  **
 90  **
 80  **
 70  **
 60  **
 50  **
 40  **
 30  **
 20  **
 10  **
     0....5....1....1....2....2....3....3....4....4....5....5....6....6....7..
              0    5    0    5    0    5    0    5    0    5    0    5    0
              CPU% per hour (last 72 hours)
```

```
        * = maximum CPU%    # = average CPU%
```

The output from the **show processes cpu history** command above shows long-term CPU utilization in a graph format for the last 60 seconds, 60 minutes, and 72 hours. This router CPU has been recently heavily loaded and is CPU bound at 99% utilization. Percent CPU utilization can hit 90% occasionally, but consistently high utilization over time can point to processing problems, such as access lists and large file transfers.

Display Memory Usage and Process Statistics

```
R3#show processes memory sorted
Processor Pool Total:   101226944 Used:   24015448 Free:    77211496
         I/O Pool Total:    17825792 Used:    5446544 Free:    12379248

  PID TTY  Allocated       Freed      Holding    Getbufs    Retbufs Process
    0   0   62860036    36235836     23615956          0          0 *Init*

   55   0     659528        1328       640200          0          0 USB Startup

    1   0     466000           0       473204          0          0 Chunk Manager

  219   0     469124       18304       436776          0          0 VLAN Manager

    0   0          0           0       420380          0          0 *MallocLite*

   25   0     260308           0       270512      99792          0 EEM ED Syslog

  170   0     218420         504       215916          0          0 Crypto HW Proc

  221   0     196192           0       203396          0          0 EEM Server

  183   0     114384         528       123060          0          0 Crypto WUI

  167   0      76544         252        83496          0          0 HTTP Process

   40   0      66536      153420        73340          0          0 IF-MGR control p

    3   0    7352228     7237092        66908          0          0 Exec
```

`<output omitted>`

The output from the **show processes memory sorted** command above shows memory utilization (used and free) for the processor and I/O memory pools. The holding amount is the amount of memory that the process is currently using. The entries are sorted by the highest amount of holding memory first.

```
R3#show processes memory sorted | include EIGRP
  265   0    1676448     7910464        24464          0          0 IP-EIGRP: PDM

  264   0          0           0        18200          0          0 IP-EIGRP Router

  266   0   19720032    13337320         7116          0          0 IP-EIGRP: HELLO
```

The list of processes output from this command can be lengthy. Use the pipe (|), as shown above, to filter the output and focus on specific processes. Search strings are case-sensitive.

```
R3#show memory statistics
```

	Head	Total(b)	Used(b)	Free(b)	Lowest(b)	Largest(b)
Processor	64E76640	101226944	23964420	77262524	76880040	76910312
I/O	EAF00000	17825792	5421732	12404060	12376432	1240031

The output from the **show memory statistics** command above shows a summary of memory utilization (total, used, and free) for the processor and I/O memory pools. The lowest column is the smallest amount of free memory since the last boot. The largest column shows the size of the largest available free block.

Reflection Questions

1. Which lab trouble tickets did you have the most difficulty with? _____

_____

_____

_____

2. Would you change anything about the process that you used for any of the trouble tickets now that you see the resolution of the problem? _____

_____

_____

_____

3. Which commands did you find most useful in diagnosing router performance issues? Add these to your toolbox for future use. Which commands did you find least useful?

_____

_____

_____

References

If you need more information on the commands and their options, see the following references:

- IP Routing Protocol Command Reference

  http://www.cisco.com/cisco/web/support/index.html

- Cisco IOS IP Switching Reference http://www.cisco.com/en/US/docs/ios/ipswitch/command/reference/isw_book.html

- TTCP information (also see Appendix A)
  http://www.cisco.com/en/US/tech/tk801/tk36/technologies_tech_note09186a0080094694.shtml

Router Interface Summary Table

Router Interface Summary				
Router Model	Ethernet Interface #1	Ethernet Interface #2	Serial Interface #1	Serial Interface #2
1700	Fast Ethernet 0 (FA0)	Fast Ethernet 1 (FA1)	Serial 0 (S0)	Serial 1 (S1)
1800	Fast Ethernet 0/0 (FA0/0)	Fast Ethernet 0/1 (FA0/1)	Serial 0/0/0 (S0/0/0)	Serial 0/0/1 (S0/0/1)
2600	Fast Ethernet 0/0 (FA0/0)	Fast Ethernet 0/1 (FA0/1)	Serial 0/0 (S0/0)	Serial 0/1 (S0/1)
2800	Fast Ethernet 0/0 (FA0/0)	Fast Ethernet 0/1 (FA0/1)	Serial 0/0/0 (S0/0/0)	Serial 0/0/1 (S0/0/1)
Note: To find out how the router is configured, look at the interfaces to identify the type of router and how many interfaces the router has. Rather than try to list all the combinations of configurations for each router class, this table includes identifiers for the possible combinations of Ethernet and serial interfaces in the device. The table does not include any other type of interface, even though a specific router might contain one. An example of this is an ISDN BRI interface. The string in parenthesis is the legal abbreviation that can be used in Cisco IOS commands to represent the interface.				

Appendix A—Using a Windows PC as a TTCP End Device

a. Download the TTCP for Windows ttcpw program from the link provided at http://www.cisco.com/en/US/ tech/tk801/tk36/technologies_tech_note09186a0080094694.shtml.

b. Expand the ZIP file in a folder to access the .exe and readme files.

c. Start the ttcpw program on the PC (in a DOS window), running as a receiver. Refer to the Readme file provided with the windows TTCP software for the appropriate syntax. An example is provided here.

```
C:\Cisco\TTCP>ttcpw -r -s ttcp-r: buflen=8192, nbuf=2048, align=16364/0,
port=5001 tcp ttcp-r: socket
```

d. Start the ttcp program on DLS2 running as a transmitter and specify the target IP address of the PC.

```
DLS2#ttcp

transmit or receive [receive]: transmit

Target IP address: 10.1.80.254

calculate checksum during buffer write [y]:

perform tcp half close [n]:

send buflen [32768]:

send nbuf [2048]:

bufalign [16384]:

bufoffset [0]:

port [5001]:

sinkmode [y]:

buffering on writes [y]:

show tcp information at end [n]:
```

e. When the transfer completes, you should see the results on the transmitter and receiver. The following output is from DLS2, the transmitter.

```
ttcp-t: buflen=32768, nbuf=2048, align=16384/0, port=5001  tcp  ->
10.1.80.254

ttcp-t: connect

ttcp-t: 67108864 bytes in 47622 ms (47.622 real seconds) (~1375 kB/s) +++

ttcp-t: 2048 I/O calls

ttcp-t: 0 sleeps (0 ms total) (0 ms average)
```

Chapter 8 Troubleshooting Converged Networks

There are no labs for this chapter.

Chapter 9 Maintaining and Troubleshooting Network Security Implementations

Lab 9-1, Management Plane Security

Lab Topology

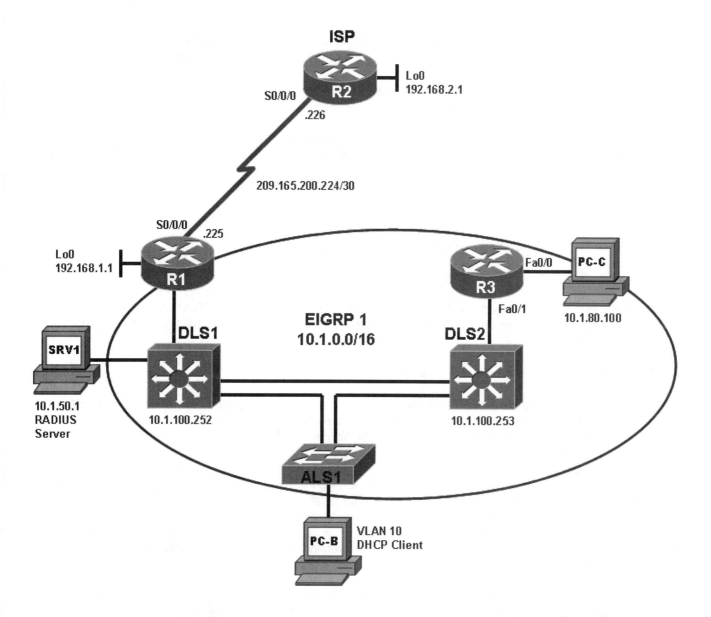

Objectives

- Load the device configuration files for each trouble ticket.
- Diagnose and resolve problems related to router and Layer 3 switch management plane security.
- Document the troubleshooting progress, configuration changes, and problem resolution.

Background

Routers and Layer 3 switches are typically segmented into three planes of operation, each with a clearly identified objective. The data plane (also called the forwarding plane) forwards user data packets. The control plane routes data correctly, and the management plane manages the network devices.

The management plane deals with the traffic used to access, manage, and monitor all the network elements. It supports all required provisioning, maintenance, and monitoring functions for the network. Like the other IP traffic planes, management plane traffic is handled in-band with all other IP traffic. Most service providers and many large enterprises also build separate, out-of-band (OOB) management networks to provide alternate reachability when the primary in-band IP path is not reachable.

Processes and protocols that are associated with this plane include Telnet, AAA, SSH, FTP, TFTP, SNMP, syslog, TACACS+, RADIUS, DNS, NetFlow, ROMMON, and other management protocols.

This lab focuses on management plane security issues related to SSH, AAA, and RADIUS for management access to routers and Layer 3 switches.

For each task or trouble ticket, the trouble scenario and problem symptom are described. While troubleshooting, you will discover the cause of the problem, correct it, and then document the process and results.

Lab Structure

This lab is divided into two main sections.

Section 1—Trouble Tickets and Troubleshooting Logs

This section includes two tasks. Each task is associated with a trouble ticket (TT) and introduces one or more errors on one or more devices. If time is a consideration, each task or trouble ticket can be performed independently.

Section 2—Troubleshooting Reference Information

This section provides general troubleshooting information that can be applied to any of the trouble tickets in this lab. Examples of useful commands and output are provided. If time permits, it is recommended that you read through Section 2 prior to starting on the trouble tickets.

Note: This lab uses Cisco 1841 routers with Cisco IOS Release 12.4(24)T1 and the Advanced IP Services image c1841-advipservicesk9-mz.124-24.T1.bin. The switches are Cisco WS-C2960-24TT-L with the Cisco IOS image c2960-lanbasek9-mz.122-46.SE.bin and Catalyst 3560-24PS with the Cisco IOS image c3560-advipservicesk9-mz.122-46.SE.bin. Other routers (such as 2801 and 2811), switches (such as 2950 or 3550), and Cisco IOS Software versions can be used if they have comparable capabilities and features. Depending on the router or switch model and Cisco IOS Software version, the commands available and output produced might vary from what is shown in this lab.

Any changes made to configurations or topology (other than errors introduced) are noted in the lab and trouble tickets so that you are aware of them prior to beginning the troubleshooting process.

Required Resources

- 3 routers (Cisco 1841 with Cisco IOS Release 12.4(24)T1 Advanced IP Service or comparable)

- 1 switch (Cisco 2960 with the Cisco IOS Release 12.2(46)SE C2960-LANBASEK9-M image or comparable)

- 2 switches (Cisco 3560 with the Cisco IOS Release 12.2(46)SE C3560-advipservicesk9-mz image or comparable)

- SRV1 (Windows PC with static IP address) with TFTP and syslog servers plus an SSH client (PuTTY or comparable) and WireShark software

- PC-B (Windows PC DHCP client) with PuTTY and WireShark software

- PC-C (Windows PC DHCP client) with PuTTY and WireShark software

- Serial and Ethernet cables

Section 1—Trouble Tickets and Troubleshooting Logs

Task 1: Trouble Ticket Lab 9-1 TT-A

Step 1: Review trouble ticket Lab 9-1 TT-A.

As a security measure, your company has decided to implement centralized server-based AAA authentication for key network devices, such as routers and switches. The implementation plan specifies that RADIUS server software is to be installed on SRV1 (see Appendix A for the installation procedure). As a pilot, Layer 3 core switch DLS1 is to be configured with AAA to access the RADIUS server for login authentication. The implementation plan specifies RADIUS as the primary method of authentication, with local authentication as the backup method.

Your colleague has configured the RADIUS server on SRV1 and AAA login authentication on DLS1 but is having trouble accessing DLS1 when attempting to log in via Telnet from PC-B. On the RADIUS server, he has created a test username **raduser** with a password of **RadUserpass**.

He has asked for your help in diagnosing and solving the problem.

Note: The freeware server WinRadius is used for this trouble ticket.

Step 2: Load the device trouble ticket configuration files for TT-A.

Using the procedure described in Lab 3-1, verify that the lab configuration files are present in flash. Load the proper configuration files as indicated in the Device Configuration File table.

Note: The following device access methods are in effect after installing RADIUS on SRV1 and loading the configuration files:

- Console access requires no username or password.

- Telnet and SSH require username **admin** and password **adminpa55** (except for DLS1, which uses RADIUS).

- The enable password is **ciscoenpa55**.

Device Configuration File Table

Device Name	File to Load	Notes
ALS1	Lab91-ALS1-TT-A-Cfg.txt	
DLS1	Lab91-DLS1-TT-A-Cfg.txt	
DLS2	Lab91-DLS2-TT-A-Cfg.txt	
R1	Lab91-R1-TT-A-Cfg.txt	
R2	Lab91-R2-TT-A-Cfg.txt	
R3	Lab91-R3-TT-A-Cfg.txt	
SRV1	N/A	Static IP: 10.1.50.1/24 Default gateway: 10.1.50.254

PC-B	N/A	DHCP
PC-C	N/A	Static IP: 10.1.80.100/24 Default gateway: 10.1.80.1

Step 3: Configure SRV1 and start the RADIUS server.

a. Configure SRV1 with the static IP address 10.1.50.1/24 and default gateway 10.1.50.254.

b. Start the WinRadius server application on SRV1. If the WinRadius server is not installed, contact your instructor.

c. From the menu, select **Operation > Add User** and create a new user named **raduser** with a password of **RadUserpass**. Click **OK**.

    Note: Passwords are case-sensitive.

d. To clear the log on the WinRadius server, select **Log > Clear** from the main menu.

    Note: If you exit the WinRadius server application and restart it, you must recreate the user **raduser**. A maximum of five users can be created using the free version of the software.

Step 4: Release and renew the DHCP lease on PC-B.

a. Ensure that PC-B is configured as a DHCP client in the OFFICE VLAN.

b   After loading all TT-A device configuration files, issue the `ipconfig /release` and `ipconfig /renew` commands on PC-B.

Step 5: Outline the troubleshooting approach and validation steps.

Use this space to identify your troubleshooting approach and the key steps to verify that the problem is resolved. Troubleshooting approaches to select from include the follow-the-path, spot-the-differences, bottom-up, top-down, divide-and-conquer, shoot-from-the-hip, and move-the-problem methods.

Note: In addition to a specific approach, you can use the generic troubleshooting process described at the beginning of Section 2 of this lab.

_____

_____

_____

_____

_____

_____

Step 6: Record the troubleshooting process and configuration changes.

Note: Section 2 of this lab includes useful commands and examples of output.

Use this log to document your actions and results during the troubleshooting process. List the commands you used to gather information. As you progress, record what you think the problem might be and the actions you take to correct the problem.

Device	Actions and Results

Step 7: Document trouble ticket debrief notes.

Use this space to make notes of the key learning points that you picked up during the discussion of this trouble ticket with your instructor. The notes can include problems encountered, solutions applied, useful commands employed, alternate solutions, methods, and processes, and procedure and communication improvements.

_____

_____

_____

_____

_____

_____

Task 2: Trouble Ticket Lab 9-1 TT-B

Step 1: Review trouble ticket Lab 9-1 TT-B.

As a further security measure, your company has decided to implement SSH and only allow vty access to key networking devices from specific management workstations. As a pilot, router R3 will be configured to allow SSH access from only PC-C (on the R3 LAN) and prevent remote access from any host other than PC-C. For testing purposes, host PC-C will be used as a management workstation and will be assigned a static address of 10.1.80.100. Login from PC-C to R3 must be authenticated by the RADIUS server running on SRV1. No other hosts in the network should be able to access R3 via SSH.

A colleague of yours configured an ACL and SSH access on R3, but due to sporadic hardware issues with R3, she decided to replace R3 with a comparable router. She says that she backed up the configuration from the old router to a USB flash drive and loaded it into the new router. Now she is unable to connect to R3 using SSH from PC-C.

On the RADIUS server, she created a test user named **raduser** with a password of **RadUserpass**. The implementation plan specifies RADIUS as the primary method of authentication with local authentication as the backup method.

She has asked for your help in diagnosing and solving the problem.

Step 2: Load the device trouble ticket configuration files for TT-B.

Using the procedure described in Lab 3-1, verify that the lab configuration files are present in flash. Load the proper configuration files as indicated in the Device Configuration File table.

Note: The following device access methods are in effect after installing RADIUS on SRV1 and loading the configuration files:

- Console access requires no username or password.

- Telnet and SSH require username **admin** and password **adminpa55** (except for R3).

- The enable password is **ciscoenpa55**.

Device Configuration File Table

Device Name	File to Load	Notes
ALS1	Lab91-ALS1-TT-B-Cfg.txt	
DLS1	Lab91-DLS1-TT-B-Cfg.txt	
DLS2	Lab91-DLS2-TT-B-Cfg.txt	
R1	Lab91-R1-TT-B-Cfg.txt	
R2	Lab91-R2-TT-B-Cfg.txt	
R3	Lab91-R3-TT-B-Cfg.txt	
SRV1	N/A	Static IP: 10.1.50.1/24 Default gateway: 10.1.50.254
PC-B	N/A	DHCP
PC-C	N/A	Static IP: 10.1.80.100/24 Default gateway: 10.1.80.1

Step 3: Configure SRV1 and start the RADIUS server.

a. Configure SRV1 with static IP address 10.1.50.1/24 and default gateway 10.1.50.254.

b. Start the WinRadius server application on SRV1. If the WinRadius server is not installed, contact your instructor.

c. Select **Operation > Add User** from the menu and create a new user named **raduser** with a password of **RadUserpass**. Click **OK**.

    Note: Passwords are case-sensitive.

d. To clear the log on the WinRadius server, select **Log > Clear** from the main menu.

    Note: If you exit the WinRadius server application and restart it, you must recreate the user **raduser**. A maximum of five users can be created using the free version of the software.

Step 4: Configure a static IP address on PC-C.

a. Configure PC-C with static IP address 10.1.80.100, subnet mask 255.255.255.0, and default gateway 10.1.80.1.

b. Verify that PC-C has PuTTY (or comparable) SSH client software installed. If it does not, contact your instructor.

Step 5: Outline the troubleshooting approach and validation steps.

Use this space to identify your troubleshooting approach and the key steps to verify that the problem is resolved. Troubleshooting approaches to select from include the follow-the-path, spot-the-differences, bottom-up, top-down, divide-and-conquer, shoot-from-the-hip, and move-the-problem methods.

Note: In addition to a specific approach, you can use the generic troubleshooting process described at the beginning of Section 2 of this lab.

_____

_____

_____

_____

_____

Step 6: Record the troubleshooting process and configuration changes.

Note: Section 2 of this lab includes useful commands and examples of output.

Use this log to document your actions and results during the troubleshooting process. List the commands you used to gather information. As you progress, record what you think the problem might be and the actions you take to correct the problem.

Device	Actions and Results

Step 7: Document trouble ticket debrief notes.

Use this space to make notes of the key learning points that you picked up during the discussion of this trouble ticket with your instructor. The notes can include problems encountered, solutions applied, useful commands employed, alternate solutions, methods, and processes, and procedure and communication improvements.

_____

_____

_____

_____

_____

_____

_____

Section 2—Troubleshooting Reference Information

General Troubleshooting Process

As a general guideline, you can use the following general troubleshooting process described in the course.

1. Define the problem (symptoms).
2. Gather information.
3. Analyze the information.
4. Propose a hypothesis (possible cause).
5. Test the hypothesis.
6. Eliminate or accept the hypothesis.
7. Solve the problem.
8. Document the problem.

Command Summary

The table lists useful commands for this lab. The sample output is shown on following pages.

Command	Key Information Displayed
`show line vty 0`	Displays the physical serial interface characteristics of a vty line as well as the transport input and output allowed (for example: Telnet or SSH).
`show users`	Displays device lines in use (for example: con, vty 0, vty 1), the username logged in, and the IP address of the connected host.
`show radius server-group all`	Displays the RADIUS servers defined in the group specified (default group is radius). The server IP address and port numbers are listed.
`show radius statistics`	Displays the RADIUS message statistics for authentication and accounting communication between the network device and the RADIUS server. Output includes packets with and without responses, response delay, and timeouts. Source port numbers are also listed.
`debug radius authentication`	Displays real-time interaction and message exchange between the network device, the calling station, and the RADIUS server. Authentication success or failure is indicated.
`show aaa servers`	Displays AAA server host information, including type (RADIUS or TACACS), IP address, port numbers in use, and AAA requests, successes, and failures.
`show aaa method-lists all`	Displays the names of AAA method lists currently defined, the type of validation in use, and the sequence of application (for example: server group, local, or none).
`debug aaa authentication`	Displays the method list defined and being used for AAA authentication (for example: TELNET_LINES).
`debug aaa authorization`	Displays the method list defined and being used for AAA authorization.
`debug aaa accounting`	Displays the method list defined and being used for AAA accounting.

`show ip ssh`	Displays SSH status (enabled or disabled), version number, timeout, retries, and key size in use (for example: 1024 bits).
`show ssh`	Displays active SSH connections with username, version, mode, encryption, HMAC, and state of the connection.
`sh access-lists`	Displays currently configured ACLs with type (for example: standard, extended) and name if one is assigned. ACL statements are listed with the number of matches for each one.
`show ip interface fa0/0`	Displays IP-related interface information, including any inbound or outbound access lists configured.

Sample Troubleshooting Output

VTY Line-related Commands

The following commands and outputs are samples from the devices in this lab.

```
DLS1#show line vty 0
   Tty Typ     Tx/Rx      A Modem  Roty AccO AccI   Uses   Noise  Overruns   Int
     1 VTY                 -    -     -    -    -      4      0     0/0        -

Line 1, Location: "", Type: ""
Length: 24 lines, Width: 80 columns
Baud rate (TX/RX) is 9600/9600
Status: Ready, No Exit Banner
Capabilities: none
Modem state: Ready
Special Chars: Escape  Hold  Stop  Start  Disconnect  Activation
               ^^x     none  -     -      none
Timeouts:      Idle EXEC    Idle Session    Modem Answer  Session   Dispatch
               01:00:00        never                        none    not set
                            Idle Session Disconnect Warning
                               never
                            Login-sequence User Response
                             00:00:30
                            Autoselect Initial Wait
                               not set
Modem type is unknown.
Session limit is not set.
Time since activation: never
Editing is enabled.
History is enabled, history size is 20.
DNS resolution in show commands is enabled
Full user help is disabled
Allowed input transports are ssh.
Allowed output transports are telnet ssh.
Preferred transport is telnet.
No output characters are padded
No special data dispatching characters
```

In the above example, DLS1 allows only SSH as an input transport protocol on vty lines, but it allows both SSH and Telnet on output.

```
R3#show users
      Line        User       Host(s)            Idle        Location
 *  0 con 0                   idle               00:00:00
    194 vty 0     raduser     idle               00:22:52 10.1.80.100
    195 vty 1     admin       idle               00:00:22 10.1.50.1
```

In the above example, two users are logged in to R3 using the vty lines (could be Telnet or SSH), one from host 10.1.80.100 and one from host 10.1.50.1.

RADIUS-related Commands

```
DLS1#show radius server-group all
Sever group radius
    Sharecount = 1   sg_unconfigured = FALSE
    Type = standard  Memlocks = 1
    Server(10.1.50.1:1645,1646) Transactions:
    Authen: Not Available  Author:Not Available  Acct:Not Available
```

In the above example, DLS1 is configured to access a RADIUS server at IP address 10.1.50.1, using ports 1645 and 1646. No transaction have taken place.

```
DLS1#show radius statistics
                                   Auth.       Acct.        Both
          Maximum inQ length:       NA          NA           1
        Maximum waitQ length:       NA          NA           1
        Maximum doneQ length:       NA          NA           1
         Total responses seen:       0           0           0
       Packets with responses:       0           0           0
    Packets without responses:       4           0           4
    Average response delay(ms):      0           0           0
    Maximum response delay(ms):      0           0           0
     Number of Radius timeouts:     16           0          16
         Duplicate ID detects:       0           0           0
    Buffer Allocation Failures:      0           0           0
Maximum Buffer Size (bytes):        82           0          82
 Source Port Range: (2 ports only)
1645 - 1646
Last used Source Port/Identifier:
1645/4
1646/0
```

In the above example, DLS1 has attempted to contact the server 16 times (four attempted logins with four retries each), and all attempts have timed out due to lack of accessibility of the server.

```
DLS1#debug radius authentication
Radius protocol debugging is on
Radius protocol brief debugging is off
Radius protocol verbose debugging is off
Radius packet hex dump debugging is off
Radius packet protocol debugging is on
Radius packet retransmission debugging is off
Radius server fail-over debugging is off
Radius elog debugging is off
```

Login attempt with incorrect RADIUS ports specified on DLS1:

```
DLS1#
Dec  4 16:06:50.142: RADIUS/ENCODE(00000005): ask "Username: "
DLS1#
Dec  4 16:06:59.430: RADIUS/ENCODE(00000005): ask "Password: "
DLS1#
Dec  4 16:07:05.487: RADIUS/ENCODE(00000005):Orig. component type = EXEC
Dec  4 16:07:05.487: RADIUS:  AAA Unsupported Attr: interface          [170] 4

Dec  4 16:07:05.487: RADIUS:   74 74                 [ tt]
Dec  4 16:07:05.487: RADIUS/ENCODE(00000005): dropping service type, "radius-server
attribute 6 on-for-login-auth" is off
Dec  4 16:07:05.487: RADIUS(00000005): Config NAS IP: 0.0.0.0
Dec  4 16:07:05.487: RADIUS/ENCODE(00000005): acct_session_id: 5
Dec  4 16:07:05.487: RADIUS(00000005): sending
Dec  4 16:07:05.487: RADIUS/ENCODE: Best Local IP-Address 10.1.50.252 for Radius
-Server 10.1.50.1
Dec  4 16:07:05.487: RADIUS(00000005): Send Access-Request to 10.1.50.1:1645 id
1645/5, len 82
Dec  4 16:07:05.487: RADIUS:  authenticator B5 DF D2 00 81 8A C0 08 - 5E 68 DA A
9 59 01 7A 00
Dec  4 16:07:05.487: RADIUS:   User-Name          [1]   9   "raduser"
Dec  4 16:07:05.487: RADIUS:   User-Password      [2]   18  *
Dec  4 16:07:05.487: RADIUS:   NAS-Port           [5]   6   1

DLS1#
Dec  4 16:07:05.487: RADIUS:   NAS-Port-Id        [87]  6   "tty1"
Dec  4 16:07:05.487: RADIUS:   NAS-Port-Type      [61]  6   Virtual
     [5]
Dec  4 16:07:05.487: RADIUS:   Calling-Station-Id [31]  11  "10.1.10.1"
Dec  4 16:07:05.487: RADIUS:   NAS-IP-Address     [4]   6   10.1.50.252

DLS1#
Dec  4 16:07:10.370: RADIUS: Retransmit to (10.1.50.1:1645,1646) for id 1645/5
DLS1#
Dec  4 16:07:15.269: RADIUS: Retransmit to (10.1.50.1:1645,1646) for id 1645/5
DLS1#
Dec  4 16:07:20.403: RADIUS: Retransmit to (10.1.50.1:1645,1646) for id 1645/5
DLS1#
Dec  4 16:07:25.370: %RADIUS-4-RADIUS_DEAD: RADIUS server 10.1.50.1:1645,1646 is
 not responding.
Dec  4 16:07:25.370: %RADIUS-4-RADIUS_ALIVE: RADIUS server 10.1.50.1:1645,1646 h
as returned.
DLS1#
Dec  4 16:07:25.370: RADIUS: No response from (10.1.50.1:1645,1646) for id 1645/
5
Dec  4 16:07:25.370: RADIUS/DECODE: parse response no app start; FAIL
Dec  4 16:07:25.370: RADIUS/DECODE: parse response; FAIL
DLS1#
Dec  4 16:07:27.375: RADIUS/ENCODE(00000005): ask "Username: "
```

The above example shows the exchange between the RADIUS client and server when the client is using port numbers that do not match the server. Note the retransmits and the server dead messages.

Successful login from PC-B (using valid username raduser on the RADIUS server):

```
DLS1(config)#
Dec  6 17:04:47.577: RADIUS/ENCODE(0000000F): ask "Username: "
```

```
DLS1(config)#
Dec  6 17:04:55.715: RADIUS/ENCODE(0000000F): ask "Password: "
DLS1(config)#
Dec  6 17:05:05.439: RADIUS/ENCODE(0000000F):Orig. component type = EXEC
Dec  6 17:05:05.439: RADIUS:  AAA Unsupported Attr: interface      [170] 4

Dec  6 17:05:05.439: RADIUS:   74 74                    [ tt]
Dec  6 17:05:05.439: RADIUS/ENCODE(0000000F): dropping service type, "radius-ser
ver attribute 6 on-for-login-auth" is off
Dec  6 17:05:05.439: RADIUS(0000000F): Config NAS IP: 0.0.0.0
Dec  6 17:05:05.439: RADIUS/ENCODE(0000000F): acct_session_id: 15
Dec  6 17:05:05.439: RADIUS(0000000F): se
DLS1(config)#nding
Dec  6 17:05:05.439: RADIUS/ENCODE: Best Local IP-Address 10.1.50.252 for Radius
-Server 10.1.50.1
Dec  6 17:05:05.439: RADIUS(0000000F): Send Access-Request to 10.1.50.1:1812 id
1645/12, len 82
Dec  6 17:05:05.439: RADIUS:  authenticator 7E D1 DF 37 75 69 EC 91 - 42 FC 2E 7
8 D7 9B 5B 3B
Dec  6 17:05:05.439: RADIUS:  User-Name          [1]    9   "raduser"
Dec  6 17:05:05.439: RADIUS:  User-Password      [2]    18  *
Dec  6 17:05:05.439: RADIUS:  NAS-Port           [5]    6   1
DLS1(config)#
Dec  6 17:05:05.439: RADIUS:  NAS-Port-Id        [87]   6   "tty1"
Dec  6 17:05:05.439: RADIUS:  NAS-Port-Type      [61]   6   Virtual
     [5]
Dec  6 17:05:05.439: RADIUS:  Calling-Station-Id [31]   11  "10.1.10.1"
Dec  6 17:05:05.439: RADIUS:  NAS-IP-Address     [4]    6   10.1.50.252

Dec  6 17:05:05.447: RADIUS: Received from id 1645/12 10.1.50.1:1812, Access-Acc
ept, len 26
Dec  6 17:05:05.447: RADIUS:  authenticator 75 81 E4 CD 45 1D F6 14 - 5D 1F AD F
4 D4 83 D
DLS1(config)#5 FE
Dec  6 17:05:05.447: RADIUS:  Session-Timeout    [27]   6   9999999

Dec  6 17:05:05.447: RADIUS(0000000F): Received from id 1645/12
```

The above example shows the exchange between the RADIUS client and server when the client is using the same port numbers as the server and a legitimate user attempts to login. Note the Access-Accept message.

```
Unsuccessful login from PC-B (using invalid username baduser):

DLS1(config)#
Dec  6 17:10:00.346: RADIUS/ENCODE(00000010): ask "Username: "
DLS1(config)#
Dec  6 17:10:06.722: RADIUS/ENCODE(00000010): ask "Password: "
DLS1(config)#
Dec  6 17:10:16.580: RADIUS/ENCODE(00000010):Orig. component type = EXEC
Dec  6 17:10:16.580: RADIUS:  AAA Unsupported Attr: interface      [170] 4

Dec  6 17:10:16.580: RADIUS:   74 74                    [ tt]
Dec  6 17:10:16.580: RADIUS/ENCODE(00000010): dropping service type, "radius-ser
ver attribute 6 on-for-login-auth" is off
Dec  6 17:10:16.580: RADIUS(00000010): Config NAS IP: 0.0.0.0
Dec  6 17:10:16.580: RADIUS/ENCODE(00000010): acct_session_id: 16
Dec  6 17:10:16.580: RADIUS(00000010): se
```

```
DLS1(config)#nding
Dec  6 17:10:16.580: RADIUS/ENCODE: Best Local IP-Address 10.1.50.252 for Radius
-Server 10.1.50.1
Dec  6 17:10:16.580: RADIUS(00000010): Send Access-Request to 10.1.50.1:1812 id
1645/13, len 82
Dec  6 17:10:16.580: RADIUS:  authenticator 17 3A 1D 34 81 4C F1 6F - 89 62 05 1
3 14 8F 33 4B
Dec  6 17:10:16.580: RADIUS:  User-Name          [1]    9   "baduser"
Dec  6 17:10:16.580: RADIUS:  User-Password      [2]    18  *
Dec  6 17:10:16.580: RADIUS:  NAS-Port           [5]    6   1
Dec  6 17:10:16.580: RADIUS:  NAS-Port-Id        [87]   6   "tty1"
Dec  6 17:10:16.580: RADIUS:  NAS-Port-Type      [61]   6   Virtual
     [5]
Dec  6 17:10:16.580: RADIUS:  Calling-Station-Id [31]   11  "10.1.10.1"
Dec  6 17:10:16.580: RADIUS:  NAS-IP-Address     [4]    6   10.1.50.252

Dec  6 17:10:16.588: RADIUS: Received from id 1645/13 10.1.50.1:1812, Access-Rej
ect, len 20
Dec  6 17:10:16.588: RADIUS:  authenticator 81 34 66 76 58 03 AF 9B - CF D5 93 F
2 C6 13 6
DLS1(config)#7 7D
Dec  6 17:10:16.588: RADIUS(00000010): Received from id 1645/13
Dec  6 17:10:18.593: RADIUS/ENCODE(00000010): ask "Username: "
```

The above example shows the exchange between the RADIUS client and server when the client is using the same port numbers as the server and a bad login is attempted (nonexistent username and bad password). Note the Access-Reject message. Switch DLS1 then prompts immediately to allow entry of a correct username and password combination.

AAA-related Commands

Incorrect RADIUS port numbers:

```
DLS1#show aaa servers

RADIUS: id 2, priority 1, host 10.1.50.1, auth-port 1645, acct-port 1646
    State: current UP, duration 13752s, previous duration 0s
    Dead: total time 0s, count 0
    Quarantined: No
    Authen: request 8, timeouts 8
         Response: unexpected 0, server error 0, incorrect 0, time 0ms
         Transaction: success 0, failure 2

<output omitted>
```

The above example shows that the AAA server is RADIUS and lists the IP address and ports defined on the client. Note the eight requests and eight timeouts, resulting in two failed authentication attempts.

Correct RADIUS port numbers:

```
R3#show aaa servers
RADIUS: id 1, priority 1, host 10.1.50.1, auth-port 1812, acct-port 1813
    State: current UP, duration 23188s, previous duration 0s
    Dead: total time 0s, count 0
    Quarantined: No
    Authen: request 0, timeouts 0, failover 0, retransmission 0
```

```
                    Response: accept 0, reject 0, challenge 0
                    Response: unexpected 0, server error 0, incorrect 0, time 0ms
                    Transaction: success 2, failure 0
                    Throttled: transaction 0, timeout 0, failure 0
        Author: request 0, timeouts 0, failover 0, retransmission 0
                    Response: accept 0, reject 0, challenge 0
                    Response: unexpected 0, server error 0, incorrect 0, time 0ms
                    Transaction: success 0, failure 0
                    Throttled: transaction 0, timeout 0, failure 0
     Account: request 0, timeouts 0, failover 0, retransmission 0
                    Request: start 0, interim 0, stop 0
                    Response: start 0, interim 0, stop 0
                    Response: unexpected 0, server error 0, incorrect 0, time 0ms
                    Transaction: success 0, failure 0
                    Throttled: transaction 0, timeout 0, failure 0
```

The above example shows that the AAA server is RADIUS and lists the IP address and ports defined on the client. Note the two successful authentication transactions.

```
R3#show aaa method-lists all
authen queue=AAA_ML_AUTHEN_LOGIN
  name=default valid=TRUE id=0 :state=ALIVE : LOCAL
  name=CONSOLE valid=TRUE id=2B000001 :state=ALIVE : NONE
  name=VTY_LINES valid=TRUE id=87000002 :state=ALIVE : SERVER_GROUP radius LOCAL

authen queue=AAA_ML_AUTHEN_ENABLE
authen queue=AAA_ML_AUTHEN_PPP
authen queue=AAA_ML_AUTHEN_SGBP
authen queue=AAA_ML_AUTHEN_ARAP
authen queue=AAA_ML_AUTHEN_DOT1X
authen queue=AAA_ML_AUTHEN_EAPOUDP
authen queue=AAA_ML_AUTHEN_8021X
permanent lists
  name=Permanent Enable None valid=TRUE id=0 :state=ALIVE : ENABLE  NONE
  name=Permanent Enable valid=TRUE id=0 :state=ALIVE : ENABLE
  name=Permanent None valid=TRUE id=0 :state=ALIVE : NONE
  name=Permanent Local valid=TRUE id=0 :state=ALIVE : LOCAL
author queue=AAA_ML_AUTHOR_SHELL
  name=VTY_LINES valid=TRUE id=61000003 :state=ALIVE : SERVER_GROUP radius LOCAL
<output omitted>
```

The above example shows the names of the AAA method lists currently defined, the type of validation in use, and the sequence of application (for example: server group, local, or none).

```
DLS1#debug aaa authentication
AAA Authentication debugging is on
DLS1#
Dec  7 15:48:21.869: AAA/BIND(0000000C): Bind i/f
Dec  7 15:48:21.869: AAA/AUTHEN/LOGIN (0000000C): Pick method list 'TELNET_LINES
'
```

The above example shows the method list defined and being used for AAA authentication (TELNET_LINES).

```
DLS1#debug aaa authorization
AAA Authorization debugging is on
DLS1#
```

```
Dec  7 16:06:34.836: AAA/AUTHOR (0xD): Pick method list 'default' - FAIL
Dec  7 16:06:34.844: AAA/AUTHOR/EXEC(0000000D): Authorization FAILED
```

The above example shows the method list defined and being used for AAA authorization (default). Note that the authorization attempt failed.

SSH-related Commands

```
R3#show ip ssh
SSH Enabled - version 1.99
Authentication timeout: 120 secs; Authentication retries: 3
Minimum expected Diffie Hellman key size : 1024 bits


R3#show ip ssh
SSH Disabled - version 1.99
%Please create RSA keys (of at least 768 bits size) to enable SSH v2.
Authentication timeout: 120 secs; Authentication retries: 3
Minimum expected Diffie Hellman key size : 1024 bits
```

The first example above shows the output when the RSA keys have been created and SSH is enabled. The second example shows the output when there are no RSA keys and SSH is disabled.

```
R3#show ssh
Connection Version Mode Encryption  Hmac       State            Username
0          2.0     IN   aes256-cbc  hmac-sha1  Session started  raduser
0          2.0     OUT  aes256-cbc  hmac-sha1  Session started  raduser
1          2.0     IN   aes256-cbc  hmac-sha1  Session started  admin
1          2.0     OUT  aes256-cbc  hmac-sha1  Session started  admin
%No SSHv1 server connections running.
```

The above example shows active SSH connections with the username, version, mode, encryption, HMAC, and state of the connection.

ACL-related Commands

```
R3#show access-lists
Standard IP access list 1
    10 permit 10.1.80.100 (77 matches)
```

The above example shows the currently configured ACLs with the type, number (if one is assigned), statements, and the number of matches for each one.

```
R3#show ip interface fa0/0
FastEthernet0/0 is up, line protocol is up
  Internet address is 10.1.80.1/24
  Broadcast address is 255.255.255.255
  Address determined by non-volatile memory
  MTU is 1500 bytes
  Helper address is not set
  Directed broadcast forwarding is disabled
  Multicast reserved groups joined: 224.0.0.10
  Outgoing access list is not set
  Inbound  access list is 1
  Proxy ARP is enabled
  Local Proxy ARP is disabled
  Security level is default
```

```
Split horizon is enabled
ICMP redirects are always sent
ICMP unreachables are always sent
ICMP mask replies are never sent
IP fast switching is enabled
IP fast switching on the same interface is disabled
IP Flow switching is disabled
IP CEF switching is enabled
IP CEF switching turbo vector
```

`<output omitted>`

The above example shows IP-related interface information, including any inbound or outbound access lists configured

Reflection Questions

1. Which lab trouble tickets did you have the most difficulty with? _____

_____

_____

_____

2. Would you change anything about the process that you used for any of the trouble tickets now that you see the

resolution of the problem? _____

_____

_____

_____

3. Which commands did you find most useful in diagnosing management plane security issues? Add these to your

toolbox for future use. Which commands did you find least useful?

_____

_____

_____

References

If you need more information on the commands and their options, see the following references:

- IP Routing Protocol

  http://www.cisco.com/cisco/web/support/index.html

- Cisco IOS IP Switching http://www.cisco.com/en/US/docs/ios/ipswitch/command/reference/isw_book.html

- Configuring SSH on Routers and Switches Running Cisco IOS Software

  http://www.cisco.com/en/US/tech/tk583/tk617/technologies_tech_note09186a00800949e2.shtml

- SSH FAQ http://www.cisco.com/en/US/tech/tk583/tk617/technologies_q_and_a_item09186a0080267e0f.shtml

Router Interface Summary Table

Router Interface Summary				
Router Model	Ethernet Interface #1	Ethernet Interface #2	Serial Interface #1	Serial Interface #2
1700	Fast Ethernet 0 (FA0)	Fast Ethernet 1 (FA1)	Serial 0 (S0)	Serial 1 (S1)
1800	Fast Ethernet 0/0 (FA0/0)	Fast Ethernet 0/1 (FA0/1)	Serial 0/0/0 (S0/0/0)	Serial 0/0/1 (S0/0/1)
2600	Fast Ethernet 0/0 (FA0/0)	Fast Ethernet 0/1 (FA0/1)	Serial 0/0 (S0/0)	Serial 0/1 (S0/1)
2800	Fast Ethernet 0/0 (FA0/0)	Fast Ethernet 0/1 (FA0/1)	Serial 0/0/0 (S0/0/0)	Serial 0/0/1 (S0/0/1)
Note: To find out how the router is configured, look at the interfaces to identify the type of router and how many interfaces the router has. Rather than try to list all the combinations of configurations for each router class, this table includes identifiers for the possible combinations of Ethernet and serial interfaces in the device. The table does not include any other type of interface, even though a specific router might contain one. An example of this is an ISDN BRI interface. The string in parenthesis is the legal abbreviation that can be used in Cisco IOS commands to represent the interface.				

Appendix A—WinRadius Server Installation

Note: A WinRadius (or comparable) server should be installed on server SRV1 for this lab. If it is not, you can use the following procedure to download and install it. Check with your instructor if you have questions regarding the RADIUS server installation.

Step 1: Download the WinRadius software.

A number of RADIUS servers are available, both freeware and for sale. This lab uses WinRadius, a freeware standards-based RADIUS server that runs on Windows XP and most other Windows operating systems.

Note: The free version of the software can support only five usernames.

Step 2: Install the WinRadius software.

a. Create a folder named WinRadius on your desktop or other location in which to store the files.

b. Search the web for **winradius** and download the latest version from a trusted website.

c. Save the downloaded zip file in the folder created in Step 2a, and extract the zipped files to the same folder. There is no installation setup. The extracted WinRadius.exe file is executable.

d. You can create a shortcut on your desktop for WinRadius.exe.

Step 3: Configure the WinRadius server database.

a. Start the WinRadius.exe application. WinRadius uses a local database in which it stores user information. When the application is started for the first time, the following messages are displayed:

```
Please go to "Settings/Database and create the ODBC for your RADIUS database.

Launch ODBC failed.
```

b. From the main menu, select **Settings > Database**.

c. Click the **Configure ODBC automatically** button and then click **OK**. You should see a message that the ODBC was created successfully. Exit WinRadius and restart the application for the changes to take effect.

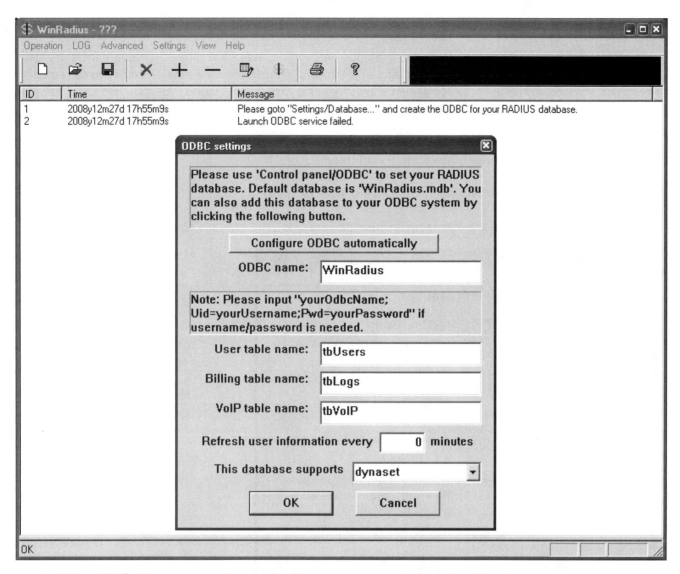

d.   When WinRadius starts again, you should see messages similar to the following:

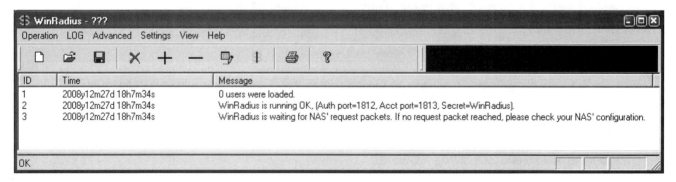

Step 4: Configure users and passwords on the WinRadius server.

Note: The free version of WinRadius can support only five usernames at a time. The usernames are lost if you exit the application and restart it. Any usernames created in previous sessions must be recreated. The first message in the previous screen shows that zero users were loaded. No users had been created prior to this, but this message is displayed each time WinRadius is started, regardless of whether users were created or not.

a. From the main menu, select **Operation > Add User.**

b. Enter the username **raduser** with a password of **RadUserpass.**

Note: The lab specifies the username **raduser** in lowercase. The example here creates user **RadUser**.

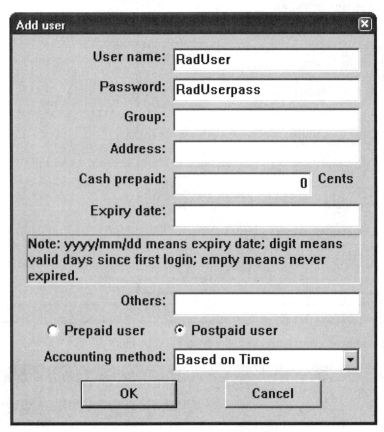

c. Click **OK**. You should see a message on the log screen that the user was added successfully.

Step 5: Clear the log display.

From the main menu, select **Log > Clear**.

Step 6: Test the new user added using the WinRadius test utility.

a. A WinRadius testing utility is included in the downloaded zip file. Navigate to the folder where you unzipped the WinRadius.zip file and locate the file named RadiusTest.exe.

b. Start the RadiusTest application, and enter the IP address of the RADIUS server. For this lab, the RADIUS server is SRV1, and the IP address is 10.1.50.1. The IP address of the RADIUS server in the example shown here is 192.168.1.3.

c.   Enter username **raduser** and password **RadUserpass**. Do not change the default RADIUS port number of 1813 nor the RADIUS password of WinRadius.

Note: Be sure to use the IP address of SRV1 in this lab (10.1.50.1) when testing.

d.   Click **Send** and you should see a Send Access_Request message indicating that the server at 10.1.50.1, port number 1813, received 44 hexadecimal characters. On the WinRadius log display, you should also see a message indicating that user raduser was authenticated successfully.

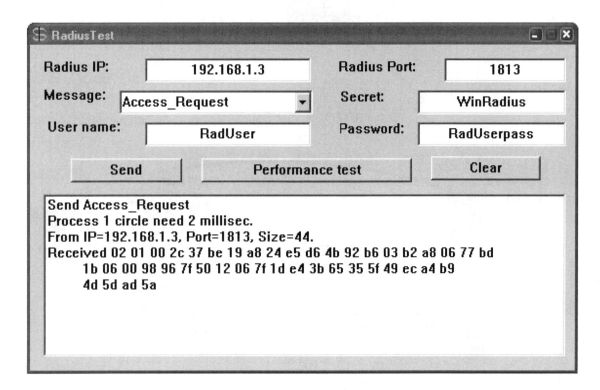

e.   Close the RadiusTest application.

Lab 9-2, Control Plane Security

Lab Topology

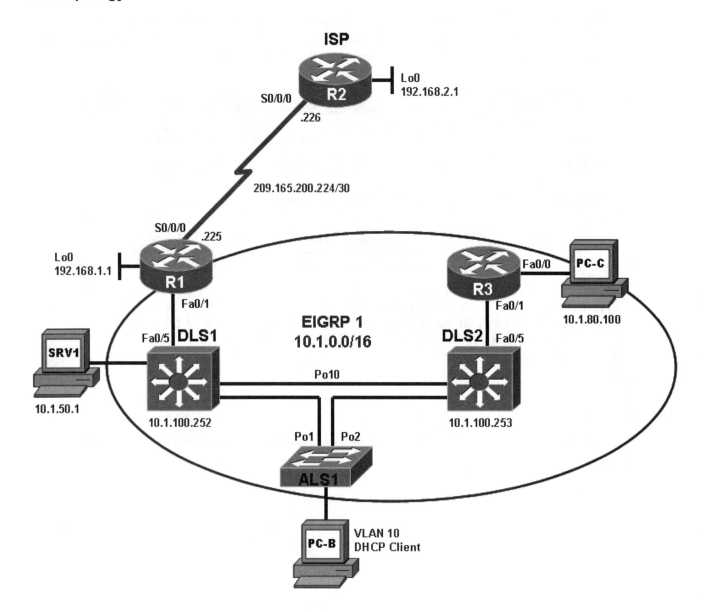

Objectives

- Load the device configuration files for each trouble ticket.
- Diagnose and resolve problems related to router and switch control plane security.
- Document the troubleshooting progress, configuration changes, and problem resolution.

Background

Routers and Layer 3 switches are typically segmented into three planes of operation, each with a clearly identified objective. The data plane (also called the forwarding plane) forwards user data packets. The control plane routes data correctly, and the management plane manages the network devices.

The control plane is typically associated with packets generated by the network elements themselves. End users typically do not interact with the control plane. Examples of Layer 3 control plane protocols and related security functions include neighbor authentication for routing protocols and HSRP. Examples of security-related Layer 2 control plane protocols include root guard, BPDU guard, DHCP snooping, Dynamic ARP Inspection, IP source guard, and the use of special VLANs for trunks and unused ports.

This lab focuses on control plane security issues related to DHCP snooping and EIGRP authentication for routers and Layer 3 switches.

For each task or trouble ticket, the trouble scenario and problem symptom is described. While troubleshooting, you will discover the cause of the problem, correct it, and then document the process and results.

Lab Structure

This lab is divided into two main sections.

Section 1—Trouble Tickets and Troubleshooting Logs

This section includes two tasks. Each task is associated with a trouble ticket (TT) and introduces one or more errors on one or more devices. If time is a consideration, each task or trouble ticket can be performed independently.

Section 2—Troubleshooting Reference Information

This section provides general troubleshooting information that can be applied to any of the trouble tickets in this lab. Examples of useful commands and output are provided. If time permits, it is recommended that you read through Section 2 prior to starting on the trouble tickets.

Note: This lab uses Cisco 1841 routers with Cisco IOS Release 12.4(24)T1 and the Advanced IP Services image c1841-advipservicesk9-mz.124-24.T1.bin. The switches are Cisco WS-C2960-24TT-L with the Cisco IOS image c2960-lanbasek9-mz.122-46.SE.bin and Catalyst 3560-24PS with the Cisco IOS image c3560-advipservicesk9-mz.122-46.SE.bin. Other routers (such as 2801 and 2811), switches (such as 2950 or 3550), and Cisco IOS Software versions can be used if they have comparable capabilities and features. Depending on the router or switch model and Cisco IOS Software version, the commands available and output produced might vary from what is shown in this lab.

Any changes made to configurations or topology (other than errors introduced) are noted in the lab and trouble tickets so that you are aware of them prior to beginning the troubleshooting process.

Required Resources

- 3 routers (Cisco 1841 with Cisco IOS Release 12.4(24)T1 Advanced IP Service or comparable)
- 1 switch (Cisco 2960 with the Cisco IOS Release 12.2(46)SE C2960-LANBASEK9-M image or comparable)
- 2 switches (Cisco 3560 with the Cisco IOS Release 12.2(46)SE C3560-advipservicesk9-mz image or comparable)
- SRV1 (Windows PC with static IP address) with TFTP and syslog servers plus an SSH client (PuTTY or comparable) and WireShark software
- PC-B (Windows PC DHCP client) with PuTTY and WireShark software
- PC-C (Windows PC DHCP client) with PuTTY and WireShark software
- Serial and Ethernet cables

Section 1—Trouble Tickets and Troubleshooting Logs

Task 1: Trouble Ticket Lab 9-2 TT-A

Step 1: Review trouble ticket Lab 9-2 TT-A.

As a security measure, your company has decided to implement DHCP snooping on access switches to prevent DHCP spoofing by unauthorized DHCP servers. For the pilot, the implementation plan specifies that the user VLAN 10 (OFFICE VLAN) on ASL1 be configured for DHCP snooping, and DHCP client PC-B be used as a test station. The test plan requires that the redundant switch topology failover allows VLAN 10 users to obtain an IP address from the DHCP server (DLS1) if one of the trunk links from ALS1 to DLS1 or DLS2 goes down.

Your colleague has configured DHCP snooping on ASL1, but now PC-B cannot access SRV1 or the Internet. He has asked for your help in diagnosing and solving the problem.

Step 2: Load the device trouble ticket configuration files for TT-A.

Using the procedure described in Lab 3-1, verify that the lab configuration files are present in flash. Load the proper configuration files as indicated in the Device Configuration File table.

Note: The following device access methods are in effect after loading the configuration files:

- Console access requires no username or password.

- Telnet and SSH require username **admin** and password **adminpa55**.

- The enable password is **ciscoenpa55**.

Device Configuration File Table

Device Name	File to Load	Notes
ALS1	Lab92-ALS1-TT-A-Cfg.txt	
DLS1	Lab92-DLS1-TT-A-Cfg.txt	
DLS2	Lab92-DLS2-TT-A-Cfg.txt	
R1	Lab92-R1-TT-A-Cfg.txt	
R2	Lab92-R2-TT-A-Cfg.txt	
R3	Lab92-R3-TT-A-Cfg.txt	
SRV1	N/A	Static IP: 10.1.50.1 Default gateway: 10.1.50.254
PC-B	N/A	DHCP
PC-C	N/A	Static IP: 10.1.80.100 Default gateway: 10.1.80.1

Step 3: Configure SRV1.

a. Configure SRV1 with static IP address 10.1.50.1/24 and default gateway 10.1.50.254.

Step 4: Release and renew the DHCP lease on PC-B.

a. Ensure that PC-B is configured as a DHCP client in the OFFICE VLAN.

b   After loading all TT-A device configuration files, issue the `ipconfig /release` and `ipconfig /renew` commands on PC-B.

Step 5: Outline the troubleshooting approach and validation steps.

Use this space to identify your troubleshooting approach and the key steps to verify that the problem is resolved. Troubleshooting approaches to select from include the follow-the-path, spot-the-differences, bottom-up, top-down, divide-and-conquer, shoot-from-the-hip, and move-the-problem methods.

Note: In addition to a specific approach, you can use the generic troubleshooting process described at the beginning of Section 2 of this lab.

_____

_____

_____

_____

_____

_____

Step 6: Record the troubleshooting process and configuration changes.

Note: Section 2 of this lab includes useful commands and examples of output.

Use this log to document your actions and results during the troubleshooting process. List the commands you used to gather information. As you progress, record what you think the problem might be and the actions you take to correct the problem.

Device	Actions and Results

Device	Actions and Results

Step 7: Document trouble ticket debrief notes.

Use this space to make notes of the key learning points that you picked up during the discussion of this trouble ticket with your instructor. The notes can include problems encountered, solutions applied, useful commands employed, alternate solutions, methods, and processes, and procedure and communication improvements.

_____

_____

_____

_____

_____

_____

_____

Task 2: Trouble Ticket Lab 9-2 TT-B

Step 1: Review trouble ticket Lab 9-2 TT-B.

As another control plane security measure, your company has decided to implement MD5 authentication between EIGRP routers and Layer 3 switches. As a pilot, a colleague of yours configured MD5 authentication on Layer 3 switch DLS2 and router R3. Now branch office users on the R3 LAN (PC-C) cannot access SRV1 or the Internet. He has asked for your help in diagnosing and solving the problem.

Step 2: Load the device trouble ticket configuration files for TT-B.

Using the procedure described in Lab 3-1, verify that the lab configuration files are present in flash. Load the proper configuration files as indicated in the Device Configuration File table.

Note: The following device access methods are in effect after loading the configuration files:

- Console access requires no username or password.

- Telnet and SSH require username **admin** and password **adminpa55**.

- The enable password is **ciscoenpa55**.

Device Configuration File Table

Device Name	File to Load	Notes
ALS1	Lab92-ALS1-TT-B-Cfg.txt	
DLS1	Lab92-DLS1-TT-B-Cfg.txt	
DLS2	Lab92-DLS2-TT-B-Cfg.txt	
R1	Lab92-R1-TT-B-Cfg.txt	
R2	Lab92-R2-TT-B-Cfg.txt	
R3	Lab92-R3-TT-B-Cfg.txt	
SRV1	N/A	Static IP: 10.1.50.1 Default gateway: 10.1.50.254
PC-B	N/A	DHCP
PC-C	N/A	Static IP: 10.1.80.100 Default gateway: 10.1.80.1

Step 3: Configure SRV1.

Configure SRV1 with static IP address 10.1.50.1/24 and default gateway 10.1.50.254.

Step 4: Configure a static IP address on PC-C.

Configure PC-C with static IP address 10.1.80.100, subnet mask 255.255.255.0, and default gateway 10.1.80.1.

Step 5: Outline the troubleshooting approach and validation steps.

Use this space to identify your troubleshooting approach and the key steps to verify that the problem is resolved. Troubleshooting approaches to select from include the follow-the-path, spot-the-differences, bottom-up, top-down, divide-and-conquer, shoot-from-the-hip, and move-the-problem methods.

Note: In addition to a specific approach, you can use the generic troubleshooting process described at the beginning of Section 2 of this lab.

_____

_____

_____

_____

_____

_____

Step 6: Record the troubleshooting process and configuration changes.

Note: Section 2 of this lab includes useful commands and examples of output.

Use this log to document your actions and results during the troubleshooting process. List the commands you used to gather information. As you progress, record what you think the problem might be and the actions you take to correct the problem.

Device	Actions and Results

Step 7: Document trouble ticket debrief notes.

Use this space to make notes of the key learning points that you picked up during the discussion of this trouble ticket with your instructor. The notes can include problems encountered, solutions applied, useful commands employed, alternate solutions, methods, and processes, and procedure and communication improvements.

_____

_____

_____

_____

_____

_____

Section 2 Troubleshooting Reference Information

General Troubleshooting Process

As a general guideline, you can use the following general troubleshooting process described in the course.

1. Define the problem (symptoms).

2. Gather information.

3. Analyze the information.

4. Propose a hypothesis (possible cause).

5. Test the hypothesis.

6. Eliminate or accept the hypothesis.

7. Solve the problem.

8. Document the problem.

Command Summary

The table lists useful commands for this lab. The sample output is shown on following pages.

Command	Key Information Displayed
`show ip dhcp snooping`	Displays snooping status (enabled or not) and, if enabled, on which VLANs. Also shows which interfaces are trusted.
`debug ip dhcp snooping packet`	Displays real-time information on DHCP snooping activity and the client/server exchange.
`debug ip dhcp server packet`	Displays real-time information on DHCP on the client/ server exchange from the server perspective.
`show ip eigrp neighbors`	Displays the IP address of EIGRP neighbors and the interface on which they were learned.
`sh ip eigrp interfaces`	Displays all interfaces participating in EIGRP for each AS and the number of peers associated with each interface.
`show ip eigrp interfaces detail`	Displays all interfaces participating in EIGRP for each AS along with the number of peers, hello interval, and the type of authentication (if configured).
`debug eigrp packets`	Displays real-time information on types of EIGRP packets exchange, which include authentication information.

Sample Troubleshooting Output

DHCP Snooping-related Commands

The following commands and outputs are provided as samples from the devices in this lab.

```
ALS1#show ip dhcp snooping
Switch DHCP snooping is enabled
DHCP snooping is configured on following VLANs:
10
DHCP snooping is operational on following VLANs:
10
DHCP snooping is configured on the following L3 Interfaces:
```

```
Insertion of option 82 is enabled
   circuit-id format: vlan-mod-port
    remote-id format: MAC
Option 82 on untrusted port is not allowed
Verification of hwaddr field is enabled
Verification of giaddr field is enabled
DHCP snooping trust/rate is configured on the following Interfaces:

Interface                    Trusted    Rate limit (pps)
-----------------------      -------    ----------------
FastEthernet0/1              yes        unlimited
FastEthernet0/2              yes        unlimited
FastEthernet0/3              yes        unlimited
FastEthernet0/4              yes        unlimited
Port-channel1                yes        unlimited
Port-channel2                yes        unlimited
```

In the above example, DHCP snooping is operational on ALS1 VLAN 10, and Fa0/1 through Fa0/4 (port channels Po1 and Po2) are trusted.

```
DLS1#show ip dhcp snooping
Switch DHCP snooping is disabled
DHCP snooping is configured on following VLANs:
none
DHCP snooping is operational on following VLANs:
none
DHCP snooping is configured on the following L3 Interfaces:

Insertion of option 82 is enabled
   circuit-id format: vlan-mod-port
    remote-id format: MAC
Option 82 on untrusted port is not allowed
Verification of hwaddr field is enabled
Verification of giaddr field is enabled
DHCP snooping trust/rate is configured on the following Interfaces:

Interface                    Trusted    Rate limit (pps)
-----------------------      -------    ----------------
```

In the above example, Option 82 on untrusted port is not allowed, and no interfaces are trusted.

```
ALS1#debug ip dhcp snooping packet
DHCP Snooping Packet debugging is on
ALS1#
*Mar  1 09:04:48.215: DHCPSNOOP(hlfm_set_if_input): Setting if_input to Fa0/18 f
or pak.  Was not set
*Mar  1 09:04:48.215: DHCPSNOOP(hlfm_set_if_input): Clearing if_input for pak.
Was Fa0/18
*Mar  1 09:04:48.215: DHCPSNOOP(hlfm_set_if_input): Setting if_input to Fa0/18 f
or pak.  Was not set
*Mar  1 09:04:48.215: DHCP_SNOOPING: received new DHCP packet from input interfa
ce (FastEthernet0/18)
*Mar  1 09:04:48.215: DHCP_SNOOPING: process new DHCP packet, message type: DHCP
DISCOVER, input interface: Fa0/18, MAC da: ffff.ffff.ffff, MAC sa: 000b.db04.a5cd,
IP da: 255.255.255.255
, IP sa: 0.0.0.0, DHCP ciaddr: 0.0.0.0, DHCP yiaddr: 0.0.0.0, DHCP siaddr: 0.0.0
.0, DHCP giaddr: 0.0.0.0, DHCP chaddr: 000b.db04.a5cd
```

```
*Mar  1 09:04:48.215: DHCP_SNOOPING: add relay information option.
*Mar  1 09:04:48.215: DHCP_SNOOPING_SW: Encoding opt82 CID in vlan-mod-port form
at
*Mar  1 09:04:48.215: DHCP_SNOOPING_SW: Encoding opt82 RID in MAC address format

*Mar  1 09:04:48.215: DHCP_SNOOPING: binary dump of relay info option, length: 20
data:
0x52 0x12 0x1 0x6 0x0 0x4 0x0 0xA 0x1 0x12 0x2 0x8 0x0 0x6 0x0 0x1B 0xC 0x6D 0x8
F 0x0
*Mar  1 09:04:48.215: DHCP_SNOOPING_SW: bridge packet get invalid mat entry: FFF
F.FFFF.FFFF, packet is flooded to ingress VLAN: (10)
ALS1#
```

In the above example, a DHCP DISCOVER message with option 82 and GIADDR of 0.0.0.0 was sent to DLS1 but, because DLS1 does not trust this relay information a reply was not received from the DLS1 DHCP server.

```
ALS1#debug ip dhcp snooping packet
DHCP Snooping Packet debugging is on
ALS1#
*Mar  1 09:10:36.904: DHCPSNOOP(hlfm_set_if_input): Setting if_input to Fa0/18 f
or pak.  Was not set
*Mar  1 09:10:36.904: DHCPSNOOP(hlfm_set_if_input): Clearing if_input for pak.
Was Fa0/18
*Mar  1 09:10:36.904: DHCPSNOOP(hlfm_set_if_input): Setting if_input to Fa0/18 f
or pak.  Was not set
*Mar  1 09:10:36.904: DHCP_SNOOPING: received new DHCP packet from input interfa
ce (FastEthernet0/18)
*Mar  1 09:10:36.904: DHCP_SNOOPING: process new DHCP packet, message type: DHCP
DISCOVER, input interface: Fa0/18, MAC da: ffff.ffff.ffff, MAC sa: 000b.db04.a5cd,
IP da: 255.255.255.255
, IP sa: 0.0.0.0, DHCP ciaddr: 0.0.0.0, DHCP yiaddr: 0.0.0.0, DHCP siaddr: 0.0.0
.0, DHCP giaddr: 0.0.0.0, DHCP chaddr: 000b.db04.a5cd
*Mar  1 09:10:36.904: DHCP_SNOOPING: add relay information option.
*Mar  1 09:10:36.904: DHCP_SNOOPING_SW: Encoding opt82 CID in vlan-mod-port form
at
*Mar  1 09:10:36.904: DHCP_SNOOPING_SW: Encoding opt82 RID in MAC address format

*Mar  1 09:10:36.904: DHCP_SNOOPING: binary dump of relay info option, length: 20
data:
0x52 0x12 0x1 0x6 0x0 0x4 0x0 0xA 0x1 0x12 0x2 0x8 0x0 0x6 0x0 0x1B 0xC 0x6D 0x8
F 0x0
*Mar  1 09:10:36.904: DHCP_SNOOPING_SW: bridge packet get invalid mat entry: FFF
F.FFFF.FFFF, packet is flooded to ingress VLAN: (10)
*Mar  1 09:10:36.912: DHCPSNOOP(hlfm_set_if_input): Setting if_input to Po1 for
pak.  Was not set
*Mar  1 09:10:36.912: DHCPSNOOP(hlfm_set_if_input): Clearing if_input for pak.
Was Po1
*Mar  1 09:10:36.912: DHCPSNOOP(hlfm_set_if_input): Setting if_input to Po1 for pak.
Was not set
*Mar  1 09:10:36.912: DHCP_SNOOPING: received new DHCP packet from input interfa
ce (Port-channel1)
*Mar  1 09:10:36.912: DHCP_SNOOPING: process new DHCP packet, message type: DHCP
OFFER, input interface: Po1, MAC da: ffff.ffff.ffff, MAC sa: 0017.5a5b.b443, IP
da: 255.255.255.255, IP sa: 10.1.10.252, DHCP ciaddr: 0.0.0.0, DHCP yiaddr: 10.1
.10.1, DHCP siaddr: 0.0.0.0, DHCP giaddr: 0.0.0.0, DHCP chaddr: 000b.db04.a5cd
*Mar  1 09:10:36.912: DHCP_SNOOPING: binary dump of option 82, length:
```

```
ALS1#20 data:
0x52 0x12 0x1 0x6 0x0 0x4 0x0 0xA 0x1 0x12 0x2 0x8 0x0 0x6 0x0 0x1B 0xC 0x6D 0x8
F 0x0
*Mar  1 09:10:36.912: DHCP_SNOOPING: binary dump of extracted circuit id, length
: 8 data:
0x1 0x6 0x0 0x4 0x0 0xA 0x1 0x12
*Mar  1 09:10:36.912: DHCP_SNOOPING: binary dump of extracted remote id, length:
 10 data:
0x2 0x8 0x0 0x6 0x0 0x1B 0xC 0x6D 0x8F 0x0
*Mar  1 09:10:36.912: DHCP_SNOOPING_SW: opt82 data indicates local packet
*Mar  1 09:10:36.912: DHCP_SNOOPING: remove relay information option.
*Mar
ALS1# 1 09:10:36.912: DHCP_SNOOPING: direct forward dhcp reply to output port: F
astEthernet0/18.
*Mar  1 09:10:36.912: DHCPSNOOP(hlfm_set_if_input): Setting if_input to Fa0/18 f
or pak.  Was not set
*Mar  1 09:10:36.912: DHCPSNOOP(hlfm_set_if_input): Clearing if_input for pak.
Was Fa0/18
*Mar  1 09:10:36.912: DHCPSNOOP(hlfm_set_if_input): Setting if_input to Fa0/18 f
or pak.  Was not set
*Mar  1 09:10:36.912: DHCP_SNOOPING: received new DHCP packet from input interfa
ce (FastEthernet0/18)
*Mar  1 09:10:36.91
ALS1#2: DHCP_SNOOPING: process new DHCP packet, message type: DHCPREQUEST, input
 interface: Fa0/18, MAC da: ffff.ffff.ffff, MAC sa: 000b.db04.a5cd, IP da: 255.2
55.255.255, IP sa: 0.0.0.0, DHCP ciaddr: 0.0.0.0, DHCP yiaddr: 0.0.0.0, DHCP sia
ddr: 0.0.0.0, DHCP giaddr: 0.0.0.0, DHCP chaddr: 000b.db04.a5cd
*Mar  1 09:10:36.912: DHCP_SNOOPING: add relay information option.
*Mar  1 09:10:36.912: DHCP_SNOOPING_SW: Encoding opt82 CID in vlan-mod-port form
at
*Mar  1 09:10:36.912: DHCP_SNOOPING_SW: Encoding opt82 RID
ALS1#in MAC address format
*Mar  1 09:10:36.912: DHCP_SNOOPING: binary dump of relay info option, length: 2
0 data:
0x52 0x12 0x1 0x6 0x0 0x4 0x0 0xA 0x1 0x12 0x2 0x8 0x0 0x6 0x0 0x1B 0xC 0x6D 0x8
F 0x0
*Mar  1 09:10:36.921: DHCP_SNOOPING_SW: bridge packet get invalid mat entry: FFF
F.FFFF.FFFF, packet is flooded to ingress VLAN: (10)
*Mar  1 09:10:36.921: DHCPSNOOP(hlfm_set_if_input): Setting if_input to Po1 for
pak.  Was not set
*Mar  1 09:10:36.921: DHCPSNOOP(hlfm_set_if_input): Clearing if_input for pak.
ALS1#  Was Po1
*Mar  1 09:10:36.921: DHCPSNOOP(hlfm_set_if_input): Setting if_input to Po1 for
pak.  Was not set
*Mar  1 09:10:36.921: DHCP_SNOOPING: received new DHCP packet from input interfa
ce (Port-channel1)
*Mar  1 09:10:36.921: DHCP_SNOOPING: process new DHCP packet, message type: DHCP
ACK, input interface: Po1, MAC da: ffff.ffff.ffff, MAC sa: 0017.5a5b.b443, IP da
: 255.255.255.255, IP sa: 10.1.10.252, DHCP ciaddr: 0.0.0.0, DHCP yiaddr: 10.1.1
0.1, DHCP siaddr: 0.0.0.0, DHCP giaddr: 0.0.0.0, DHCP chaddr:
ALS1# 000b.db04.a5cd
*Mar  1 09:10:36.921: DHCP_SNOOPING: binary dump of option 82, length: 20 data:
0x52 0x12 0x1 0x6 0x0 0x4 0x0 0xA 0x1 0x12 0x2 0x8 0x0 0x6 0x0 0x1B 0xC 0x6D 0x8
F 0x0
*Mar  1 09:10:36.921: DHCP_SNOOPING: binary dump of extracted circuit id, length
: 8 data:
0x1 0x6 0x0 0x4 0x0 0xA 0x1 0x12
*Mar  1 09:10:36.921: DHCP_SNOOPING: binary dump of extracted remote id, length:
```

```
 10 data:
0x2 0x8 0x0 0x6 0x0 0x1B 0xC 0x6D 0x8F 0x0
*Mar  1 09:10:36.921: DHCP_SNOOPING_SW: opt82 data indicates lo
ALS1#cal packet
*Mar  1 09:10:36.921: DHCP_SNOOPING_SW: opt82 data indicates local packet
*Mar  1 09:10:36.921: DHCP_SNOOPING: remove relay information option.
*Mar  1 09:10:36.921: DHCP_SNOOPING: direct forward dhcp reply to output port: F
astEthernet0/18.
ALS1#u all
All possible debugging has been turned off
ALS1#
```

In the above example, the **ip dhcp relay information trust-all** command was issued on DLS1. The DHCP DISCOVER message received on ALS1 interface Fa0/18 (from PC-B) and was forwarded to DLS1 to complete the DHCP exchange between PC-B and DLS1.

```
DLS1#debug ip dhcp server packet
DHCP server packet debugging is on.
Dec 11 14:14:25.024: DHCPD: Reload workspace interface Vlan10 tableid 0.
Dec 11 14:14:25.024: DHCPD: tableid for 10.1.10.252 on Vlan10 is 0
Dec 11 14:14:25.024: DHCPD: client's VPN is .
Dec 11 14:14:25.024: DHCPD: inconsistent relay information.
Dec 11 14:14:25.024: DHCPD: relay information option exists, but giaddr is zero
```

In the above example, with dhcp relay information from ALS1 and a GIADDR of 0.0.0.0, the relay information is inconsistent and DLS1 rejects the DHCP DISCOVER message from PC-B.

```
DLS1#debug ip dhcp server packet
DHCP server packet debugging is on.
Dec 11 14:28:13.118: DHCPD: Reload workspace interface Vlan10 tableid 0.
Dec 11 14:28:13.118: DHCPD: tableid for 10.1.10.252 on Vlan10 is 0
Dec 11 14:28:13.118: DHCPD: client's VPN is .
Dec 11 14:28:13.118: DHCPD: DHCPRELEASE message received from client 0100.0bdb.0
4a5.cd (10.1.10.1).
Dec 11 14:28:15.542: DHCPD: Reload workspace interface Vlan10 tableid 0.
Dec 11 14:28:15.542: DHCPD: tableid for 10.1.10.252 on Vlan10 is 0
Dec 11 14:28:15.542: DHCPD: client's VPN is .
Dec 11 14:28:15.542: DHCPD: using received relay info.
Dec 11 14:28:15.542: DHCPD: DHCPDISCOVER received from client 0100.0bdb.04a5.cd
on interface Vlan10.
Dec 11 14:28:15.542: DHCPD: using received relay info.
Dec 11 14:28:17.556: DHCPD: Sending DHCPOFFER to client 0100.0bdb.04a5.cd (10.1.
10.1).
Dec 11 14:28:17.556: DHCPD: Check for IPe on Vlan10
Dec 11 14:28:17.556: DHCPD: creating ARP entry (10.1.10.1, 000b.db04.a5cd).
Dec 11 14:28:17.556: DHCPD: unicasting BOOTREPLY to client 000b.db04.a5cd (10.1.
10.1).
Dec 11 14:28:17.556: DHCPD: Reload workspace interface Vlan10 tableid 0.
Dec 11 14:28:17.556: DHCPD: tableid for 10.1.10.252 on Vlan10 is 0
Dec 11 14:28:17.556: DHCPD: client's VPN is .
Dec 11 14:28:17.556: DHCPD: DHCPREQUEST received from client 0100.0bdb.04a5.cd.
Dec 11 14:28:17.556: DHCPD: Sending DHCPACK to client 0100.0bdb.04a5.cd (10.1.10
.1).
Dec 11 14:28:17.556: DHCPD: Check for IPe on Vlan10
Dec 11 14:28:17.556: DHCPD: creating ARP entry (10.1.10.1, 000b.db04.a5cd).
Dec 11 14:28:17.556: DHCPD: unicasting BOOTREPLY to client 000b.db04.a5cd (10.1.
```

`10.1).`

In the above example, with the `ip dhcp relay information trust-all` command issued on DLS1, the entire DHCP conversation between PC-B and the DLS1 server takes place, and PC-B is provided with an IP address.

EIGRP Authentication-related Commands

DLS2#`show ip eigrp neighbors`
```
EIGRP-IPv4:(1) neighbors for process 1
H   Address                  Interface       Hold Uptime   SRTT   RTO  Q   Seq
                                             (sec)         (ms)        Cnt Num
1   10.1.2.14                Fa0/5           13 00:20:59   1      200  0   29
0   10.1.200.252             Vl200           14 05:31:25   2      200  0   45
```

In the above example, DLS2 has two EIGRP neighbors, R3 (10.1.2.14) via Fa0/5 and DLS1 (10.1.200.252) via VLAN 200.

DLS2#`show ip eigrp interfaces`
```
EIGRP-IPv4:(1) interfaces for process 1

                    Xmit Queue   Mean  Pacing Time  Multicast    Pending
Interface    Peers  Un/Reliable  SRTT  Un/Reliable  Flow Timer   Routes
Vl200        1      0/0          2     0/1          50           0
Fa0/5        1      0/0          1     0/1          50           0
```

In the above example, DLS2 has two interfaces participating in the EIGRP process, VLAN 200 and Fa0/5. Both interfaces have a peer attached.

DLS2#`show ip eigrp interfaces detail`
```
EIGRP-IPv4:(1) interfaces for process 1

                    Xmit Queue   Mean  Pacing Time  Multicast    Pending
Interface    Peers  Un/Reliable  SRTT  Un/Reliable  Flow Timer   Routes
Vl200        1      0/0          1     0/1          50           0
  Hello interval is 5 sec
  Next xmit serial <none>
  Un/reliable mcasts: 0/18  Un/reliable ucasts: 22/9
  Mcast exceptions: 1  CR packets: 1  ACKs suppressed: 1
  Retransmissions sent: 1  Out-of-sequence rcvd: 0
  Topology-ids on interface - 0
  Authentication mode is not set

Fa0/5        0      0/0          0     0/1          50           0
  Hello interval is 5 sec
  Next xmit serial <none>
  Un/reliable mcasts: 0/18  Un/reliable ucasts: 9/25
  Mcast exceptions: 2  CR packets: 2  ACKs suppressed: 3
  Retransmissions sent: 6  Out-of-sequence rcvd: 1
  Topology-ids on interface - 0
  Authentication mode is md5,  key-chain is "EIGRPCHAIN"
```

In the above example, no authentication is configured on DLS2 interface VLAN 200. MD5 authentication is configured on interface Fa0/5 using key chain EIGRPCHAIN.

DLS2#`debug eigrp packets`

```
EIGRP Packets debugging is on
    (UPDATE, REQUEST, QUERY, REPLY, HELLO, IPXSAP, PROBE, ACK, STUB, SIAQUERY,
SIAREPLY)
DLS2#
Dec 14 18:21:51.626: EIGRP: Sending HELLO on FastEthernet0/5
Dec 15 18:21:51.626:   AS 1, Flags 0x0, Seq 0/0 interfaceQ 0/0 iidbQ un/rely 0/0
Dec 15 18:21:51.895: EIGRP: FastEthernet0/5: ignored packet from 10.1.2.14, opcode =
5 (missing authentication)
Dec 15 18:21:52.255: EIGRP: Sending HELLO on Vlan200
Dec 15 18:21:52.255:   AS 1, Flags 0x0, Seq 0/0 interfaceQ 0/0 iidbQ un/rely 0/0
Dec 15 18:21:54.495: EIGRP: Received HELLO on Vlan200 nbr 10.1.200.252
Dec 15 18:21:54.495:   AS 1, Flags 0x0, Seq 0/0 interfaceQ 0/0 iidbQ un/rely 0/0
 peerQ un/rely 0/0

DLS2#debug eigrp packets
EIGRP Packets debugging is on
    (UPDATE, REQUEST, QUERY, REPLY, HELLO, IPXSAP, PROBE, ACK, STUB, SIAQUERY,
SIAREPLY)

Dec 15 18:28:38.442: EIGRP: Sending UPDATE on FastEthernet0/5 tid 0
Dec 15 18:28:38.442:   AS 1, Flags 0x2, Seq 21/0 interfaceQ 2/0 iidbQ un/rely 0/
0 serno 1-10
Dec 15 18:28:38.442: EIGRP: received packet with MD5 authentication, key id = 1
Dec 15 18:28:38.442: EIGRP: Received HELLO on FastEthernet0/5 nbr 10.1.2.14
```

In the first debug example above, authentication is configured on DLS2 Fa0/5. However, it is not configured on R3 Fa0/1, and DLS2 ignores packets from R3. No authentication is required on VLAN 200, so DLS2 is able to send and receive hello messages with DLS1.

In the second debug example above, authentication is now configured on R3 Fa0/1, and DLS2 accepts hello packets from R3.

```
R3#show ip route
Codes: C - connected, S - static, R - RIP, M - mobile, B - BGP
       D - EIGRP, EX - EIGRP external, O - OSPF, IA - OSPF inter area
       N1 - OSPF NSSA external type 1, N2 - OSPF NSSA external type 2
       E1 - OSPF external type 1, E2 - OSPF external type 2
       i - IS-IS, su - IS-IS summary, L1 - IS-IS level-1, L2 - IS-IS level-2
       ia - IS-IS inter area, * - candidate default, U - per-user static route
       o - ODR, P - periodic downloaded static route

Gateway of last resort is 10.1.2.13 to network 0.0.0.0

     10.0.0.0/8 is variably subnetted, 9 subnets, 3 masks
D       10.1.10.0/24 [90/28416] via 10.1.2.13, 00:01:43, FastEthernet0/1
C       10.1.2.12/30 is directly connected, FastEthernet0/1
D       10.1.2.0/30 [90/30976] via 10.1.2.13, 00:01:43, FastEthernet0/1
D       10.1.30.0/24 [90/28416] via 10.1.2.13, 00:01:43, FastEthernet0/1
D       10.1.20.0/24 [90/28416] via 10.1.2.13, 00:01:43, FastEthernet0/1
D       10.1.50.0/24 [90/28416] via 10.1.2.13, 00:01:43, FastEthernet0/1
D       10.1.100.0/24 [90/28416] via 10.1.2.13, 00:01:43, FastEthernet0/1
C       10.1.203.1/32 is directly connected, Loopback0
D       10.1.200.0/24 [90/28416] via 10.1.2.13, 00:01:43, FastEthernet0/1
D    192.168.1.0/24 [90/158976] via 10.1.2.13, 00:01:43, FastEthernet0/1
D*EX 0.0.0.0/0 [170/2175232] via 10.1.2.13, 00:01:43, FastEthernet0/1
```

In the above example, all expected routes are present in the R3 routing table. This does not prove that authentication is occurring. However, it does indicate that either authentication is configured correctly for both adjacent interfaces, or it is not configured at all for both adjacent interfaces.

Reflection Questions

1. Which lab trouble tickets did you have the most difficulty with? _____

_____

_____

_____

2. Would you change anything about the process that you used for any of the trouble tickets now that you see the resolution of the problem? _____

_____

_____

_____

3. Which commands did you find most useful in diagnosing control plane security issues? Add these to your toolbox for future use. Which commands did you find least useful?

_____

_____

_____

References

If you need more information on the commands and their options, see the following references

*   IP Routing Protocol
    http://www.cisco.com/cisco/web/support/index.html

*   Cisco IOS IP Switching
    http://www.cisco.com/en/US/docs/ios/ipswitch/command/reference/isw_book.html

*   Configuring DHCP Features on a Cisco 2960 Switch http://www.cisco.com/en/US/docs/switches/lan/
    catalyst2960/software/release/12.2_37_se/configuration/guide/swdhcp82.html

*   Configuring EIGRP Message Authentication http://www.cisco.com/en/US/tech/tk365/technologies_
    configuration_example09186a00807f5a63.shtml

Router Interface Summary Table

Router Interface Summary				
Router Model	Ethernet Interface #1	Ethernet Interface #2	Serial Interface #1	Serial Interface #2
1700	Fast Ethernet 0 (FA0)	Fast Ethernet 1 (FA1)	Serial 0 (S0)	Serial 1 (S1)
1800	Fast Ethernet 0/0 (FA0/0)	Fast Ethernet 0/1 (FA0/1)	Serial 0/0/0 (S0/0/0)	Serial 0/0/1 (S0/0/1)
2600	Fast Ethernet 0/0 (FA0/0)	Fast Ethernet 0/1 (FA0/1)	Serial 0/0 (S0/0)	Serial 0/1 (S0/1)
2800	Fast Ethernet 0/0 (FA0/0)	Fast Ethernet 0/1 (FA0/1)	Serial 0/0/0 (S0/0/0)	Serial 0/0/1 (S0/0/1)
Note: To find out how the router is configured, look at the interfaces to identify the type of router and how many interfaces the router has. Rather than try to list all the combinations of configurations for each router class, this table includes identifiers for the possible combinations of Ethernet and serial interfaces in the device. The table does not include any other type of interface, even though a specific router might contain one. An example of this is an ISDN BRI interface. The string in parenthesis is the legal abbreviation that can be used in Cisco IOS commands to represent the interface.				

Lab 9-3, Data Plane Security

Lab Topology

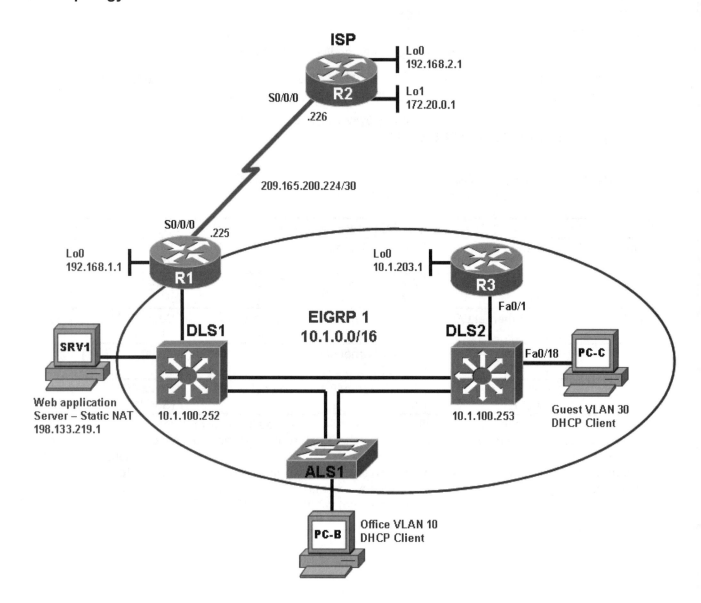

Objectives

- Load the device configuration files for each trouble ticket.
- Diagnose and resolve problems related to router and switch data plane security.
- Document the troubleshooting progress, configuration changes, and problem resolution.

Background

Routers and Layer 3 switches are typically segmented into three planes of operation, each with a clearly identified objective. The data plane (also called the forwarding plane) forwards user data packets. The control plane routes data correctly. The management plane provides administrative access to network devices.

The data plane encompasses all "customer" application traffic. Customer traffic refers to traffic generated by hosts, clients, servers, and applications that are intended to use the network for the purpose of transport only. Data plane traffic should never have destination IP addresses that belong to any networking devices (routers or switches). Instead, data plane traffic should be sourced from and destined to other devices, such as PCs and servers, that are supported by the network. The primary job of the router or Layer 3 switch is to forward these packets downstream as quickly as possible. Routers and switches can inspect and filter traffic as part of the implementation of a security policy.

Examples of security features implemented on the data plane include ACLs, NAT, firewalls, IPS, switch port security, VLAN ACLs (VACLs), IP Source Guard, private VLANs, Storm Control, and VPNs.

This lab focuses on data plane security issues related to Cisco IOS stateful firewalls and VLAN ACLs for routers and Layer 3 switches.

For each task or trouble ticket, the trouble scenario and problem symptom are described. While troubleshooting, you will discover the cause of the problem, correct it, and then document the process and results.

Lab Structure

This lab is divided into two main sections.

Section 1—Trouble Tickets and Troubleshooting Logs

This section includes two tasks. Each task is associated with a trouble ticket (TT) and introduces one or more errors on one or more devices. If time is a consideration, each task or trouble ticket can be performed independently.

Section 2—Troubleshooting Reference Information

This section provides general troubleshooting information that can be applied to any of the trouble tickets in this lab. Examples of useful commands and output are provided. If time permits, it is recommended that you read through Section 2 prior to starting on the trouble tickets.

Note: This lab uses Cisco 1841 routers with Cisco IOS Release 12.4(24)T1 and the Advanced IP Services image c1841-advipservicesk9-mz.124-24.T1.bin. The switches are Cisco WS-C2960-24TT-L with the Cisco IOS image c2960-lanbasek9-mz.122-46.SE.bin and Catalyst 3560-24PS with the Cisco IOS image c3560-advipservicesk9-mz.122-46.SE.bin. Other routers (such as 2801 and 2811), switches (such as 2950 or 3550), and Cisco IOS Software versions can be used if they have comparable capabilities and features. Depending on the router or switch model and Cisco IOS Software version, the commands available and output produced might vary from what is shown in this lab.

Any changes made to configurations or topology (other than errors introduced) are noted in the lab and trouble tickets so that you are aware of them prior to beginning the troubleshooting process.

Required Resources

- 3 routers (Cisco 1841 with Cisco IOS Release 12.4(24)T1 Advanced IP Service or comparable)

- 1 switch (Cisco 2960 with the Cisco IOS Release 12.2(46)SE C2960-LANBASEK9-M image or comparable)

- 2 switches (Cisco 3560 with the Cisco IOS Release 12.2(46)SE C3560-LANBASEK9-M image or comparable)

- SRV1 (Windows PC with static IP address) with TFTP and syslog servers plus an SSH client (PuTTY or comparable) and WireShark software

- PC-B (Windows PC DHCP client) with PuTTY and WireShark software

- PC-C (Windows PC DHCP client) with PuTTY and WireShark software

- Serial and Ethernet cables

Section 1—Trouble Tickets and Troubleshooting Logs

Task 1: Trouble Ticket Lab 9-3 TT-A

Step 1: Review trouble ticket Lab 9-3 TT-A.

As a security measure, your company has decided to implement stateful packet inspection using a Cisco IOS firewall on edge router R1. The firewall will allow traffic from external hosts only if it is a response to a legitimate request from an internal host. The only exception is that Internet access to the internal SRV1 web-based application will be allowed. Internal users should be able to access the Internet (simulated by Lo1 on R2) using various protocols, such as ICMP, FTP, Telnet, DNS, and HTTP. The firewall implementation must work in conjunction with the dynamic NAT currently being employed on R1. In addition, internal network devices must be able to obtain the correct time from the ISP (R2).

You colleague has configured the firewall and the necessary access lists on R1. However, users on the office VLAN cannot access Internet websites, and remote users on the Internet cannot access the web-based application on SRV1. Your colleague has asked for your help in diagnosing and solving the problem.

Step 2: Load the device trouble ticket configuration files for TT-A.

Using the procedure described in Lab 3-1, verify that the lab configuration files are present in flash. Load the proper configuration files as indicated in the Device Configuration File table.

Note: The following device access methods are in effect after loading the configuration files:

- Console access requires no username or password.

- Telnet and SSH require username **admin** and password **adminpa55**.

- The enable password is **ciscoenpa55**.

Device Configuration File Table

Device Name	File to Load	Notes
ALS1	Lab93-ALS1-TT-A-Cfg.txt	
DLS1	Lab93-DLS1-TT-A-Cfg.txt	
DLS2	Lab93-DLS2-TT-A-Cfg.txt	
R1	Lab93-R1-TT-A-Cfg.txt	
R2	Lab93-R2-TT-A-Cfg.txt	
R3	Lab93-R3-TT-A-Cfg.txt	
SRV1	N/A	Static IP: 10.1.50.1 Default gateway: 10.1.50.254
PC-B	N/A	DHCP
PC-C	N/A	DHCP

Step 3: Configure SRV1.

Configure SRV1 with static IP address 10.1.50.1/24 and default gateway 10.1.50.254.

Step 4: Release and renew the DHCP lease on PC-B.

a. Ensure that PC-B is configured as a DHCP client in the OFFICE VLAN.

b. After loading all TT-A device configuration files, issue the `ipconfig /release` and `ipconfig /renew` commands on PC-B.

Step 5: Outline the troubleshooting approach and validation steps.

Use this space to identify your troubleshooting approach and the key steps to verify that the problem is resolved. Troubleshooting approaches to select from include the follow-the-path, spot-the-differences, bottom-up, top-down, divide-and-conquer, shoot-from-the-hip, and move-the-problem methods.

Note: In addition to a specific approach, you can use the generic troubleshooting process described at the beginning of Section 2 of this lab.

_____

_____

_____

_____

_____

_____

Step 6: Record the troubleshooting process and configuration changes.

Note: Section 2 of this lab includes useful commands and examples of output.

Use this log to document your actions and results during the troubleshooting process. List the commands you used to gather information. As you progress, record what you think the problem might be and the actions you take to correct the problem.

Device	Actions and Results

Device	Actions and Results

Step 7: Document trouble ticket debrief notes.

Use this space to make notes of the key learning points that you picked up during the discussion of this trouble ticket with the instructor. The notes can include problems encountered, solutions applied, useful commands employed, alternate solutions, methods, and processes, and procedure and communication improvements.

_____

_____

_____

_____

_____

_____

Task 2: Trouble Ticket Lab 9-3 TT-B

Step 1: Review trouble ticket Lab 9-3 TT-B.

In a continuing effort to improve network data plane security, your company has decided to limit access for users on the guest VLAN 30 subnet (10.1.30.0/24). Guest VLAN users should not have access to any Office VLAN 10 or Server VLAN 50 resources. In addition, it will be necessary to prevent guests from pinging internal network switches. Although they will not have access to internal resources, guest users must be able to access the Internet from VLAN 30. Guest user PCs are DHCP clients (simulated by PC-C) that connect to the network from Layer 3 core switch DLS2 and obtain their IP addresses from DLS1.

Your colleague has configured a VLAN access control list (VACL) on DLS2 to limit guest access. After the VACL implementation, guests are prevented from accessing Office VLAN and Server VLAN resources, as expected. However, guest users are unable to access the Internet (simulated by R2 Lo1). Your colleague has asked for your help in diagnosing and solving the problem.

Step 2: Load the device trouble ticket configuration files for TT-B.

Using the procedure described in Lab 3-1, verify that the lab configuration files are present in flash. Load the proper configuration files as indicated in the Device Configuration File table.

Note: The following device access methods are in effect after loading the configuration files:

- Console access requires no username or password.

- Telnet and SSH require username **admin** and password **adminpa55**.

- The enable password is **ciscoenpa55**.

Device Configuration File Table

Device Name	File to Load	Notes
ALS1	Lab93-ALS1-TT-B-Cfg.txt	
DLS1	Lab93-DLS1-TT-B-Cfg.txt	
DLS2	Lab93-DLS2-TT-B-Cfg.txt	
R1	Lab93-R1-TT-B-Cfg.txt	
R2	Lab93-R2-TT-B-Cfg.txt	
R3	Lab93-R3-TT-B-Cfg.txt	
SRV1	N/A	Static IP: 10.1.50.1 Default gateway: 10.1.50.254
PC-B	N/A	DHCP
PC-C	N/A	DHCP

Step 3: Configure SRV1.

Configure SRV1 with static IP address 10.1.50.1/24 and default gateway 10.1.50.254.

Step 4: Release and renew the DHCP lease on PC-C.

After loading all TT-B device configuration files, issue the `ipconfig /release` and `ipconfig /renew` commands on PC-C.

Step 5: Outline the troubleshooting approach and validation steps.

Use this space to identify your troubleshooting approach and the key steps to verify that the problem is resolved. Troubleshooting approaches to select from include the follow-the-path, spot-the-differences, bottom-up, top-down, divide-and-conquer, shoot-from-the-hip, and move-the-problem methods.

Note: In addition to a specific approach, you can use the generic troubleshooting process described at the beginning of Section 2 of this lab.

_____

_____

Step 6: Record the troubleshooting process and configuration changes.

Note: Section 2 of this lab includes useful commands and examples of output.

Use this log to document your actions and results during the troubleshooting process. List the commands you used to gather information. As you progress, record what you think the problem might be and the actions you take to correct the problem.

Device	Actions and Results

Step 7: Document trouble ticket debrief notes.

Use this space to make notes of the key learning points that you picked up during the discussion of this trouble ticket with the instructor. The notes can include problems encountered, solutions applied, useful commands employed, alternate solutions, methods, and processes, and procedure and communication improvements.

_____

_____

_____

_____

_____

Section 2 Troubleshooting Reference Information

General Troubleshooting Process

As a general guideline, you can use the following general troubleshooting process described in the course.

1. Define the problem (symptoms).

2. Gather information.

3. Analyze the information.

4. Propose a hypothesis (possible cause).

5. Test the hypothesis.

6. Eliminate or accept the hypothesis.

7. Solve the problem.

8. Document the problem.

Command Summary

The table lists useful commands for this lab. The sample output is shown on following pages.

Command	Key Information Displayed
`show ip inspect sessions`	Displays established sessions with the source IP address and port number, protocol name, and destination IP address and port number.
`show ip inspect config`	Displays inspection rule configuration information, including rule name, session parameters, and protocols being inspected.
`show ip inspect interfaces`	Displays interfaces configured for inspection and inbound/outbound inspection rules, if set, and inbound/outbound access lists, if applied. Also displays protocols being inspected.
`show access-lists` *ACL#/name*	Displays all ACLs configured on a device, including the ACL number and name, the type of ACL (standard or extended), the statements in each ACL, and the number of matches accumulated for each statement.
`show vlan access-map`	Displays the name of any configured VLAN access maps, including the match clauses in each. An implied **deny all** match clause is in effect at the end of the access map.
`show vlan filter`	Displays the name of any configured VLAN access maps and the VLANs for which they are filtering traffic.
`show clock`	Displays the time and date kept by the device internal clock.
`show ntp associations`	Displays the configured NTP server IP address, reference clock in use, stratum level, and sync status.
`show ntp status`	Displays the clock synchronization status, stratum level, and reference clock IP address. Also shows the number of seconds since the last update was received from the reference clock.

Sample Troubleshooting Output

The following commands and outputs are provided as samples from the devices in this lab.

Cisco IOS Stateful Firewall-related Commands

```
R1#show ip inspect sessions
Established Sessions
 Session 657D5B98 (10.1.10.1:8)=>(172.20.0.1:0) icmp SIS_OPEN
 Session 657D5608 (10.1.10.1:1041)=>(172.20.0.1:23) telnet SIS_OPEN
```

In the example above, PC-B (10.1.10.1) has established two sessions to R2 Lo1 through the firewall, one for ping (ICMP) and one for Telnet.

```
R1#show ip inspect config
Session audit trail is disabled
Session alert is enabled
one-minute (sampling period) thresholds are [unlimited : unlimited] connections
max-incomplete sessions thresholds are [unlimited : unlimited]
max-incomplete tcp connections per host is unlimited. Block-time 0 minute.
tcp synwait-time is 30 sec -- tcp finwait-time is 5 sec
tcp idle-time is 3600 sec -- udp idle-time is 30 sec
tcp reassembly queue length 16; timeout 5 sec; memory-limit 1024 kilo bytes
dns-timeout is 5 sec
Inspection Rule Configuration
 Inspection name FW-inspect
    ftp alert is on audit-trail is off timeout 3600
    http alert is on audit-trail is off timeout 3600
    smtp max-data 20000000 alert is on audit-trail is off timeout 3600
    tftp alert is on audit-trail is off timeout 30
    dns alert is on audit-trail is off timeout 30
    icmp alert is on audit-trail is off timeout 10
    telnet alert is on audit-trail is off timeout 3600
    http alert is on audit-trail is off timeout 3600
    ntp alert is on audit-trail is off timeout 30
```

In the example above, a stateful firewall rule named FW-inspect has been configured that inspects FTP, HTTP, SMTP, TFTP, DNS, ICMP, HTTP, NTP, and Telnet traffic.

```
R1#show ip inspect interfaces
Interface Configuration
 Interface Serial0/0/0
  Inbound inspection rule is not set
  Outgoing inspection rule is FW-inspect
    ftp alert is on audit-trail is off timeout 3600
    http alert is on audit-trail is off timeout 3600
    smtp max-data 20000000 alert is on audit-trail is off timeout 3600
    tftp alert is on audit-trail is off timeout 30
    dns alert is on audit-trail is off timeout 30
    icmp alert is on audit-trail is off timeout 10
    telnet alert is on audit-trail is off timeout 3600
  Inbound access list is FW-ACL
  Outgoing access list is not set
```

In the example above, an outgoing inspection rule named FW-inspect has been configured on S0/0/0, and an access list FW-ACL is applied inbound on S0/0/0.

The example below shows the use of the Cisco IOS help function to display a partial listing of the protocols that can be inspected.

```
R1(config)#ip inspect name FW-inspect ?
  802-11-iapp        IEEE 802.11 WLANs WG IAPP
  ace-svr            ACE Server/Propagation
  appfw              Application Firewall
  appleqtc           Apple QuickTime
  bgp                Border Gateway Protocol
  biff               Bliff mail notification
  bittorrent         bittorrent
  bootpc             Bootstrap Protocol Client
  bootps             Bootstrap Protocol Server
  cddbp              CD Database Protocol
  cifs               CIFS
  cisco-fna          Cisco FNATIVE
  cisco-net-mgmt     cisco-net-mgmt
  cisco-svcs         cisco license/perf/GDP/X.25/ident svcs
  cisco-sys          Cisco SYSMAINT
  cisco-tdp          Cisco TDP
  cisco-tna          Cisco TNATIVE
  citrix             Citrix IMA/ADMIN/RTMP
  citriximaclient    Citrix IMA Client
  clp                Cisco Line Protocol
  creativepartnr     Creative Partnr
  creativeserver     Creative Server
  cuseeme            CUSeeMe Protocol
  daytime            Daytime (RFC 867)
  dbase              dBASE Unix
  dbcontrol_agent    Oracle dbControl Agent po
  ddns-v3            Dynamic DNS Version 3
  dhcp-failover      DHCP Failover
  directconnect      Direct Connect Version 2.0
  discard            Discard port
  dns                Domain Name Server
  dnsix              DNSIX Securit Attribute Token Map
  echo               Echo port
  edonkey            eDonkey
  entrust-svc-hdlr   Entrust KM/Admin Service Handler
  entrust-svcs       Entrust sps/aaas/aams
  esmtp              Extended SMTP
  exec               Remote Process Execution
  fasttrack          FastTrack Traffic - KaZaA, Morpheus, Gro
  fcip-port          FCIP
  finger                 Finger
  fragment           IP fragment inspection
  ftp                File Transfer Protocol
  ftps               FTP over TLS/SSL
  gdoi               GDOI
  giop               Oracle GIOP/SSL
  gnutella           Gnutella Version2 Traffic - BearShare, S
  gopher             Gopher
  gtpv0              GPRS Tunneling Protocol Version 0
  gtpv1              GPRS Tunneling Protocol Version 1
  h323               H.323 Protocol (e.g, MS NetMeeting, Intel Video Phone)
  h323-annexe        H.323 Protocol AnnexE (e.g, MS NetMeetin
  h323-nxg           H.323 Protocol AnnexG
  hp-alarm-mgr       HP Performance data alarm manager
  hp-collector       HP Performance data collector
  hp-managed-node    HP Performance data managed node
  hsrp               Hot Standby Router Protocol
```

```
http                    HTTP Protocol
https                   Secure Hypertext Transfer Protocol
ica                     ica (Citrix)
icabrowser              icabrowser (Citrix)
icmp                    ICMP Protocol
<output omitted>
```

ACL-related Commands

```
R1#show access-lists
Standard IP access list 1
    10 permit 10.1.0.0, wildcard bits 0.0.255.255 (18 matches)

Extended IP access list FW-ACL
    10 deny ip any any (29 matches)
```

In the above example, two ACLs are configured on R1: a standard numbered ACL that identities internal NAT hosts, and an extended named ACL that blocks all traffic for a given direction (inbound or outbound). Statements in both are accumulating matches.

```
R1#show access-lists FW-ACL
Extended IP access list FW-ACL
    10 permit icmp any host 198.133.219.1 (13 matches)
    20 permit tcp any host 198.133.219.1 eq www
       30 permit udp host 192.168.2.1 host 192.168.1.1 eq ntp
    40 deny ip any any log (299 matches)
```

In the above example, a specific named ACL is displayed. Note the log option on the **deny ip any any** statement. The use of this option produces logged message output on the console and syslog server, similar to that shown below. In this example, an NTP packet (port 123) from R2 to R1 is being denied.

```
Dec 19 20:23:29.691: %SEC-6-IPACCESSLOGP: list FW-ACL denied udp 192.168.2.1(123) ->
192.168.1.1(123), 1 packet
```

VACL-related Commands

```
DLS2#show vlan access-map
Vlan access-map "BLOCK-GUEST"  10
  Match clauses:
    ip  address: GUEST-ACCESS-CTRL
  Action:
    drop
Vlan access-map "BLOCK-GUEST"  20
  Match clauses:
  Action:
    Forward
```

In the above example, access map BLOCK-GUEST has been configured with two match clauses. The first drops all traffic that matches the IP addresses specified in named ACL GUEST-ACCESS-CTRL. The second forwards all traffic that does not match the IP addresses specified in named ACL GUEST-ACCESS-CTRL. An implied **deny all** match clause is in effect at the end of the access map.

```
DLS2#show vlan filter
VLAN Map BLOCK-GUEST is filtering VLANs:
  30
```

In the above example, access map BLOCK-GUEST has been applied to VLAN 30 and is filtering traffic.

NAT-related Commands

```
R1#show ip nat translations
Pro Inside global       Inside local      Outside local       Outside global
icmp 198.133.219.20:512 10.1.10.1:512     172.20.0.1:512      172.20.0.1:512
tcp 198.133.219.20:1043 10.1.10.1:1043    172.20.0.1:23       172.20.0.1:23
tcp 198.133.219.20:1046 10.1.10.1:1046    172.20.0.1:80       172.20.0.1:80
--- 198.133.219.1       10.1.50.1         ---                 ---
udp 198.133.219.17:123 10.1.100.1:123     192.168.2.1:123     192.168.2.1:123
udp 198.133.219.18:123 10.1.100.252:123   192.168.2.1:123     192.168.2.1:123
udp 198.133.219.16:123 10.1.100.253:123   192.168.2.1:123     192.168.2.1:123
```

In the above example, PC-B (inside local 10.1.10.1) has initiated a ping (ICMP port 512), a Telnet session (TCP port 23), and a browser (HTTP) session (TCP port 80) to the external R2 Lo1 IP address 172.20.0.1. In addition, several internal devices have initiated NTP requests (UDP port 123) to NTP server R2 (192.168.2.1). Server SRV1 with IP address 10.1.50.1 has a NAT static mapping to public address 198.133.219.1.

NTP-related Commands

```
R2#show clock
*19:19:48.350 UTC Wed Dec 21 2009
```

```
R1#show ntp associations
  address         ref clock       st   when    poll reach  delay  offset    disp
~192.168.2.1      .INIT.          16   2258     256     0  0.000   0.000 15937.
 * sys.peer, # selected, + candidate, - outlyer, x falseticker, ~ configured
```

```
R1#show ntp associations
  address         ref clock       st   when    poll reach  delay  offset    disp
*~192.168.2.1     127.127.1.1      3      3      64   377  0.000  -0.393   3.038
 * sys.peer, # selected, + candidate, - outlyer, x falseticker, ~ configured
```

In the first example above, R1 is configured to contact the NTP server R2 at 192.168.2.1, but the reference clock is in the INIT state, and R1 has not peered with R2. In the second example, R1 has peered with the NTP server R2 at 192.168.2.1, and the reference clock is now R1's internal clock (127.127.1.1).

```
R1#show ntp status
Clock is unsynchronized, stratum 16, no reference clock
nominal freq is 250.0000 Hz, actual freq is 250.0002 Hz, precision is 2**24
reference time is CED4F227.B352D730 (18:08:39.700 UTC Thu Dec 17 2009)
clock offset is 0.0000 msec, root delay is 0.00 msec
root dispersion is 0.02 msec, peer dispersion is 0.00 msec
loopfilter state is 'CTRL' (Normal Controlled Loop), drift is -0.000000961 s/s
system poll interval is 64, last update was 2278 sec ago.
```

```
R1#show ntp status
Clock is synchronized, stratum 4, reference is 192.168.2.1
nominal freq is 250.0000 Hz, actual freq is 250.0002 Hz, precision is 2**24
reference time is CED63F93.9C972B04 (17:51:15.611 UTC Fri Dec 18 2009)
```

```
clock offset is -0.0003 msec, root delay is 0.01 msec
root dispersion is 0.00 msec, peer dispersion is 0.00 msec
loopfilter state is 'CTRL' (Normal Controlled Loop), drift is -0.000000977 s/s
system poll interval is 64, last update was 20 sec ago.
```

In the first example above, the R1 clock is unsynchronized, and there is no reference clock. The stratum level defaults to 16 (the highest) when no NTP server is reachable. The last update occurred before the firewall was applied and blocked NTP. In the second example, the R1 clock is synchronized, and the reference clock is R2 192.168.2.1. The stratum level is now 4. The last update occurred very recently after the firewall was adjusted to allow NTP.

Reflection Questions

1. Which lab trouble tickets did you have the most difficulty with? _____

_____

_____

_____

2. Would you change anything about the process that you used for any of the trouble tickets now that you see the resolution of the problem? _____

_____

_____

_____

3. Which commands did you find most useful in diagnosing data plane security issues? Add these to your toolbox for future use. Which commands did you find least useful?

_____

_____

_____

References

If you need more information on the commands and their options, see the following references:

- **IP Routing Protocol**

  http://www.cisco.com/cisco/web/support/index.html

- **Cisco IOS IP Switching**
  http://www.cisco.com/en/US/docs/ios/ipswitch/command/reference/isw_book.html

- **Configuring Cisco IOS Firewall with NAT** http://www.cisco.com/en/US/products/sw/secursw/ps1018/products_configuration_example09186a008009445f.shtml

- **Configuring VLAN ACLs (VACLs)** http://www.cisco.com/en/US/docs/routers/7600/ios/12.2SXF/configuration/guide/vacl.html#wp1039754

Router Interface Summary Table

Router Interface Summary				
Router Model	Ethernet Interface #1	Ethernet Interface #2	Serial Interface #1	Serial Interface #2
1700	Fast Ethernet 0 (FA0)	Fast Ethernet 1 (FA1)	Serial 0 (S0)	Serial 1 (S1)
1800	Fast Ethernet 0/0 (FA0/0)	Fast Ethernet 0/1 (FA0/1)	Serial 0/0/0 (S0/0/0)	Serial 0/0/1 (S0/0/1)
2600	Fast Ethernet 0/0 (FA0/0)	Fast Ethernet 0/1 (FA0/1)	Serial 0/0 (S0/0)	Serial 0/1 (S0/1)
2800	Fast Ethernet 0/0 (FA0/0)	Fast Ethernet 0/1 (FA0/1)	Serial 0/0/0 (S0/0/0)	Serial 0/0/1 (S0/0/1)

Note: To find out how the router is configured, look at the interfaces to identify the type of router and how many interfaces the router has. There is no way to effectively list all the combinations of configurations for each router class. This table includes identifiers for the possible combinations of Ethernet and Serial interfaces in the device. The table does not include any other type of interface, even though a specific router may contain one. An example of this might be an ISDN BRI interface. The string in parenthesis is the legal abbreviation that can be used in Cisco IOS commands to represent the interface.

Chapter 10 Review and Preparation for Troubleshooting Complex Enterprise Networks

Lab 10-1, Troubleshooting Complex Environments

Lab Topology

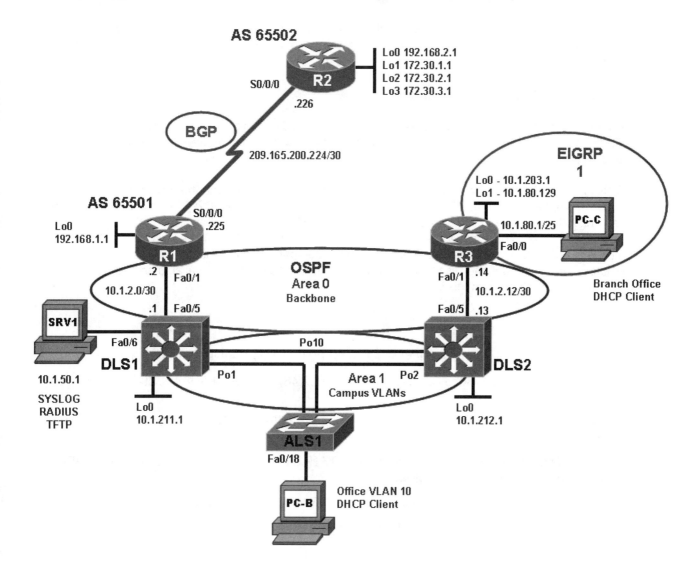

Objectives

- Load the device configuration files for each trouble ticket.

- Diagnose and resolve problems related to features, protocols, or technology that could be encountered in a complex, integrated enterprise network.

- Document the troubleshooting progress, configuration changes, and problem resolution.

Background

This lab covers a range of problems and requires that you make use of the troubleshooting skills acquired throughout this course to resolve the routing and switching problems introduced. These trouble tickets are based on scenarios from previous labs. This lab focuses on routing and switching connectivity issues related to EtherChannel, STP, OSPF, EIGRP, and ACLs.

For each task or trouble ticket, the trouble scenario and problem symptom are described. While troubleshooting, you will discover the cause of the problem, correct it, and then document the process and results.

Trouble Tickets and Troubleshooting Logs

This lab includes four tasks. Each task is associated with a trouble ticket (TT) and introduces one or more errors on one or more devices. If time is a consideration, each task or trouble ticket can be performed independently.

Troubleshooting Reference Information

A generic troubleshooting flow is provided for analysis. Suggested commands are provided for each trouble ticket. Refer to previous labs for specific troubleshooting flows, examples of additional commands and command output.

Note: This lab uses Cisco 1841 routers with Cisco IOS Release 12.4(24)T1 and the Advanced IP Services image c1841-advipservicesk9-mz.124-24.T1.bin. The switches are Cisco WS-C2960-24TT-L with the Cisco IOS image c2960-lanbasek9-mz.122-46.SE.bin and Catalyst 3560-24PS with the Cisco IOS image c3560-advipservicesk9-mz.122-46.SE.bin. Other routers (such as 2801 and 2811), switches (such as 2950 or 3550), and Cisco IOS Software versions can be used if they have comparable capabilities and features. Depending on the router or switch model and Cisco IOS Software version, the commands available and output produced might vary from what is shown in this lab.

Required Resources

- 3 routers (Cisco 1841 with Cisco IOS Release 12.4(24)T1 Advanced IP Service or comparable)

- 1 switch (Cisco 2960 with the Cisco IOS Release 12.2(46)SE C2960-LANBASEK9-M image or comparable)

- 2 switches (Cisco 3560 with the Cisco IOS Release 12.2(46)SE C3560-advipservicesk9-mz image or comparable)

- SRV1 (Windows PC with static IP address) with TFTP and syslog servers plus an SSH client (PuTTY or comparable) and WireShark software

- PC-B (Windows PC DHCP client) with PuTTY and WireShark software

- PC-C (Windows PC DHCP client) with PuTTY and WireShark software

- Serial and Ethernet cables

Section 1—Trouble Tickets and Troubleshooting Logs

Task 1: Trouble Ticket Lab 10-1 TT-A

Step 1: Review trouble ticket Lab 10-1 TT-A.

One of your colleagues mentioned that he had established a Telnet connection to switch ALS1 from PC-B and tested connectivity to server SRV1 via ping but was not successful. All switches in the network have a management address assigned, so he should be able to ping any device in the network. He asked for your help in determining the cause and resolving the issue.

Step 2: Load the device trouble ticket configuration files for TT-A.

Using the procedure described in Lab 3-1, verify that the lab configuration files are present in flash. Load the proper configuration files as indicated in the Device Configuration File table.

Note: The following device access methods are in effect after loading the configuration files:

*   Console access requires no username or password.

*   Telnet and SSH require username **admin** and password **adminpa55**.

*   The enable password is **ciscoenpa55**.

Device Configuration File Table

Device Name	File to Load	Notes
ALS1	Lab101-ALS1-TT-A-Cfg.txt	
DLS1	Lab101-DLS1-TT-A-Cfg.txt	
DLS2	Lab101-DLS2-TT-A-Cfg.txt	
R1	Lab101-R1-TT-A-Cfg.txt	
R2	Lab101-R2-TT-A-Cfg.txt	
R3	Lab101-R3-TT-A-Cfg.txt	
SRV1	N/A	Static IP: 10.1.50.1 Default gateway: 10.1.50.254
PC-B	N/A	DHCP
PC-C	N/A	DHCP

Step 3: Configure SRV1 and start the syslog and TFTP servers.

a. Configure SRV1 with the static IP address 10.1.50.1/24 and default gateway 10.1.50.254.

b. Start the syslog server on SRV1 to monitor console messages from multiple devices.

c. Start the TFTP server on SRV1 to record device configuration changes.

Step 4: Release and renew the DHCP lease on PC-B and PC-C.

a. Ensure that PC-B is configured as a DHCP client in the OFFICE VLAN.

b. Ensure that PC-C is configured as a DHCP client in the R3 branch office LAN.

c. After loading all TT-A device configuration files, issue the `ipconfig /release` and `ipconfig /renew` commands on PC-B and PC-C.

Step 5: Outline the troubleshooting approach and validation steps.

Use this space to identify your troubleshooting approach and the key steps to verify that the problem is resolved. Troubleshooting approaches to select from include the follow-the-path, spot-the-differences, bottom-up, top-down, divide-and-conquer, shoot-from-the-hip, and move-the-problem methods.

Note: In addition to a specific approach, you can use the generic troubleshooting process described at the beginning of Section 2 of this lab.

_____

_____

_____

_____

_____

_____

Step 6: Record the troubleshooting process and configuration changes.

Use this log to document your actions and results during the troubleshooting process. List the commands you used to gather information. As you progress, record what you think the problem might be and the actions you take to correct the problem.

Note: Refer to the table of commands following this log, which might be helpful in troubleshooting this problem. You can also refer to Lab 4-1 for sample troubleshooting flows and additional commands.

Device	Actions and Results

Device	Actions and Results

Command	Key Information Displayed
`show interfaces status`	Displays link status, speed, duplex, trunk or VLAN membership, and interface descriptions.
`show cdp neighbors [detail]`	Displays detailed information about a neighbor (or neighbors) including network address, enabled protocols, hold time, and software version.
`show spanning-tree vlan vlan#`	Displays all essential parameters that affect the topology, such as root port, designated ports, port state, and port type, as well as the spanning-tree mode implemented.
`show spanning-tree summary`	Displays the spanning-tree mode and the VLANs for which this switch is the root bridge. VLANs are listed along with the number of ports in various STP states.
`show vlan brief`	Displays an overview of all existing VLANs and the ports within them. Trunk ports are not listed.
`show vlan id vlan#`	Displays whether the VLAN exists and which ports are assigned to it. Includes which trunk ports that the VLAN is allowed on.
`show interfaces trunk`	Displays all trunk ports, the operational status, trunk encapsulation, and native VLAN, as well as the list of allowed VLANs, active VLANs, and the VLANs in Spanning Tree Forwarding state for the trunk.
`show interfaces type/# switchport`	Checks all VLAN-related parameters for a specific interface (access ports and trunk ports).
`show etherchannel summary`	Displays port channels, member ports, and flags indicating status.

Step 7: Document trouble ticket debrief notes.

Use this space to make notes of the key learning points that you picked up during the discussion of this trouble ticket with the instructor. The notes can include problems encountered, solutions applied, useful commands employed, alternate solutions, methods, and processes, and procedure and communication improvements.

_____

_____

_____

_____

_____

_____

Task 2: Trouble Ticket Lab 10-1 TT-B

Step 1: Review trouble ticket Lab 10-1 TT-B.

Many users on the network are experiencing problems when accessing the Internet. An office user who uses client PC-B reports that he cannot browse to a website at IP address 172.30.3.1 (simulated by R2 Lo3).

Your task is to restore connectivity from client PC-B to the Internet and ensure that the user can connect to 172.30.3.1 using ping or a web browser.

Step 2: Load the device trouble ticket configuration files for TT-B.

Using the procedure described in Lab 3-1, verify that the lab configuration files are present in flash. Load the proper configuration files as indicated in the Device Configuration File table.

Note: The following device access methods are in effect after loading the configuration files:

- Console access requires no username or password.

- Telnet and SSH require username **admin** and password **adminpa55**.

- The enable password is **ciscoenpa55**.

Device Configuration File Table

Device Name	File to Load	Notes
ALS1	Lab101-ALS1-TT-B-Cfg.txt	
DLS1	Lab101-DLS1-TT-B-Cfg.txt	
DLS2	Lab101-DLS2-TT-B-Cfg.txt	
R1	Lab101-R1-TT-B-Cfg.txt	
R2	Lab101-R2-TT-B-Cfg.txt	
R3	Lab101-R3-TT-B-Cfg.txt	
SRV1	N/A	Static IP: 10.1.50.1 Default gateway: 10.1.50.254
PC-B	N/A	DHCP
PC-C	N/A	DHCP

Step 3: Configure SRV1 and start the syslog and TFTP servers.

a. Configure SRV1 with the static IP address 10.1.50.1/24 and default gateway 10.1.50.254.

b. Start the syslog server on SRV1 to monitor console messages from multiple devices.

c. Start the TFTP server on SRV1 to record device configuration changes.

Step 4: Release and renew the DHCP lease on PC-B and PC-C.

    a.   Ensure that PC-B is configured as a DHCP client in the OFFICE VLAN.

    b.   Ensure that PC-C is configured as a DHCP client in the R3 branch office LAN.

    c.   After loading all TT-B device configuration files, issue the `ipconfig /release` and `ipconfig /renew` commands on PC-B and PC-C.

Step 5: Outline the troubleshooting approach and validation steps.

Use this space to identify your troubleshooting approach and the key steps to verify that the problem is resolved. Troubleshooting approaches to select from include the follow-the-path, spot-the-differences, bottom-up, top-down, divide-and-conquer, shoot-from-the-hip, and move-the-problem methods.

Note: In addition to a specific approach, you can use the generic troubleshooting process described at the beginning of Section 2 of this lab.

_____

_____

_____

_____

_____

_____

Step 6: Record the troubleshooting process and configuration changes.

Use this log to document your actions and results during the troubleshooting process. List the commands you used to gather information. As you progress, record what you think the problem might be and the actions you take to correct the problem.

Note: In addition to the commands listed for TT-A, the table of commands following this log might be helpful in troubleshooting this problem. You can also refer to Labs 5-2 and 5-3 for sample troubleshooting flows and additional commands.

Device	Actions and Results

Device	Actions and Results

Command	Key Information Displayed

`show ip route`
or
`show ip route ip-addr`
	Displays the entire routing table or information for a particular destination address.

`show ip ospf interface brief`	Displays interfaces that are participating in the OSPF routing process. An interface does not need to be operational to be listed in the command output.
`show ip ospf neighbor`	Displays the OSPF neighbor table to verify that all expected neighbor relationships are operational.
`show ip bgp`	Displays local and learned network entries in the BGP table with next hop, metric, local preference, weight, and AS path.
`show ip bgp summary`	Displays a summary of the BGP neighbor table. Lists important BGP parameters, such as the AS number and router ID, statistics about the memory consumption of the various BGP data structures, and a brief overview of the configured neighbors and their state.
`show ip bgp neighbors`	Displays parameters and extensive statistics about the peering session for all BGP neighbors.
`show ip ospf database`	Verifies the link types and link IDs for all areas in which this device participates.

Step 7: Document trouble ticket debrief notes.

Use this space to make notes of the key learning points that you picked up during the discussion of this trouble ticket with the instructor. The notes can include problems encountered, solutions applied, useful commands employed, alternate solutions, methods, and processes, and procedure and communication improvements.

_____

_____

_____

_____

_____

_____

Task 3: Trouble Ticket Lab 10-1 TT-C

Step 1: Review trouble ticket Lab 10-1 TT-C.

The user of PC-C on the branch office network called the help desk and reported that she is unable to access SRV1 or the Internet. Your task is to restore connectivity from client PC-C to SRV1 and the Internet and ensure that the user can connect to 172.30.3.1 using ping or a web browser. The branch office administrator did some preliminary testing and reported that he cannot ping or use Telnet to DLS2 or any other network devices from R3. The capability to ping other devices from remote router R3 is a connectivity requirement for the network.

Step 2: Load the device trouble ticket configuration files for TT-C.

Using the procedure described in Lab 3-1, verify that the lab configuration files are present in flash. Load the proper configuration files as indicated in the Device Configuration File table.

Note: The following device access methods are in effect after loading the configuration files:

- Console access requires no username or password.

- Telnet and SSH require username **admin** and password **adminpa55**.

- The enable password is **ciscoenpa55**.

Device Configuration File Table

Device Name	File to Load	Notes
ALS1	Lab101-ALS1-TT-C-Cfg.txt	
DLS1	Lab101-DLS1-TT-C-Cfg.txt	
DLS2	Lab101-DLS2-TT-C-Cfg.txt	
R1	Lab101-R1-TT-C-Cfg.txt	
R2	Lab101-R2-TT-C-Cfg.txt	
R3	Lab101-R3-TT-C-Cfg.txt	
SRV1	N/A	Static IP: 10.1.50.1 Default gateway: 10.1.50.254
PC-B	N/A	DHCP
PC-C	N/A	DHCP

Step 3: Configure SRV1 and start the syslog and TFTP servers.

a. Configure SRV1 with the static IP address 10.1.50.1/24 and default gateway 10.1.50.254.

b. Start the syslog server on SRV1 to monitor console messages from multiple devices.

c. Start the TFTP server on SRV1 to record device configuration changes.

Step 4: Release and renew the DHCP lease on PC-B and PC-C.

a. Ensure that PC-B is configured as a DHCP client in the OFFICE VLAN.

b. Ensure that PC-C is configured as a DHCP client in the R3 branch office LAN.

c. After loading all TT-C device configuration files, issue the `ipconfig /release` and `ipconfig /renew` commands on PC-B and PC-C.

Step 5: Outline the troubleshooting approach and validation steps.

Use this space to identify your troubleshooting approach and the key steps to verify that the problem is resolved. Troubleshooting approaches to select from include follow-the-path, spot-the-differences, bottom-up, top-down, divide-and-conquer, shoot-from-the-hip, and move-the-problem methods.

Note: In addition to a specific approach, you can use the generic troubleshooting process described at the beginning of Section 2 of this lab.

_____

_____

_____

_____

_____

_____

Step 6: Record the troubleshooting process and configuration changes.

Use this log to document your actions and results during the troubleshooting process. List the commands that you used to gather information. As you progress, record what you think the problem might be and the actions you take to correct the problem.

Note: In addition to the commands listed for TT-A and TT-B, the table of commands following this log might help you troubleshoot this problem. You can also refer to Lab 5-1 and the Chapter 9 labs for sample troubleshooting flows and additional commands.

Device	Actions and Results

Device	Actions and Results

Command	Key Information Displayed
`show ip cef ip-addr detail`	Displays the next hop and interface used for a particular destination address from the CEF table.
`show standby brief`	Verifies active and standby roles and IP addresses for all VLANs on an HSRP router.
`show ip eigrp interfaces`	Displays interfaces that are participating in the EIGRP routing process. An interface does not need to be operational to be listed in the output.
`show ip eigrp neighbors`	Displays the EIGRP neighbor table to verify that all expected neighbor relationships are operational.
`show access-lists ACL#/name`	Displays all ACLs configured on a device, including the ACL number and name, the type (standard or extended), the statements, and the number of matches accumulated for each statement.
`show ntp status`	Displays the clock synchronization status, stratum level, and reference clock IP address. Also shows the number of seconds since the last update was received from the reference clock.

Step 7: Document trouble ticket debrief notes.

Use this space to make notes of the key learning points that you picked up during the discussion of this trouble ticket with the instructor. The notes can include problems encountered, solutions applied, useful commands employed, alternate solutions, methods, and processes, and procedure and communication improvements.

_____

_____

_____

_____

_____

_____

Task 4: Trouble Ticket Lab 10-1 TT-D

Step 1: Review trouble ticket Lab 10-1 TT-D.

The user of PC-C on the branch office network called the help desk again and reported that she is unable to access SRV1 or the Internet and she is pretty upset. You must restore access to these resources for this user.

Step 2: Load the device trouble ticket configuration files for TT-D.

Using the procedure described in Lab 3-1, verify that the lab configuration files are present in flash. Load the proper configuration files as indicated in the Device Configuration File table.

Note: The following device access methods are in effect after loading the configuration files:

- Console access requires no username or password.

- Telnet and SSH require username **admin** and password **adminpa55**.

- The enable password is **ciscoenpa55**.

Step 3: Restart router R3 after the TT-D file is loaded.

After loading the TT-D file into the running config for router R3 and then copying it to the startup config, use the `reload` command to restart the router.

Device Configuration File Table

Device Name	File to Load	Notes
ALS1	Lab101-ALS1-TT-D-Cfg.txt	
DLS1	Lab101-DLS1-TT-D-Cfg.txt	
DLS2	Lab101-DLS2-TT-D-Cfg.txt	
R1	Lab101-R1-TT-D-Cfg.txt	
R2	Lab101-R2-TT-D-Cfg.txt	
R3	Lab101-R3-TT-D-Cfg.txt	
SRV1	N/A	Static IP: 10.1.50.1 Default gateway: 10.1.50.254
PC-B	N/A	DHCP
PC-C	N/A	DHCP

Step 4: Configure SRV1 and start the syslog and TFTP servers.

a. Configure SRV1 with the static IP address 10.1.50.1/24 and default gateway 10.1.50.254.

b. Start the syslog server on SRV1 to monitor console messages from multiple devices.

c. Start the TFTP server on SRV1 to record device configuration changes.

Step 5: Release and renew the DHCP lease on PC-B and PC-C.

a.   Ensure that PC-B is configured as a DHCP client in the OFFICE VLAN.

b.   Ensure that PC-C is configured as a DHCP client in the R3 branch office LAN.

c.   After loading all TT-D device configuration files, issue the `ipconfig /release` and `ipconfig /renew` commands on PC-B and PC-C.

Step 6: Outline the troubleshooting approach and validation steps.

Use this space to identify your troubleshooting approach and the key steps to verify that the problem is resolved. Troubleshooting approaches to select from include the follow-the-path, spot-the-differences, bottom-up, top-down, divide-and-conquer, shoot-from-the-hip, and move-the-problem methods.

Note: In addition to a specific approach, you can use the generic troubleshooting process described at the beginning of Section 2 of this lab.

_____

_____

_____

_____

_____

_____

Step 7: Record the troubleshooting process and configuration changes.

Use this log to document your actions and results during the troubleshooting process. List the commands that you used to gather information. As you progress, record what you think the problem might be and the actions you take to correct the problem.

Note: The table of commands following this log might help you troubleshoot this problem.

Device	Actions and Results

Device	Actions and Results

Command	Key Information Displayed
`show version`	Displays the device hardware and software status.
`dir flash:`	Displays the files and directories in flash memory.

Step 7: Document trouble ticket debrief notes.

Use this space to make notes of the key learning points that you picked up during the discussion of this trouble ticket with the instructor. The notes can include problems encountered, solutions applied, useful commands employed, alternate solutions, methods, and processes, and procedure and communication improvements.

_____

_____

_____

_____

_____

_____

_____

Section 2 Troubleshooting Reference Information

This lab covers all the technologies that were practiced in the previous labs. Therefore, no specific additional troubleshooting flows are provided for this lab. Refer to the Sample Troubleshooting Flows sections in previous labs for examples of procedures for specific technologies.

General Troubleshooting Process

As a general guideline, you can use the following general troubleshooting process described in the course.

1. Define the problem (symptoms).

2. Gather information.

3. Analyze the information.

4. Propose a hypothesis (possible cause).

5. Test the hypothesis.

6. Eliminate or accept the hypothesis.

7. Solve the problem.

8. Document the problem.

Reflection Questions

1. Which lab trouble tickets did you have the most difficulty with? _____

_____

_____

_____

2. Would you change anything about the process that you used for any of the trouble tickets now that you see the resolution of the problem? _____

_____

_____

3. Which commands did you find most useful in diagnosing issues?

_____

_____

_____

Router Interface Summary Table

Router Interface Summary				
Router Model	Ethernet Interface #1	Ethernet Interface #2	Serial Interface #1	Serial Interface #2
1700	Fast Ethernet 0 (FA0)	Fast Ethernet 1 (FA1)	Serial 0 (S0)	Serial 1 (S1)
1800	Fast Ethernet 0/0 (FA0/0)	Fast Ethernet 0/1 (FA0/1)	Serial 0/0/0 (S0/0/0)	Serial 0/0/1 (S0/0/1)
2600	Fast Ethernet 0/0 (FA0/0)	Fast Ethernet 0/1 (FA0/1)	Serial 0/0 (S0/0)	Serial 0/1 (S0/1)
2800	Fast Ethernet 0/0 (FA0/0)	Fast Ethernet 0/1 (FA0/1)	Serial 0/0/0 (S0/0/0)	Serial 0/0/1 (S0/0/1)

Note: To find out how the router is configured, look at the interfaces to identify the type of router and how many interfaces the router has. There is no way to effectively list all the combinations of configurations for each router class. This table includes identifiers for the possible combinations of Ethernet and Serial interfaces in the device. The table does not include any other type of interface, even though a specific router may contain one. An example of this might be an ISDN BRI interface. The string in parenthesis is the legal abbreviation that can be used in Cisco IOS commands to represent the interface.